Trade, Employment and Labour Standards

A Study of Core Workers' Rights and International Trade

ORGANISATION FOR ECONOMIC CO-OPERATION AND DEVELOPMENT

ORGANISATION FOR ECONOMIC CO-OPERATION AND DEVELOPMENT

Pursuant to Article 1 of the Convention signed in Paris on 14th December 1960, and which came into force on 30th September 1961, the Organisation for Economic Co-operation and Development (OECD) shall promote policies designed:

- to achieve the highest sustainable economic growth and employment and a rising standard of living in Member countries, while maintaining financial stability, and thus to contribute to the development of the world economy;
- to contribute to sound economic expansion in Member as well as non-member countries in the process of economic development; and
- to contribute to the expansion of world trade on a multilateral, non-discriminatory basis in accordance with international obligations.

The original Member countries of the OECD are Austria, Belgium, Canada, Denmark, France, Germany, Greece, Iceland, Ireland, Italy, Luxembourg, the Netherlands, Norway, Portugal, Spain, Sweden, Switzerland, Turkey, the United Kingdom and the United States. The following countries became Members subsequently through accession at the dates indicated hereafter: Japan (28th April 1964), Finland (28th January 1969), Australia (7th June 1971), New Zealand (29th May 1973), Mexico (18th May 1994), the Czech Republic (21st December 1995) and Hungary (7th May 1996). The Commission of the European Communities takes part in the work of the OECD (Article 13 of the OECD Convention).

Publié en français sous le titre :
LE COMMERCE, L'EMPLOI ET LES NORMES DU TRAVAIL
Une étude sur les droits fondamentaux des travailleurs et l'échange international

FOREWORD

This study has been prepared in response to a request given to the Organisation by OECD Ministers to undertake an analysis of areas where further progress with liberalisation and the strengthening of the multilateral system may be required. One such area was trade, employment and internationally recognised labour standards, including basic concepts, empirical evidence on trade and investment patterns, and current mechanisms for promoting higher labour standards world-wide.

The study begins with a Report agreed by the two OECD Committees which oversaw the work, i.e. the Employment, Labour and Social Affairs Committee and the Trade Committee. The agreed Report reflects the findings of a detailed analytical report of the OECD Secretariat as well as extensive discussions by the two Committees and other Committees involved in the work, notably the Committee on Investment and Multinational Enterprises. The Secretariat's analytical report itself is presented after the agreed Report and is published under the responsibility of the Secretary-General of the OECD.

This report was prepared by Corinne Deléchat, Mariarosa Lunati, Anne Richards and Raymond Torres, with specific contributions from Rolf Alter, Stéphanie Baile, Crawford Falconer, Evdokia Moïsé, Nicholas Vanston and Craig VanGrasstek, under the general supervision of John Martin and Jacques de Miramon.

CONTENTS

ABBREVIATIONS

AFL-CIO	American Federation of Labor and Congress of Industrial Organizations
BIAC	Business and Industry Advisory Committee to the OECD
BICE	Bureau International Catholique de l'Enfance
CEACR	Committee of Experts on the Application of Conventions and Recommendations (ILO)
CEDC	Programme on Children in Especially Difficult Circumstances
CFA	Committee on Freedom of Association (ILO)
CIME	Committee on International Investment and Multinational Enterprises (OECD)
CWIN	Child Workers in Nepal Concerned Center
DAC	Development Assistance Committee (OECD)
DNME	dynamic non-member economy
EBRD	European Bank for Reconstruction and Development
EC	European Community
EPZ	export-processing zone
EU	European Union
FDI	foreign direct investment
GATT	General Agreement on Tariffs and Trade
GDP	gross domestic product
GSP	Generalised System of Preferences
ILC	Conference Committee on the Application of Conventions and Recommendations (ILO)
ILO	International Labour Organisation
ILRERF	International Labour Rights Education and Research Fund
IMF	International Monetary Fund
IO	input/output

IPEC	International Programme on the Elimination of Child Labour (ILO)
ISO	International Organisation for Standardisation
ITO	International Trade Organisation
MFN	most-favoured nation
MNE	multinational enterprise
MOU	memorandum of understanding
NAALC	North American Agreement on Labor Cooperation
NAFTA	North American Free Trade Agreement
NAO	National Administrative Office
NBER	National Bureau for Economic Research
NGO	non-governmental organisation
QRs	quantitative restrictions
SITC	Standard International Trade Classification
SRI	socially responsible investing
TPRM	Trade Policy Review Mechanism (WTO)
TUAC	Trade Union Advisory Committee to the OECD
UN	United Nations
UNCTAD	United Nations Conference on Trade and Development
UNESCO	United Nations Educational, Scientific and Cultural Organisation
UNICEF	United Nations International Children's Emergency Fund
USITC	United States International Trade Commission
USTR	US Trade Representative
WTO	World Trade Organisation

JOINT REPORT ON TRADE, EMPLOYMENT AND LABOUR STANDARDS

(by the Employment, Labour and Social Affairs Committee and the Trade Committee of the OECD)

Since the end of the Uruguay Round, the issue of trade and labour standards has come to the forefront of the policy agenda. The protracted rise in unemployment in many OECD countries and in wage inequality in some countries has led some observers to look for external explanations, including claims of unfair trade practices associated with competition from firms that allegedly base their comparative advantage on low labour standards. This view is challenged by those who see internal structural rigidities as the key factor behind unemployment and growing wage inequality and who claim that differences in labour standards do not have any significant impact on trade flows or foreign direct investment.

The debate has focused on the human rights dimension of certain labour standards. It is argued that some labour standards reflect basic human rights and that all countries in the world should therefore adhere to these standards. Claims are also made that i) those labour standards that embody basic human rights can stimulate economic development and are therefore in the interest of all workers (and countries) in the world; and ii) observance of these labour standards could neutralise protectionist pressures, thus securing support for free trade.

However, there are significant differences of opinion on how such labour standards can be promoted. Some take the view that the international community should exert pressure on those countries that do not observe these standards, with the possibility of trade sanctions as a last resort. Others remain unconvinced that new international promotion mechanisms are required, in addition to those available in the International Labour Organisation (ILO), and fear that the defence of human rights would be captured by protectionist interests. More fundamentally, the issue arises as to whether economic development (associated, for example, with trade liberalisation) will gradually improve labour standards, or whether additional actions (for example, through the imposition of conditionality criteria in international trade agreements) are needed.

In June 1994, Ministers invited the OECD Secretariat to undertake an analysis of "areas where further progress with liberalisation and the strengthening of the multilateral system may be required". These areas included "trade, employment and internationally recognised labour standards, including basic concepts, empirical evidence in trade and investment patterns, and current mechanisms for promoting higher labour standards world-wide". Responding to this mandate, the Trade Committee and the Employment, Labour and Social Affairs Committee began jointly an analytical programme to examine these issues, in close co-operation with other relevant OECD Committees and Directorates as well as other international organisations, in particular the ILO. The attached study is the result of this exercise. Its purpose is to shed some light on the analytical aspects of this issue, while also evaluating mechanisms to promote core labour standards world-wide.

Selection of core labour standards and their implementation

The debate on trade and labour standards has been made more complex because of a lack of agreement on a list of the labour standards that are relevant to this issue and their definition. Part I of the study identifies a small set of labour standards, termed "core" for the purposes of the study, which are widely recognised to be of particular importance: elimination of child labour exploitation, prohibition of forced labour, freedom of association, the right to organise and bargain collectively, and non-discrimination in employment.

The choice of these labour standards is based primarily on the fact that they embody important human rights and that they derive from the Universal Declaration of Human Rights. The universality of these basic labour rights has been highlighted in the conclusions of the recent World Social Summit. In addition, three United Nations acts (the Covenant on Economic, Social and Cultural Rights, the Covenant on Civil and Political Rights and the Convention on the Rights of the Child), which contain relatively detailed provisions on core labour standards, have been ratified by over 120 countries, suggesting that these standards receive near-universal adherence. It is also important to note that all countries which are members of the ILO subscribe to the principles of freedom of association and collective bargaining by virtue of their membership.

Certain ILO Conventions provide for internationally negotiated definitions of core standards: Conventions 87 and 98 provide detailed provisions on freedom of association, the right to organise and collective bargaining; Conventions 29 and 105 establish the prohibition of all forms of forced labour; and Convention 111

10

provides for non-discrimination in employment. Although there is general agreement on the underlying principles behind these Conventions, the study suggests that certain provisions of some of these Conventions or their interpretation may find themselves at variance with national laws or regulations, thereby providing one explanation why so few ILO member countries have ratified *all* five Conventions in question. Finally, there is no ILO Convention that addresses the issue of child labour exploitation as such. Instead, Convention 138 provides for a minimum employment age, while remaining silent on the possibility of non-exploitative forms of child labour. Therefore, some OECD countries are of the view that ILO Conventions do not provide a unique and comprehensive set of definitions for the core standards selected in this report.

It is difficult to make a precise assessment of the degree of enforcement of core labour standards across countries, as available information is sparse and incomplete. The lack of reliable indicators of enforcement of standards on child labour, forced labour and non-discrimination is especially acute. Available evidence in this area is mostly anecdotal, making any attempt to analyse the economic implications of these standards problematic. But, on the basis of ILO reports and other sources, the study makes a tentative assessment of the state of freedom-of-association rights in over 70 countries throughout the world. It highlights wide cross-country differences in the degree of enforcement of freedom-of-association rights. There is a weak positive association between the degree of enforcement of these rights and the level of economic development. Finally, there seems to be a trend towards better compliance in low-standards countries.

Links between core labour standards, trade, economic development and employment

The theoretical discussion in Part II suggests that proper implementation of some core labour standards can support economic development, permitting an expansion in trade. Improved enforcement of non-discrimination standards might raise economic efficiency by ensuring that the allocation of labour resources moves closer to a free-market situation. Elimination of forced labour and child labour exploitation can also contribute to improving allocative efficiency. Child labour exploitation, moreover, is likely to undermine long-term economic prospects to the extent that it hampers children's education possibilities and degrades their health and welfare. The economic effects of freedom of association and the right to collective bargaining depend on a variety of factors. On the one hand, these rights can help upgrade production processes, while also raising workers' motivation and productivity. On the other hand, they can introduce a new distortion in the market if unionised workers succeed in raising their wages and working conditions above market levels. The net outcome on economic efficiency depends on the relative importance of these two effects. However, freedom of association as well as the other core labour standards cannot be considered primarily as a means to improve market efficiency, as they are fundamental rights of workers.

The empirical analysis presented in Part II refers almost entirely to only two core standards, freedom of association and the right to collective bargaining. This limitation of the analysis is unavoidable given the lack of data regarding the other core standards and the considerable technical difficulties encountered when trying to link the observance of labour standards with a range of economic outcomes.

Within these limitations, this analysis suggests that the output effects of greater freedom-of-association and collective bargaining rights are likely to be negligible compared with other factors such as shifts in technology, raw-material prices and terms of trade. More generally, the actual economic effects of core labour standards are likely to be small.

Part II also analyses the possible relationship between trade flows and core standards. Several points emerge:

- theoretical analysis suggests that, in general, trade improves aggregate economic welfare, irrespective of whether or not core standards are observed by all trading partners;

- standard trade models show that patterns of specialisation are likely to be determined by fundamental factors such as relative factor endowments, technology and economies of scale;

- empirical research suggests that there is no correlation at the aggregate level between real-wage growth and the degree of observance of freedom-of-association rights;

- there is no evidence that low-standards countries enjoy a better global export performance than high-standards countries;

- a detailed analysis of US imports of textile products (for which competition from low-standards countries is thought to be most intense) suggests that imports from high-standards countries account for a large share of the US market. Moreover, on average, the price of US imports of textile products does not appear to be associated with the degree of enforcement of child labour standards in exporting countries;

— some cases have been recorded where governments appear to deny core standards to workers or deliberately do not enforce them with the aim of improving sectoral trade competitiveness or attracting investment into export-processing zones (EPZs); the expected economic gains from such a strategy are, however, likely to prove short-lived and could be outweighed in the longer term by the economic costs associated with low core standards;

— an analysis of selected trade liberalisation episodes does not prove unambiguously whether trade reforms or freer association rights came first. There is no evidence that freedom-of-association rights worsened in any of the countries that liberalised trade. Nor is it apparent that the promotion of these rights impeded a subsequent trade liberalisation. The strongest finding is that there is a positive association over time between successfully sustained trade reforms and improvements in core standards;

— while core labour standards may not be systematically absent from the location decisions of OECD investors in favour of non-OECD destinations, aggregate FDI data suggest that core labour standards are not important determinants in the majority of cases. In these circumstances, host countries may be able to enforce core labour standards without risking negative repercussions on FDI flows. Observance may work as an incentive to raise productivity through investment in human and physical capital.

These results imply that concerns expressed by certain developing countries that core standards would negatively affect their economic performance or their international competitive position are unfounded; indeed, it is theoretically possible that the observance of core standards would strengthen the long-term economic performance of all countries.

The debate on trade and core standards is also motivated by concern that trade between low-standards countries and high-standards countries has led to a rise in unemployment, especially for unskilled workers, and/or growing wage inequality in the latter countries. Part II reviews research in this area, including *The OECD Jobs Study*, and shows that any shift in total employment associated with changes in trade patterns should be small. However, there is no agreement among researchers on the magnitude of the trade impact on sectoral employment patterns relative to the impact of other forces, e.g. technological progress and institutional changes. While the majority view is that trade with low-wage countries has had only a small impact on wage inequality over the past 15 years, some studies find larger impacts. It seems clear that further theoretical and empirical work is needed to resolve these issues.

Mechanisms to promote core labour standards world-wide

Even though efforts to improve observance of core standards may be facilitated by economic growth and freer trade, there are reasons to doubt that market forces alone will automatically improve core standards. Hence, the importance of more direct promotion mechanisms. Part III of the study reviews and evaluates different mechanisms that are currently in use or have been proposed to promote core labour standards. These mechanisms may take the form of either incentives or disincentives (i.e. sanctions as the most extreme form), which are channelled through government decisions at the multilateral, bilateral or unilateral level, or alternatively, through private actions.

To evaluate the effectiveness of the various mechanisms, one must first determine the extent to which they address the very issue under consideration, that is the existence of low core labour standards and its causes. Once this is done, the effectiveness of particular promotion mechanisms will depend upon the broad coverage of these mechanisms in terms of countries and economic agents, their character (e.g. legally binding versus voluntary), their political acceptability and, finally, their economic and social impacts.

In cases of systematic violations of basic worker rights by non-democratic regimes, it is up to the international community to decide what should be done. In such situations, the solution lies in political and legislative changes within the countries concerned with a view to ensuring that the effective implementation of these rights becomes an objective of national policy. For example, there are cases in recent history where serious violations of human rights have been condemned by the UN system. Trade sanctions (either unilateral or by the consensus of the international community in exceptional circumstances) and/or consumer boycotts have also been used.

Relatively few countries systematically deny core labour standards. The more common case is the non-observance of core standards in certain sectors or the inadequate enforcement of national legislation. A variety of promotion mechanisms, in effect or proposed, have been examined with respect to such cases.

Enhancing the role of the ILO

The ILO's distinguishing features -- its mandate, unique tripartite structure and quasi-universal membership -- make it an appropriate international forum for the promotion of core labour standards. It also provides the only functioning and directly relevant supervisory mechanism. Its monitoring/peer review procedures are specifically aimed at raising the level of standards and ensuring that they are universally recognised and properly implemented.

The special procedure on freedom of association appears to be relatively effective. There is some evidence that governments respond to complaints presented under this procedure. Its effectiveness could be increased if more attention were given to countries where union rights are not fully protected and if important recommendations formulated by the Freedom of Association Committee were given more publicity.

Recent proposals to promote application of the principles of prohibition of forced labour and non-discrimination in employment in all Member states include, on the one hand, the extension of the freedom-of-association procedure and, on the other, requests for regular reports on obstacles to ratification and application of fundamental ILO Conventions (a procedure now existing only for Convention 111). While the latter option is being given serious consideration, the former has met with scepticism, and discussion in the ILO has not proceeded very far at this stage.

At present there exist practical obstacles to ratification, which prevent some countries from ratifying core ILO Conventions, even when their laws and practices are consistent with the principles embodied in these Conventions. Some of these countries argue that revision and updating of the Conventions in question may help attract more ratifications.

An additional problem is that there is presently no mechanism to monitor cases of child labour exploitation. However, the ILO Governing Body has decided to place the issue of child labour on the agenda of the 1998 International Labour Conference. More generally, it would help the debate if the ILO could provide reliable and up-to-date information on the enforcement of core standards, an area where information is presently sparse and incomplete.

In sum, the current ILO monitoring system has proven to be reasonably effective, within the limits of its applicability. In particular, the ILO has an important role as a focal organisation where universal agreement on core labour standards can be reached. It can also persuade countries that it is in their own interest to promote basic labour rights and to avoid the exploitation of workers, while also informing the international community on cases of non-respect of core labour standards. In poor countries, the ILO technical assistance may also contribute to the eradication of child labour exploitation.

The ILO has also established a Working Party on the Social Dimensions of the Liberalisation of International Trade. The Working Party has decided to suspend any discussion of the link between trade and labour standards through trade sanctions. Instead, it has agreed a future work programme of (i) research and country studies on the impact of trade liberalisation on core standards; and (ii) reviewing the ILO's means of action to promote core standards.

Development co-operation and actions through other international organisations

Insofar as the non-enforcement of some core labour standards, in particular the prohibition of child labour exploitation, is linked to issues of poverty and economic development, development co-operation programmes can make a positive contribution by addressing the underlying causes. An important advantage of such positive mechanisms is that they can produce concrete and practical results -- e.g. getting children into schools, helping strengthen labour codes or enforcement capabilities -- without generating major economic distortions or political frictions. On the contrary, these measures are more likely to attract the support of all concerned countries, including developing ones. This links with the broader emphasis in today's development co-operation programmes on strengthening capacity for human rights and good governance, as embodied in the *DAC Statement on Development Partnerships in the New Global Context*. More can now be achieved in this direction by documenting and sharing experience as well as by assessing the effectiveness of different types of development co-operation in reducing the incidence of child labour and in promoting basic human rights.

Proposals have also been made to harness WTO disciplines in order to foster core labour standards. Existing WTO provisions have not been designed for promoting core standards. Some of the suggestions under discussion would imply a reinterpretation of WTO practices and procedures, while others would require to a greater or lesser extent renegotiation and amendment of WTO articles. Extending the WTO's Trade Policy Review Mechanism procedure to include labour standards would fall into the former category, while other proposals would fall into the latter. In all cases, a consensus among WTO Members on the appropriateness and effectiveness of using WTO procedures to promote core labour standards and on the institutional changes required would have to be reached. Such a consensus does not exist at present. However, while some countries continue to call for discussion of the issue in the WTO and others are opposed, this remains an issue for international consideration. The debate on this issue and on the associated conceptual and practical difficulties will continue.

Finally, it has been suggested to make international financial assistance conditional on the respect of core labour rights by borrowing countries, as there is no practical experience of such a mechanism, it is impossible to evaluate it. However, some difficulties can already be envisaged. First, it would target only those countries which apply for multilateral loans. Second, it is doubtful that restricting one important means of improving national welfare is likely to result in faster improvement of labour standards.

Other mechanisms at national or regional level

Other types of measures include unilateral or plurilateral government actions. Regarding unilateral government actions, the evidence from the US Generalised System of Preferences (GSP) Program suggests that conditioning eligibility for GSP benefits on the respect of core labour standards induced a positive change in the behaviour of some countries. This has prompted the EU to attach a similar set of conditions to its GSP, to become effective as of 1 January 1998. Both systems refer explicitly to internationally recognised labour standards, thus enhancing their credibility and ensuring their consistency with other international actions to promote core labour standards.

Compared with unilateral measures, making the respect of core labour standards part of regional trade agreements, as in the case of the NAFTA side agreement on labour co-operation, has the advantage that all concerned parties must agree to a pre-established set of norms and a well-defined dispute-settlement mechanism. However, the NAFTA side agreement aims to enhance the enforcement of existing *national* labour laws, but does not explicitly refer to norms defined in relevant ILO Conventions. It is also far too early to assess the effectiveness of this particular mechanism.

In sum, the influence of these mechanisms depends not only on the sanctions but also on the review process. In any case, their effectiveness is clearly related to the size of the US and EU markets, as well as to the steady erosion of GSP preferences for developing countries under the implementation of the Uruguay Round Agreements.

International standards for the conduct of firms

International codes of conduct for firms, such as the ILO Tripartite Declaration and the OECD Guidelines for Multinational Enterprises (MNEs), can also play an important role. In a globalising environment, MNEs are a prime vehicle for the transfer of technology, innovation and modern management practices. Nevertheless, the impact of MNEs on the promotion of core labour standards should not be overstated. The most direct effect MNEs can have is on raising the labour standards of their own labour force. MNEs can also exert an indirect influence by requesting that good labour practices be applied by their suppliers and other local partners. Indeed, the variety of existing codes of conduct for firms seems to reflect the increasing importance of business ethics in the regular operation of enterprises. The fact that such codes are voluntary also makes them easier for firms to adopt. However, evidence is lacking on their effectiveness in promoting core labour standards in developing countries.

Private-sector mechanisms

In situations where non-enforcement of core labour standards is not necessarily due to poverty, but is an act of individual employers motivated by potential economic benefits, private-party mechanisms can help create counter-incentives, whereby the respect of core labour standards, and not their denial, is economically rewarded. These mechanisms take various forms:

– Ethical standards for firms have been used in the past, in particular with the aim of eliminating apartheid in South Africa. Though these private-sector codes of conduct have had certain effects, in particular with respect to the operations of large MNEs, they have not been specifically directed to the set of core labour standards under consideration in this study. In addition, they have two weaknesses: i) since they are voluntary, firms are free not to follow them; and ii) they are not subject to satisfactory review procedures.

– Another mechanism consists in persuading consumers to base their purchases not only on price but also on moral principles. This may take the form of boycotts of products which can be connected with non-observance of core labour standards. The effectiveness of these mechanisms is variable and uncertain, since they depend on widespread consumer acceptance. In addition, boycotts can have an impact on trade and run the risk of being manipulated to suit narrow domestic interests.

– "Social labelling" of products allows consumers to buy goods that meet certain criteria deemed to be socially desirable. The advantages of such a mechanism are that it takes the form of an incentive rather than a sanction and that it requires the co-operation of both manufacturers and importers. This enhances its effectiveness. But, as in the case of all labelling programmes, care must be taken that the criteria for attribution are properly defined and monitored, and that all the components/parts of a given product also comply with these criteria. It is unlikely that social labelling could deal with all cases of low core standards.

– "Socially responsible investment schemes" aim to promote firms which implement high standards of social policies. Investment fund managers either screen and select such firms for their funds or reject those firms which violate the set criteria. These schemes have, so far, been run on a limited scale and therefore their economic (and social) impact is difficult to gauge. In any case, they generally target only one or two core labour standards, such as freedom of association and child exploitation, and, by their very nature, impact only on those countries in which firms listed on the stock exchange operate or invest.

In sum, such private codes and mechanisms can help in certain specific cases, particularly if they reinforce other, more broadly based mechanisms, but they are unlikely to provide a general solution. More generally, an important question that needs to be addressed in connection with these mechanisms is that of how to ensure that the information on which private-sector actions are based is accurate and free from manipulation.

Conclusion

Combining the range of situations and objectives outlined above with a variety of existing or potential promotion mechanisms highlights the multifaceted nature of the problem. In particular, all the mechanisms reviewed in the study can potentially address at least one of the reasons for non-observance of core labour standards. However, none of them can solve all problems at the same time.

INTRODUCTION

The issue of trade and labour standards is not a new one. It first arose in the 19th century when concern was expressed about the risk of "unfair" trade associated with competition from firms producing under socially unacceptable practices (Follows, 1951). In fact, this concern was one of the motivations behind the creation of the International Labour Organisation (ILO) in 1919. More recently, the protracted rise in unemployment in many OECD countries has led some observers to look for external explanations, including claims of unfair trade practices associated with competition from countries that allegedly base their comparative advantage on low labour standards. This view is challenged by others who lay stress on internal structural rigidities in labour and product markets as the key factor behind unemployment and who claim that differences in labour standards have no significant impact on trade flows and foreign direct investment patterns, and that, consequently, trade between the North (equated to high-standards countries) and the South (equated to low-standards countries) is not a significant cause of unemployment in the OECD area.

The issue is also strongly motivated by a concern with human rights. It is argued that some labour standards reflect basic human rights which should be observed in all countries, independently of their levels of economic development and socio-cultural traditions. The universality of these basic labour rights is highlighted in the conclusions of the recent World Social Summit in Copenhagen. Claims are also made that i) those labour standards that embody basic human rights can stimulate economic development and are therefore in the interest of all workers (and countries) in the world; and ii) observance of these labour standards could neutralise protectionist pressures, thus securing support for free trade.

Attention then focuses on the choice of the most appropriate mechanisms to ensure world-wide promotion of these basic rights. Trade sanctions (or the threat of them) are sometimes advocated as a mechanism of last resort to achieve observance of these basic human rights at the workplace. Acceptance of a human rights justification for certain labour standards does not lead automatically to agreement that a link should be established between these standards and trade policies. For example, it is sometimes argued that human rights should be enforced in a manner that is consistent with the specific socio-economic conditions prevailing in each country. On the issue of trade sanctions, some argue that they could be counter-productive since free trade is a powerful engine of economic development and social progress. More generally, there is concern that the alleged human rights nature of certain labour standards could be used as an excuse for adopting protectionist solutions.

The Ministerial Mandate does not question the importance of promoting, as widely as possible, the observance of human rights and the labour standards that embody these rights. Endorsement by OECD countries and many non-OECD countries of several international conventions and declarations on human rights lends support to this view.

The aim of this report is rather i) to assess whether there is any relationship between those labour standards that are held to embody basic human rights on the one hand, and trade and foreign direct investment flows and policies on the other; and ii) to discuss current mechanisms proposed to promote those standards. Part I provides basic concepts and definitions and identifies a set of core labour standards that are likely to be important from the human rights point of view. The extent to which existing ILO Conventions embody these core standards is also discussed, and observance of these standards in a wide range of countries is described. Part II is devoted to an economic analysis of core labour standards, with a view to assessing the impact of core standards on economic development, trade and foreign investment patterns, and employment. Part III reviews a range of existing and proposed mechanisms to promote core labour standards and draws some tentative conclusions as to their effectiveness.

PART I

LABOUR STANDARDS IN OECD AND SELECTED NON-OECD COUNTRIES

PART I

LABOUR STANDARDS IN OECD

AND SELECTED NON-OECD COUNTRIES

Labour standards are norms and rules that govern working conditions and industrial relations. They embrace practically all aspects of labour markets (minimum wages, working time, health and safety, labour inspection, statistics, industrial relations, non-discrimination, child labour, etc.). They are established either at the national level, in the form of laws and government regulations, or at the international level. National labour standards are typically binding. Governments have competence to enforce them and, if necessary, they can impose sanctions in cases of non-observance. Likewise, international labour standards recognised in certain regional trading areas, such as EU Directives on social matters, have some sort of legal force. They are usually compulsory upon member countries; a variety of instruments exist to sanction countries that do not comply with these labour standards. Other international labour standards such as the ILO Conventions and several acts of the United Nations also have a binding character, but no sanctions are imposed in case of non-enforcement. However, the ILO Conventions constitute the most comprehensive set of international labour standards. As such, they are often cited in the trade and labour standards debate.

Selection of core labour standards

Despite the lack of formal international consensus in this area, there appears to be some agreement that the debate should focus on a subset of labour standards, often termed "core", as opposed to labour standards writ large. For example, a recent report by the ILO (1994a) suggests that a few labour standards such as freedom of association, collective bargaining, prohibition of forced labour and elimination of child labour are particularly important from the humanitarian point of view. Agreement on the same set of labour standards was reached at the World Social Summit in Copenhagen in March 1995.

Proposals have been made to add some other labour standards to the "core" list. For example, Fields (1994) adds to this list health and safety, i.e. the provision whereby no person should be exposed to dangerous working conditions without being appropriately informed. Other authors propose adding non-discrimination in employment and equal wage treatment to the list of core standards.

This paper suggests that the following standards, called "core" standards for convenience, should be selected for the purpose of the analysis:

- Freedom of association and collective bargaining, i.e. the right of workers to form organisations of their own choice and to negotiate freely their working conditions with their employers[1].

- Elimination of *exploitative* forms of child labour, such as bonded labour and forms of child labour that put the health and safety of children at serious risk.

- Prohibition of forced labour, in the form of slavery and compulsory labour.

- Non-discrimination in employment, i.e. the right to equal respect and treatment for all workers.

The selection of these core labour standards is based on several considerations. First, they embody basic human rights as exemplified in the Declaration of the World Social Summit. Other labour standards, such as working-time arrangements or minimum-wage laws, do not embody basic human rights. Second, some argue that core standards are framework conditions for other labour standards to be meaningful.

Core labour standards as basic human rights

Throughout the 20th century, a body of international law on human rights has developed and certain basic workers' rights have become part of this legislation. The first important international agreements on workers' rights date from the beginning of the century, when several international treaties on the elimination of slavery were signed[2]. The creation of the ILO in 1919 reflects concern with the improvement of living conditions of human beings and illustrates the growing importance of basic workers' rights. Ever since the creation of the United Nations, the promotion of human rights in general, including workers' rights, has been one of the major aims of member countries.

This is illustrated by the presence of human rights provisions in several acts of the United Nations, starting with its constitutive Charter. Article 55 of the Charter of the United Nations of 1945 states that countries should provide a higher level of living standards, full employment, and should promote respect for human rights and basic liberties for all, without distinction of race, gender, language or religion. It is important to note that the article considers these provisions as necessary conditions for the maintenance of peaceful relations between countries. Obviously, all member countries are bound by these provisions by virtue of membership. Besides the very general provisions of the Charter of the United Nations, the Universal Declaration of Human Rights of 1948 gives a more detailed description of human rights. These include civil and political rights (the right to life, liberty, freedom from torture, freedom of opinion and expression, freedom from slavery and servitude, right to peaceful assembly and association) and economic, social and cultural rights (right to join and form trade unions, right to work, right to equal pay for equal work, right to education). Again, the right to decent living standards is regarded as one important element.

This body of international law considers human rights as universal, transcending all political, economic, social and cultural situations. They are characterised as such because they involve the fundamental liberty, dignity and respect of the individual. Moreover, freedom of association, prohibition of forced labour, elimination of child labour exploitation and the principle of non-discrimination are well-established elements of international jurisprudence concerning human rights; in fact, these workers' rights are an inseparable part of human rights.

The recent World Social Summit in Copenhagen has reinforced international consensus on fundamental human and workers' rights[3]. In Commitment 3 of the Declaration from this summit, nations affirm their adhesion to certain workers' rights, which are identical to the core labour standards selected in this study. The Declaration also encourages countries that have ratified the relevant ILO Conventions to implement them and calls upon other countries to respect the principles embodied in these Conventions. It also invites governments to ratify these Conventions and, more generally, to use international labour standards as a benchmark for their national labour legislation[4].

Core labour standards as framework conditions for other labour standards

In a market economy, working conditions are generally the outcomes of supply and demand forces. For these forces to manifest themselves, however, individuals must be allowed to express their choices and act freely, and core labour standards provide basic guarantees for the expression of free choices. This issue, as well as the overall economic and labour-market implications of core standards, is explored in some detail in Part II.

Moreover, without core labour standards, other standards may not be very meaningful as their implementation requires that individuals be able to determine (or influence) these standards freely. For example, many countries have working-time standards, but if workers are forced to accept the working conditions laid down by employers because, for example, their basic human rights are not respected, then working-time standards will have little impact. More generally, it can be expected that workers will be better placed to demand improved working conditions when the economy expands rapidly; but for this to happen, they must be allowed to express these demands freely. By the same token, attempts to suppress standards will be less successful in a growing economy, as market forces put upward pressure on wages and working conditions.

Conclusions

The following core standards have been selected for the purposes of analysis: freedom of association and collective bargaining, elimination of exploitative forms of child labour, prohibition of forced labour and non-discrimination in employment. These core standards have the characteristics of human rights. Moreover, observance of these standards might pave the way for the establishment of better working conditions.

ILO Conventions

ILO Conventions are a major source of international labour standards, which are binding only on countries that have ratified them[5]. However, it is important to note that a special procedure on freedom of association is applicable to all ILO member countries. The ILO is empowered, under Article 33 of its Constitution, to take such action as may be considered wise and expedient to secure compliance by a state against which another member country has filed a complaint with the terms of the Convention which both member countries have ratified. In practice, however, the ILO relies on technical assistance, peer pressure and persuasion to encourage greater compliance[6]. It does not impose sanctions -- financial, commercial or other. An overview of ILO procedures is presented in Part III. One key issue, examined here, is whether existing ILO Conventions and instruments embody in all cases the core labour standards identified in this study.

Overview of ILO Conventions

ILO Conventions embrace numerous aspects of labour standards, ranging from minimum wages and equal pay to health and safety regulations. Given this wide coverage, the main principles contained in ILO Conventions are worth mentioning. The ILO groups existing Conventions in the following categories.

First of all, there are so-called *Fundamental Human Rights*. The right of workers and employers to create and freely to join trade unions or other types of representative organisations is established. Two Conventions call for the abolition of any form of slavery and forced labour. They also specify conditions under which some form of compulsory labour "in the public interest" can be maintained. Finally, various other Conventions affirm the principles of equal pay and working conditions. In particular, these Conventions affirm that race and sex, *inter alia*, should not motivate unequal pay, occupation or career prospects.

Conventions grouped under the *Employment* category aim at encouraging countries to pursue policies that will maximise the level of employment, by ensuring that there is work for all available persons who are actively seeking a job. Also, another Convention sets out conditions under which employment contracts can be terminated, with the aim of providing workers with a minimum level of employment security; provisions can be established by collective agreements, not necessarily by government regulations[7].

As regards *Social Policy*, two Conventions set out basic principles with the objective of improving living standards while also ensuring that every person has access to a minimum level of living conditions. The Conventions also state that education and training are key instruments to achieve better living standards.

Another category of Conventions, related to *Labour Administration*, calls for the establishment of a well-functioning administrative system, with the participation of the social partners. A Convention on labour inspection matters aims at securing the enforcement of labour laws. Another Convention asks governments to establish procedures that promote tripartite consultation.

Industrial Relations are addressed in several Conventions which call for the promotion of collective bargaining and its progressive extension to most aspects of working conditions. They also recommend that governments should consult employers' organisations and workers' groups before adopting any measure that aims at encouraging collective bargaining. The establishment of tripartite consultative procedures with the aim of improving the application of international labour standards is also recommended.

Numerous Conventions are grouped in another category termed *Conditions of Work*. First, the principle of minimum wages is established and conditions that protect wages defined. Accordingly, workers should be guaranteed a minimum wage in cases where wages are exceptionally low and collective agreements do not provide for wage floors. Second, this category also includes Conventions on working time and on health and safety matters.

Social Security constitutes another important category, comprising several general Conventions as well as specific ones on sickness benefits, pensions, compensation for work-related accidents, unemployment benefits and maternity benefits. The basic purpose of these Conventions is to establish minimum standards for social security benefits.

Conditions for *Employment of Women* are regulated in several Conventions. For instance, a Convention on maternity protection grants 12 weeks of (paid) maternity leave. Another Convention prohibits night work by women, with some exceptions. Underground work by women is also prohibited, with few possible exceptions.

The category on *Employment of Children and Young Persons* comprises several Conventions that aim at the elimination of child labour. For instance, the most recent Convention stipulates that the minimum age for admission to employment or work shall not be less than 15 years or the end of compulsory schooling, whichever is greater, with the possibility that this age can be lower for developing countries[8]. Other Conventions also regulate night work by young persons.

The last four categories deal with Old Workers, Migrant Workers, Indigenous Workers and Tribal Populations, and Particular Categories of Workers (notably seamen and fishermen).

It is important to note that a hierarchy can be discerned among these Conventions, even though the ILO does not make one. There are first-level Conventions, which deal with freedom of association, the right to organise and collective bargaining, and which set conditions governing child labour, non-discrimination in employment and the prohibition of forced labour. The principles behind these Conventions represent minimum norms which should be respected by all. Their implementation does not rely on other Conventions. Particularly important are the principles of freedom of association and collective bargaining, which are enshrined in the Preamble of the ILO Constitution and the Declaration of Philadelphia. Then there are second-level Conventions, which establish rules that help improve working conditions, minimum wages, social benefits and workers' participation in the determination of their labour conditions. Countries are encouraged to subscribe to these norms, which are not as fundamental to the rights of workers as core standards. Their enforcement does not always call for government regulation; some of the provisions of these Conventions can be enforced by collective agreement or other national practices. Therefore, freedom of association, collective bargaining rights and other first-level standards might be seen as framework conditions that permit direct determination of second-level standards by the social partners[9].

Discussion of several key ILO Conventions

Several ILO Conventions loom large in discussions of core labour standards, but no consensus exists on the extent to which these Conventions in themselves provide adequate definitions of core standards. These include Conventions 87 and 98 which establish the principles of freedom of association and collective bargaining; Conventions 29 and 105 on prohibition of forced labour; Convention 138 on the minimum age for employment; Convention 100 on equal remuneration and Convention 111 on non-discrimination in employment. The main provisions of these Conventions are as follows.

Convention 87 sets guarantees for freedom of association:

– It stipulates that workers have the right to establish and join organisations of their own choosing. These organisations have the right to draw up their own constitutions and rules, to elect their representatives in full freedom, to organise their administration and activities and to formulate their programmes. Provisions whereby only one trade union may be established at the enterprise, sectoral or national level run counter to the Convention. Likewise, regulations stating that a union may be established only if it has a minimum number of members, that minimum being set at such a high level that it effectively prevents the formation of unions, are not in agreement with the Convention.

– Workers have the right to establish organisations without prior authorisation. In certain countries, the authorities apply arbitrary registration and recognition requirements, thereby violating the spirit of the Convention.

- The ILO Committee on Freedom of Association, as well as other ILO bodies, consider the right to engage in industrial disputes and the right to strike as an inherent dimension of the principle of freedom of association[10].

In certain countries, although unions can be freely formed, they face restrictions when they seek to exert their functions. Respect for Convention 98 on the right to collective bargaining is essential to make meaningful the principle of freedom of association established in Convention 87; for this reason these two conventions are usually grouped together. Convention 98 contains three main provisions:

- It stipulates that workers should be protected against acts of anti-union discrimination, such as subjecting the establishment of an employment contract to the condition of not being unionised, or dismissing workers only because they are union members.

- The law should also provide "adequate protection against acts of interference between workers and employers organisations".

- The authorities are asked to promote collective bargaining.

The aim of Conventions 29 and 105 is to eliminate all forms of forced labour, i.e. "work exacted from any person under menace of any penalty, and for which the said person has not offered himself voluntarily". Certain forms of forced labour do not fall within the scope of Convention 29 and are therefore permitted; this is notably the case of work performed in the interest of the community when there is imminent necessity and work by convicted prisoners. However, it is important to note that the Convention prohibits prison labour when such workers are hired by (or placed at the disposal of) private agents, though not when such work is carried out under the supervision or control of a public authority (Article 2.c) or when it is voluntary. Convention 105 states that forced labour should be suppressed "as a means of political coercion or education; as a method of mobilising and using labour for purposes of economic development; as a means of labour discipline; as a punishment for having participated in strikes".

The aim of Convention 138 is to establish a minimum age for child labour. According to Article 1 of the Convention, "each Member for which [the]

Convention is in force undertakes to pursue a national policy designed to ensure the effective abolition of child labour and to raise progressively the minimum age for admission to employment or work to a level consistent with the fullest physical and mental development of young persons". The Convention stipulates that children should not enter the labour market before completion of compulsory education or having reached the age of 15. In case of work that is unhealthy or dangerous, the minimum age set by the Convention is 18. These provisions do not apply to work done by children in the context of training institutions. Likewise, light work by children aged 13 to 15 may be allowed, to the extent that it is not prejudicial to their educational activities. Finally, developing countries can, in consultation with the social partners, limit the scope of application of the Convention and lower the minimum age for employment to 14 (12 in the case of light work).

Convention 100 provides for the principle of equal remuneration for work of equal value, without discrimination based on sex. This principle may be applied by means of national law and regulations, as well as by collective bargaining or other existing machinery for wage determination.

According to Convention 111, states should take action with the aim of eliminating any form of job discrimination on the basis of "race, colour, sex, religion, political opinion, national extraction or social origin". It can be asserted that non-discrimination in pay is a special form of non-discrimination in employment: the latter establishes the principle of equal terms and conditions of employment for equal work without any sort of discrimination, while the former is specifically devoted to equal pay (one element of the terms and conditions of employment), without discrimination based on sex. Therefore, the principles behind Convention 100 are embodied in Convention 111.

ILO Conventions and core labour standards

Three of the core labour standards identified in this study are embodied in some of these key Conventions:

- Freedom of association and collective bargaining are contained in Conventions 87 and 98.

- Prohibition of forced labour is given by Conventions 29 and 105.

- Non-discrimination in employment is given by Convention 111.

– No ILO Convention is explicitly devoted to elimination of *exploitative* forms of child labour, but the ILO Committee of Experts has taken the position that Convention 29 covers exploitative forms of child labour when they constitute forced labour within the definition of that instrument.

Even if these five Conventions (29, 105, 87, 98 and 111) appear to embody core standards, they have not received universal ratification; a Convention becomes a binding obligation only for the states that ratify it. It is noteworthy that only 62 countries (including 15 OECD countries) have ratified all five key Conventions. However, these Conventions are among the most ratified ones[11]. Convention 29 on forced labour is the most ratified Convention (135 of the 173 member states had ratified it by the end of 1994); this is followed by Convention 98 on the right to organise and collective bargaining (124 ratifications), Convention 100 on equal pay (123 ratifications), Convention 111 on non-discrimination (119 ratifications), Convention 11 on the right of association in agriculture (116 ratifications), Conventions 14 and 19 on weekly rest in industry and equality of treatment for accident compensation (114 and 115 ratifications), Convention 105 on prohibition of forced labour (114 ratifications), Convention 81 on labour inspection (114 ratifications) and Convention 87 on freedom of association (112 ratifications).

It is perhaps surprising that so many ILO member states have not ratified all five of these key Conventions despite the fact that their underlying principles are likely to meet universal agreement. A recent ILO survey on the reasons for non-ratification of several important Conventions gives interesting results (GB.264/LILS/5 and GB.264/9/2). First, none of the countries that responded to the survey was in disagreement with the underlying principles of Conventions 29, 105, 87, 98 and 111, and indeed a number of them indicated that they are examining the possibility of ratifying the Conventions. Second, several countries mentioned specific aspects or details of Conventions 29, 105, 87 and 98 as the main obstacle to ratification:

– The United States indicated that the subcontracting of the operation of prison facilities appears to conflict with Convention 29. Canada argued that Convention 29 is not relevant to the situation of the country because provisions of Convention 29 are believed to be intended primarily for colonies. Several countries (e.g. Croatia) claimed that there is no substantial difference between Conventions 29 and 105, and thus there was no need to ratify both.

– Brazil and the United States observed that Conventions 87 and 98 cannot be ratified without some changes in national legislation and regulations concerning, for example, the right to strike for certain employees. For New Zealand, non-ratification was explained by the fact that the Committee on Freedom of Association finds some of its practices to be contrary to Conventions 87 and 98. India argued that the Conventions are "largely influenced by western concepts". Finally, Canada indicated that its legislation provides for exclusions from collective bargaining rights that are wider than those provided for in Convention 98.

Overall, practically no country opposes ratification of Conventions 29, 105, 87, 98 and 111 for reasons of principle. Instead, the reasons given for non-ratification refer to specific details of the Conventions or their interpretations by ILO bodies. For example, while the right to strike is not mentioned in Convention 87, the Committee on Freedom of Association regards this right as an intrinsic part of the right to freedom of association. This makes ratification problematic in countries which by and large respect the main principles of the Conventions, but not certain (relatively unimportant) provisions of either the Conventions or their interpretation. Some countries, though respecting the principles of core labour standards, feel that the provisions of ILO Conventions that are supposed to embody these standards are either too detailed or out-of-date. Also, some countries may find it difficult to apply specific provisions of Convention 29 that treat differently prison labour carried out for a private enterprise and for a government agency.

Even so, ILO member countries have decided not to revise these Conventions in the context of the current revision exercise, though this question may arise in the longer run. The ILO Governing Body is examining ways to strengthen the promotion of fundamental ILO Conventions; this includes examination of possible new review procedures (see Part III). It cannot be excluded that this process would be accompanied by a simplification of certain provisions of core Conventions or a reconsideration of their interpretation.

Convention 138 on a minimum age for child labour has been ratified by only 46 countries[12]. This Convention is not specifically devoted to any core standard as it does not contain provisions on exploitative forms of child labour (see box below). The results of the recent ILO survey on the reasons for non-ratification of certain Conventions showed that several countries explicitly oppose ratification of Convention 138 and openly criticise various substantive aspects of the Convention, including the fact that it does not provide for an effective safeguard against child labour exploitation. ILO member countries have decided "for the time being" not to consider the issue of whether Convention 138 should be revised, but the Governing Body of the ILO has decided to place the issue of child labour on the agenda of the 1998 International Labour Conference, either for a general discussion of this issue or for the adoption of standards on the elimination of "intolerable" forms of child labour.

Conclusions

The set of labour standards selected as "core" provides a basis for regarding a certain number of ILO Conventions as basic Conventions. The Constitution of the ILO mentions freedom of association as a basic principle, one that all members of the ILO have to apply by virtue of their membership. ILO Conventions 87 and 98 provide detailed provisions for freedom of association. However, some of these provisions give rise to interpretations by ILO bodies that seem to go beyond the freedom-of-association principle. None of these Conventions has received universal ratification: Convention 98 has been ratified by less than three-quarters of member countries and Convention 87 by less than two-thirds of them. ILO Conventions 29 and 105, which are two of the most ratified conventions, explicitly embody the principle of prohibition of forced labour, even though they contain more detailed provisions that do not necessarily relate to human rights. Also, these two Conventions implicitly prohibit the most abhorrent forms of child labour. Convention 138 sets out a minimum age for child labour and, as such, does not deal with the issue of child labour exploitation: some forms of child labour are consistent with observance of human rights. Finally, Convention 111 (ratified by two-thirds of member countries) seems to reflect adequately the right to non-discrimination in employment. Despite some caveats and a less-than-universal ratification record, it can be asserted that, at present, Conventions 87, 98, 29, 105 and 111 are important references for monitoring observance of core labour standards.

Child work and exploitation

"Child labour" encompasses an extremely complex set of phenomena. In many countries, including in the OECD, part-time work is a fact of life for many children and is not necessarily exploitative or detrimental to the child's development. Sometimes it can help young people acquire skills and build confidence. In combating exploitative child labour, it is necessary, therefore, to consider carefully its various forms, making a distinction between work and exploitation, and taking due account of the developmental and cultural contexts.

It is widely agreed that child labour is strongly associated with poverty, low levels of development, lack of educational opportunities and certain cultural traditions. The countries with the highest illiteracy rates, lowest school enrolment ratios and serious nutritive deficiencies are in general those that have the highest proportions of children working.

According to the criteria developed by UNICEF in 1986, child exploitation is characterised by children who work too young, too long hours, for too little pay, in hazardous conditions or under slave-like arrangements. UNICEF adds that exploitation also occurs when children's work entails too much responsibility; hampers their access to education; is detrimental to their full social and psychological development; or undermines their dignity or self-esteem. Based on these criteria, some of the most obvious and intolerable cases of exploitation stand out, such as those involving children in bonded labour, prostitution, military groups, the drugs trade and other highly dangerous occupations. But children engaged in agriculture, services or manufacturing may also be exposed to exploitative situations. Due to heavy workloads and malnutrition, children in these occupations often confront high health risks and occupational hazards with severe consequences for their physical and intellectual development.

At the same time, the phenomenon of child exploitation needs careful analysis. It is not necessarily linked to poverty alone and may be associated with children's being used to advance various kinds of family aspirations or roles[13]. Solutions such as the imposition of a minimum wage or compulsory education, unless they take proper account of the economic, social and cultural factors underlying child labour, may even risk worsening the situation of children. Unless some alternative is provided for the children and their families, many children dismissed from work could be left to fend for themselves in the streets or might take up more hazardous employment. Child work can be expected to decrease gradually with higher levels of development. However, the eradication of specific forms of child exploitation and a massive reduction in child labour can be achieved only through political commitment, targeted policies and complementary development programmes.

No existing ILO Convention contains detailed provisions on the exploitation of children as such. Several Conventions set a minimum age for employment. Cases of child exploitation are sometimes examined under the aegis of forced labour Conventions. Finally, Article 32 of the UN Convention on the Rights of the Child reflects the UNICEF criteria and prohibits the economic exploitation of children.

UN provisions on workers' rights

Several acts of the United Nations also include provisions on core labour standards. The Declaration of Human Rights is a direct source of two Covenants which have legal binding force on countries that ratify them. First, the Covenant on Economic, Social and Cultural Rights of 1966, ratified by 131 countries at the end of 1994, seeks to promote and protect the right to work in just and favourable conditions, the right to social protection and to decent standards of living, and the right to education. More specifically, concerning workers' rights, the Covenant mentions the right to "equal opportunity for everyone to be promoted in his employment to an appropriate higher level, subject to no considerations other than those of seniority and competence" (Article 7). This provision seems to be fully consistent with provisions of ILO Convention 111 on non-discrimination in employment. In addition, according to Article 8 of the Covenant, countries should ensure the right of all to join and form trade unions of their own choosing, the right of trade unions to establish national federations or confederations and the right of trade unions to function freely. This is very similar to the provisions of Convention 87 of the ILO. However, the Covenant also states that these trade union rights should not be subject to any limitations *other than* "those prescribed by law and which are necessary in a democratic society in the interest of national security or public order or *for the protection of the rights and freedoms of others*" (our emphasis). This latter provision is not mentioned in Convention 87 of the ILO, which states, however, that workers' and employers' organisations should respect the law of the land. Despite this difference, the Covenant states that countries that have ratified the Covenant as well as Convention 87 of the ILO should observe both.

Second, the Covenant on Civil and Political Rights of 1966, ratified by 129 countries at the end of 1994, deals with individual rights such as the right to life, prohibition of torture, freedom of opinion and expression, as well as freedom of association, prohibition of forced labour and equality before the law. Several articles deal with workers' rights. Article 8 prohibits slavery, servitude and other forms of forced and compulsory labour, in terms that are very similar to those of Conventions 29 and 105 of the ILO. However, according to Article 8 of the Covenant, the term forced labour does not include prison labour "in consequence of a lawful order of a court". The ILO Conventions also exclude from the prohibition on forced labour any work or service undertaken by a convicted person so long as the work is carried out under the supervision of a public authority and the convict is not placed at the disposal of private individuals or companies. This is an important nuance. Article 22 of the Covenant provides for freedom of association in terms that are very similar to

Article 8 of the Covenant on Economic, Social and Cultural Rights. It is also mentioned that trade union rights should not interfere with the freedoms and rights of other individuals, including non-unionised workers. Again, the Covenant states that countries that have ratified the Covenant as well as Convention 87 of the ILO should observe both.

A recent UN Convention on the Rights of the Child (adopted in 1989) contains general provisions on the right of children to special protection and healthy development. It affirms the right to free primary education for all children. Also, Article 32 of the Convention establishes the principle of non-exploitation of child labour: countries recognise the right of the child to be protected against economic exploitation and not to be forced to carry out dangerous or unhealthy work, or work that would hamper educational prospects; countries should determine a minimum age for child labour and regulate child labour conditions, including working time; finally abuses should be sanctioned as appropriate. In contrast to Convention 138 of the ILO, this UN Convention does not specify a minimum age for employment. Instead, it protects against child labour exploitation and abuses. It is worth noting that, by the end of 1994, the UN Convention had been ratified by 168 countries, compared with 46 countries in the case of Convention 138 of the ILO[14].

In sum, the UN acts on human rights contain provisions on core labour standards. These provisions are similar to, but less detailed than, the ones contained in the corresponding ILO Conventions. The UN acts on human rights, though adopted fairly recently, have been generally ratified by more countries than the corresponding ILO Conventions: by the end of 1994, 123 countries had ratified the three UN acts containing workers' rights provisions, compared with 62 having ratified the five ILO Conventions in question (see box next page). This suggests that, independently of whether ratified UN instruments on workers' rights are applied in practice, the principles that they contain receive near-universal acceptance.

Observance of core labour standards in selected countries

This section describes the extent to which the ILO Conventions on the selected core standards are applied in 75 countries[15]. The latter include the OECD countries, Dynamic Non-Member Economies (Argentina, Brazil, Chile, Hong Kong, Korea, Malaysia, the Philippines, Singapore, Chinese Taipei and Thailand), as well as three populous countries with considerable trade potential (China, India, Indonesia) and a range of poor countries throughout the world for which information could be collected. Taken together, these countries account for almost all of world trade. Table 1 presents basic economic indicators for these countries. Per capita GDP levels (in 1990) ranged from US$98 in Tanzania to above US$33 000 in Switzerland. As expected, per capita GDP is on average highest in the OECD area. However, in a large number of non-OECD countries, per capita GDP is higher than in Mexico and Turkey, the two lowest-income OECD economies. For example, Hong Kong and Singapore come close to the OECD average, while Korea and Chinese Taipei have similar levels of per capita GDP to Portugal and Greece, countries at the bottom end of the OECD league table.

Ratification of several Conventions of the ILO and UN

	Total	OECD Countries
ILO Convention 87 (freedom of association)	113	23
ILO Convention 98 (right to organise and collective bargaining)	125	20
ILO Convention 111 (non-discrimination in employment)	119	20
ILO Convention 29 (forced labour)	137	22
ILO Convention 105 (abolition of forced labour)	115	24
Number of countries that have ratified all above ILO Conventions	*65*	*15*
UN Covenant on Economic, Social and Cultural Rights	131	23
UN Covenant on Civil and Political Rights	129	23
UN Convention on the Rights of the Child	168	21
Number of countries that have ratified all above UN acts	*123*	*20*

Note: Situation at October 1995 for ILO Conventions, at the end of 1994 for UN acts.
Sources: ILO and UN.

Table 2 provides information on ratifications of Conventions that fall within the province of core labour standards. There are wide cross-country differences in the number of these Conventions that have been ratified in this area. Almost half of the selected countries (and 60 per cent of OECD countries) have ratified them all. At the other extreme, Botswana, China, Korea, South Africa and Zimbabwe have not ratified any of the five Conventions, while the United States has ratified only one.

Freedom to form unions and the right to strike

Tables 3 and 4 give an overview of the main restrictions to the principle of freedom of association, as established in Convention 87. In virtually all OECD countries, legislation and practice appear to be consistent with the principle of freedom of association. In most of the selected non-OECD countries, freedom of association is subject to some restrictions.

As can be seen from Table 3, there are two main avenues through which the authorities can deny the establishment and functioning of independent unions. First, there can be direct or indirect political interference in union activities. For instance, in Jordan, Kenya, Singapore and Chinese Taipei, the ruling party maintains close links with the main union federation. Political control appears to be very strict in China, Egypt, Iran, Kuwait, Syria, Tanzania and, to a lesser extent, Indonesia. In these countries, there is *de facto* a single union structure. Second, the right to form unions may be restricted through the imposition of discretionary registration and recognition requirements. Thus, the requirement that only one union may be registered in each enterprise or occupational category is imposed in several of the Latin American and Asian countries under study (see Table 3). Also, in certain countries (notably Malaysia), the authorities can deny union recognition to a workers' organisation whose objectives are judged to run counter to government policies[16]. Finally, special restrictions apply in export-processing zones in Bangladesh, Mauritius, Pakistan and Panama.

The right to strike, a crucial dimension of the principle of freedom of association, is not only complex, but it also leads to numerous controversies, as attested by the complaints examined by the ILO. Table 4 describes the main impediments to the right to strike. It shows that in many countries, legislation and government regulations seriously hamper this right. Restrictions pertaining to essential services are not indicated in the table, except in those cases where the definition of essential services can lead to abuses.

The main findings from Table 4 are the following. First, the right to strike is recognised in all countries with the sole exception of China, where there is a general prohibition of strikes. Strikes are also practically prohibited in Egypt, Iran and Syria and rendered very difficult in Pakistan and Tanzania. Second, sectoral restrictions apply in Korea (defence sector), the Philippines (so-called the strategic industries), Thailand (state enterprises), Turkey (export-processing zones) and in broadly defined essential services in Bangladesh, Colombia, Jamaica, South Africa and Zimbabwe. Third, in several countries -- the Bahamas, Guatemala, Indonesia, Kenya, Korea, Malaysia, Mauritius, Pakistan,

Peru, the Philippines, South Africa, Chinese Taipei, Turkey, Zambia and Zimbabwe -- strikes are authorised only if prior notification is given and/or a long "cooling-off" period, during which the strike is illegal, is observed. Fourth, arbitration by administrative authorities can be made compulsory in many non-OECD countries. Finally, in the United Kingdom, the ILO has raised the question of whether protection against dismissal of strikers is adequate. In Hong Kong and Jamaica, such protection is weak, according to the ILO.

Protection of union members and collective bargaining rights

In the majority of non-OECD countries, legal protection against acts of anti-union discrimination is not adequately enforced (Table 5). Lack of appropriate judicial structures as well as the authorities' unwillingness to sanction employers are factors explaining the weakness of enforcement. In several countries, legislation itself does not provide adequate protection. For instance, in Hong Kong reinstatement in the enterprise is not required by law. By contrast, protection is more satisfactory on average in the OECD area. ILO experts have raised questions about the adequacy of application procedures in the United Kingdom, but these have now been answered[17].

In several countries, legal provisions limit the right to bargain collectively. Collective bargaining is severely restricted in Egypt, Swaziland and Syria, as well as in Malaysia (so-called pioneer industries), Singapore (new firms), China and Thailand (state enterprises). Collective bargaining is inhibited by legal or practical obstacles in export-processing zones in Bangladesh, Honduras, Jamaica, Panama and Sri Lanka. Even though collective bargaining may be allowed, its scope is sometimes limited to certain issues. For example, promotions and the termination of contracts are excluded from the scope of collective bargaining in Brazil and Singapore. Third-party intervention in collective bargaining is prohibited in Korea.

In order to make a more exhaustive assessment of the situation regarding freedom-of-association rights across selected countries, the evolution of these rights over the past decade or so has been examined. It appears that in none of the selected countries did freedom-of-association rights worsen significantly. Instead, in 17 countries they improved markedly (Table 6). More generally, there seems to be a trend towards better enforcement of these rights, especially in countries where legislation is very restrictive.

Freedom of association: an assessment

Based on the above information, it is now possible to arrange countries in different groups, based on Secretariat judgement concerning the extent to which they comply with freedom of association. In group 1, comprising all OECD countries (except Mexico and Turkey), as well as the Bahamas, Barbados, Israel, Malta and Surinam, freedom of association is by and large guaranteed in law and practice. At the other extreme are group 4 countries, where freedom of association is practically non-existent (China, Egypt, Indonesia, Iran, Kuwait, Syria and Tanzania). In countries of group 2 (Argentina, Brazil, Chile, Ecuador, Ethiopia, Fiji, Hong Kong, India, Jamaica, Mexico, Niger, Papua New Guinea, Peru, South Africa, Venezuela and Zambia) some restrictions exist, but it is possible to establish independent workers' organisations and union confederations. In the remaining countries (group 3), restrictions on freedom of association are significant: the existence of stringent registration requirements, political interference or acts of anti-union discrimination make it very difficult to form independent workers' organisations or union confederations.

Given these four country groupings, Chart 1 shows that there is some association between the level of economic development, proxied by GDP per capita, on the one hand, and the degree of observance of freedom of association on the other. Most developed countries enjoy better-than-average standards, and conversely the poorest countries do not generally comply with standards. However, there are major departures from this pattern.

Chart 1
Freedom of association and level of economic development

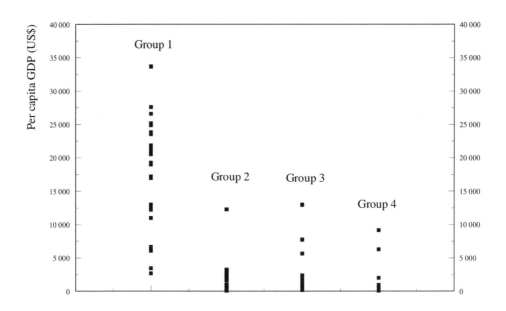

Source: OECD.

Child labour

According to Ashagrie (1993), in 1990 nearly 80 million children under age 15 were officially reported to be working around the world. This figure is likely to under-estimate considerably the real situation, as suggested by the results of a recent study by UNESCO which show that, in developing countries, 20 per cent of school-age children are working[18]. Also, an ILO study on the incidence of child labour in Ghana, India, Indonesia and Senegal shows that 25 per cent of children aged under 14 are working. Some 95 per cent of working children live in developing countries, with about half of them in Asia. However, child labour is not restricted to developing countries and has not been fully eliminated in OECD countries. The main characteristics of child labour are as follows:

- By far the greater part of the work done by children is classified by the ILO as unpaid assistance to the family (on average, 80 per cent of child labour).

- Most child labour in developing countries is rural and unpaid. In rural areas, an important distinction needs to be drawn between children working on the family plot and those employed as labourers on plantations and estates. Children working on the family farm are usually considered to be better protected by traditional systems, even when the family lives near subsistence, but in some cases, child work in this traditional context can also become highly exploitative. Such exploitation may take the form of excessively heavy loads, physically demanding tasks, long hours and work-related hazards.

- Some large estates employ entire families, and in many developing countries, there is no legal protection for agricultural employees. To keep wages low, large estates may employ children as well as their parents and other family members.

- In urban areas, most children work in the informal sector, in family business and small shops, which escape statistics and regulations. Hence, work in this sector can be very similar to the rural subsistence economy. At the same time, child labour can also operate in the context of a more open and formal economy, as in the case of many firms which rely upon networks of small subcontractors and, occasionally, family workshops to serve local, national or even international markets.

- Millions of children, particularly girls, also work as domestic servants, but figures are not available, especially since this is often not counted as work in any official estimate. Many children also work under conditions of bonded labour or are engaged in marginal and illegal activities, which are the most difficult to trace and regulate. They include the drug trade, pornography and prostitution, and the many activities performed by street children.

- Children also work in the formal sector, including export-processing zones where implementation of national regulations may be more lax. Children are mainly found in the textile, garment, shoe and carpet industries. According to the ILO, there are relatively few children working in export-related sectors and, among these sectors, the incidence of child labour is probably higher in agricultural activities than in manufacturing industries. A study of Norwegian imports finds that the incidence of child labour is the highest for agricultural and fishing products and hand-made goods (Grimsrud and Melchior, 1996). According to the study, products made with child labour account for less than 1 per cent of Norwegian imports in value terms.

– There is strong evidence of child labour exploitation in a few export-oriented industries of some countries[19].

The causes of child labour are complex. The recent ILO study on this issue mentions poverty as the main factor. Work is a matter of survival for children of poor families. It is estimated that the cost of sending a child to primary school may exceed a third of the money income of poor families, and these families often have more than one child of school age. Only 68 per cent of children complete primary education in the world as a whole. It is also argued that one of the reasons for child labour is the fact that children are paid less than adults for the same kind of job. However, according to an ILO analysis of the price of carpets and bangles, the labour-cost savings realised through the employment of children are small.

In the majority of OECD countries, legal provisions regarding child labour appear to be broadly in compliance with Convention 138, but there are some exceptions. First, in Australia and New Zealand, there is no specific legislation setting a minimum employment age. In these two countries, however, school attendance is compulsory until a certain age. Second, in Mexico as well as certain Canadian provinces, the legal minimum age for employment is less than that provided for by the Convention. In the United Kingdom, the legal minimum age for light work is 13, but education is compulsory until age 16.

Outside the OECD area, only in Chile, China, the Philippines and Chinese Taipei do legal provisions comply fully with Convention 138. However, in most countries legal requirements come close to these provisions. The minimum age for employment in Morocco and Thailand is as low as 12.

In sum, it is unlikely that the gaps in legal provisions are the main factor behind child labour. Instead, it is the lack of enforcement of the existing provisions (however low) which poses the major problem. Enforcement is typically weak in the informal sector. In several countries, the under-provision of schools makes enforcement of child labour laws problematic. This is especially the case in rural areas of many developing countries. More generally, in the face of very low living standards, child labour contributes to family income. However, there are cases where the authorities, either at the national level (Korea, Singapore and Chinese Taipei) or at the local level (Kerala state in

India), have given high priority to school enrolment and this has resulted in a drop in the levels of child labour.

Forced labour

A relatively large number of the observations of the ILO concerning Conventions 29 and 105 on prohibition of forced labour, and the corresponding requests for legislative reform, relate to OECD countries. This is all the more surprising since Conventions 29 and 105 have been ratified by the majority of ILO member countries.

In fact, most of the ILO observations on OECD countries relate to certain legal provisions of relatively minor importance. For example, according to the ILO, in Austria, France, Germany and the United Kingdom, work done by certain prisoners is performed in workshops managed by private enterprises and individuals. The ILO has repeatedly stressed that this practice is inconsistent with the provisions of Convention 29, except with the formal consent of prisoners and when guarantees and safeguards with regard to wages and social security are given so that the labour relationship can be regarded as a free one. It has therefore asked the authorities to abolish this practice, or else give the necessary guarantees to bring it into conformity with the Convention.

It can be safely asserted that, in general, forced labour is of negligible importance in the OECD area. However, in several countries outside the OECD area, forced labour appears to be a prominent problem. In China, most prisoners are systematically required to work without pay. In India and Pakistan, bonded labour is widespread. Accordingly, many families and children are forced to work almost as slaves for certain individuals in order to pay off their debts. In Brazil, according to ILO experts, thousands of workers in rural sectors and mining are subject to forced-labour conditions. It is dangerous for these workers to escape.

Non-discrimination

As with the two Conventions on forced labour, many ILO observations concerning Convention 111 refer to OECD countries (for example, in 1995, of the 32 observations made by the Committee of Experts on Convention 111, six concerned OECD countries). There is, however, a substantial difference between the issues raised by the ILO concerning OECD and non-OECD countries. Whenever OECD countries are concerned, elimination of sex discrimination in employment seems to be the major problem. Sex discrimination often takes the form of practical obstacles experienced by women in advancing to higher positions. Observations by the ILO concerning Turkey relate to the positions of public servants whose employment had been affected during the period of martial law.

In non-OECD countries, additional issues on discrimination have been detected by the ILO. For example, in Brazil the ILO has denounced cases where employers demand certificates attesting to the sterilisation of women who seek employment or wish to keep their jobs. Discrimination on the basis of social origin has been subjected to complaints in India.

Conclusions

It is difficult to make an overall assessment of the degree of enforcement of core labour standards across countries. Information on this issue is sparse and incomplete. The lack of reliable indicators on enforcement is especially acute regarding child labour, forced labour and non-discrimination in employment. Based on ILO reports and other sources, however, it is possible to make a tentative assessment of freedom-of-association rights in selected countries. It emerges that there are wide cross-country differences in the degree of enforcement of freedom-of-association rights.

Table 1. Basic economic indicators

	Per capita GDP (US$) (1990)	Growth in real per capita GDP (1980-90)	Exports (US$ billion) (1990)
Non-OECD			
Argentina	3 261	-1.7	12.3
Bahamas	12 235	n.a.	2.8
Bangladesh	200	1.7	1.6
Barbados	6 655	1.9	0.2
Bolivia	624	-2.9	0.9
Botswana	2 274	6.5	1.3
Brazil	3 178	0.6	31.4
Chile	2 110	1.5	8.6
China	326	8.2	62.1
Colombia	1 247	1.6	6.7
Ecuador	1 008	-0.7	2.7
Egypt	971	2.4	2.6
Ethiopa	121	-0.7	0.3
Fiji	1 691	0.0	0.4
Guatemala	831	-2.1	1.2
Haiti	380	-2.5	0.1
Honduras	594	-0.7	0.8
Hong Kong	12 278	5.7	82.2
India	358	3.6	17.7
Indonesia	580	2.5	25.7
Iran	9 185	-1.5	15.3
Israel	10 991	1.6	11.6

49

Table 1. Basic economic indicators *(cont.)*

	Per capita GDP *(US$)* *(1990)*	*Growth in real* *per capita GDP* *(1980-90)*	*Exports* *(US$ billion)* *(1990)*
Jamaica	1 640	0.3	1.1
Jordan	984	-0.8	1.0
Kenya	371	0.7	1.0
Korea	5 626	8.3	65.0
Kuwait	6 295	-7.0	8.0
Malaysia	2 368	2.5	29.4
Malta	6 484	2.7	1.1
Mauritius	2 374	5.2	1.2
Morocco	1 006	1.5	4.2
Niger	326	-4.4	0.3
Pakistan	336	2.8	5.5
Panama	2 047	-1.8	0.3
Papua New Guinea	827	-0.4	1.1
Peru	1 691	-2.5	3.2
Philippines	706	-1.6	8.2
Singapore	12 963	5.2	52.7
South Africa	2 686	-1.2	16.3
Sri Lanka	466	0.7	1.9
Surinam	3 419	-4.3	0.5
Swaziland	938	0.0	0.6
Syria	2 009	-1.9	4.0
Chinese Taipei	7 760	6.9	67.2
Tanzania	98	-0.6	0.4

Table 1. Basic economic indicators *(cont.)*

	Per capita GDP *(US$)* *(1990)*	Growth in real per capita GDP *(1980-90)*	Exports *(US$ billion)* *(1990)*
Thailand	1 466	5.9	23.1
Uruguay	2 677	0.4	1.7
Venezuela	2 515	-1.4	17.5
Zambia	518	-2.8	0.9
Zimbabwe	610	0.0	1.7
OECD			
Australia	17 199	1.8	39.6
Austria	20 510	1.9	41.5
Belgium	19 294	1.9	118.3
Canada	21 273	2.3	127.4
Denmark	25 150	2.4	35.1
Finland	27 608	2.9	26.7
France	21 020	1.7	210.2
Germany	23 522	2.0	398.4
Greece	6 587	1.2	8.0
Ireland	12 278	3.0	23.8
Italy	18 986	2.2	169.3
Japan	23 802	3.3	286.9
Mexico	2 814	-1.4	26.5
Netherlands	18 975	1.4	131.8
New Zealand	12 970	0.8	9.1
Norway	24 895	2.5	34.0
Portugal	6 048	2.6	16.4

Table 1. Basic economic indicators *(cont.)*

	Per capita GDP (US$) (1990)	Growth in real per capita GDP (1980-90)	Exports (US$ billion) (1990)
Spain	12 609	2.7	55.6
Sweden	26 605	1.9	57.4
Switzerland	33 674	1.6	63.9
Turkey	1 939	3.0	12.9
United Kingdom	16 968	2.9	186.0
United States	21 861	1.9	393.6
World	4 221		3 416.6

Source: UNCTAD, *Handbook of International Trade and Development Statistics,* 1992.

Table 2. Ratification of key ILO Conventions
(Situation at 31 December 1994)

	Freedom of association (Conv. 87)	Right to organise and collective bargaining (Conv. 98)	Forced labour (Conv. 29)	Abolition of forced labour (Conv. 105)	Non-discrimination (Conv. 111)
Non-OECD					
Argentina	r	r	r	r	r
Bahamas		r	r	r	
Bangladesh	r	r	r	r	r
Barbados	r	r	r	r	r
Bolivia	r	r		r	r
Botswana					
Brazil		r	r	r	r
Chile			r		r
China					
Colombia	r	r	r	r	r
Ecuador	r	r	r	r	r
Egypt	r	r	r	r	r
Ethiopia	r	r			r
Fiji		r	r	r	
Guatemala	r	r	r	r	r
Haiti	r	r	r	r	r
Honduras	r	r	r	r	r
Hong Kong[a]					
India			r		r
Indonesia		r	r		
Iran			r	r	r
Israel	r	r	r	r	r
Jamaica	r	r	r	r	r

Table 2. Ratification of key ILO Conventions *(cont.)*
(Situation at 31 December 1994)

	Freedom of association *(Conv. 87)*	Right to organise and collective bargaining *(Conv. 98)*	Forced labour *(Conv. 29)*	Abolition of forced labour *(Conv. 105)*	Non-discrimina-tion *(Conv .111)*
Jordan		r	r	r	r
Kenya		r	r	r	
Korea					
Kuwait	r		r	r	r
Malaysia[b]		r	r		
Malta	r	r	r	r	r
Mauritius		r	r	r	
Morocco		r	r	r	r
Niger	r	r	r	r	r
Pakistan	r	r	r	r	r
Panama	r	r	r	r	r
Papua New Guinea		r	r	r	
Peru	r	r	r	r	r
Philippines	r	r		r	r
Singapore		r	r	r	
South Africa					
Sri Lanka		r	r		
Surinam	r		r	r	
Swaziland	r	r	r	r	r
Syria	r	r	r	r	r
Tanzania		r	r	r	
Thailand			r	r	
Uruguay	r	r		r	r
Venezuela	r	r	r	r	r
Zambia			r	r	r
Zimbabwe					

Table 2. Ratification of key ILO Conventions *(cont.)*
(Situation at 31 December 1994)

	Freedom of association (Conv. 87)	*Right to organise and collective bargaining (Conv. 98)*	*Forced labour (Conv. 29)*	*Abolition of forced labour (Conv. 105)*	*Non-discrimina-tion (Conv. 111)*
OECD					
Australia	r	r	r	r	r
Austria	r	r	r	r	r
Belgium	r	r	r	r	r
Canada	r			r	r
Denmark	r	r	r	r	r
Finland	r	r	r	r	r
France	r	r	r	r	r
Germany	r	r	r	r	r
Greece	r	r	r	r	r
Iceland	r	r	r	r	r
Ireland	r	r	r	r	
Italy	r	r	r	r	r
Japan	r	r	r		
Luxembourg	r	r	r	r	
Mexico	r		r	r	r
Netherlands	r	r	r	r	r
New Zealand			r	r	r
Norway	r	r	r	r	r
Portugal	r	r	r	r	r
Spain	r	r	r	r	r
Sweden	r	r	r	r	r
Switzerland	r		r	r	r

Table 2. Ratification of key ILO Conventions *(cont.)*
(Situation at 31 December 1994)

	Freedom of association (Conv. 87)	Right to organise and collective bargaining (Conv. 98)	Forced labour (Conv. 29)	Abolition of forced labour (Conv. 105)	Non-discrimina-tion (Conv. 111)
Turkey	r	r		r	r
United Kingdom	r	r	r	r	
United States				r	

a) The United Kingdom has made declarations of application of Conventions in Hong Kong. In the case of Convention 87, the declaration contains certain reservations.
b) Malaysia has denounced Convention 105.

Source: ILO, *Listes des ratifications par convention et par pays*, Rapport III (Partie 5), Conférence du Travail, 1995.

Table 3. Restrictions on the right to establish free unions

Non-OECD	
Argentina	Only one organisation can be granted representative status at the enterprise level. Bargaining rights and fiscal privileges are accorded only to representative organisations.
Bahamas	Requirements consistent with ILO Conventions.
Bangladesh	Professional and industry unions are prohibited in export-processing zones.
Barbados	Requirements consistent with ILO Conventions.
Bolivia	Only one union can be granted legal status at the enterprise level. Authorities can de-register unions, but rarely do so.
Botswana	Union officials must work full-time in the industry they represent.
Brazil	According to the system of *unicidade*, no more than one union for the same professional category is allowed in each geographical district. In practice, there is increasing union pluralism.
Chile	The minimum number of workers required by law to establish an enterprise union, as well as the percentage it must represent in relation to the total of workers employed in the enterprise, make difficult the establishment in an enterprise of more than one union.
China	There is only one officially recognised national union. The establishment of a union at the enterprise or professional level must be submitted for approval to the single existing union, which always denies it. Non-recognised unions are illegal; leaders of such unions have often been arrested.
Colombia	According to ILO, government officials can attend union meetings.
Ecuador	According to ILO, the minimum number of workers required by law to establish an enterprise union is too high, making it difficult to establish unions in small enterprises.
Egypt	There is only one legally recognised union federation, which is closely related to the ruling party. Only one union per workplace is permitted. Authorities intervene in the election of union officers.
Ethiopia	In 1993, the single union system, in vigour since 1975, was repealed.
Fiji	Until 1992, the only union federation was closely associated with the ruling party.
Guatemala	According to ILO (Committee on Freedom of Association, case 1734), union rights are hampered by interference of employers' associations in union activities in the food and beverages sector. Registration procedures are also long and bureaucratic.
Haiti	Union rights have often been severely repressed.
Honduras	Employers' associations reportedly intefere in the functioning of unions (see CFA, case 1568). Only one union per workplace is permitted.

Table 3. Restrictions on the right to establish free unions *(cont.)*

Hong Kong	The right to form unions is recognised.
India	Freedom of association is guaranteed. Enforcement is difficult in a few states, as registration of certain organisations is hampered by bureaucratic hurdles.
Indonesia	Only recognised unions can bargain collectively and represent workers before the courts. To be recognised, a union must have offices in no less than five provinces, branch offices in no less than 27 districts. Plant-level units must exceed 100 in number. A union representing an industry located in a small geographical area must claim at least 10 000 members for it to be registered. Finally, labour authorities deny recognition to organisations that include lawyers, human rights activists or other so-called non-workers. There is a *de facto* union monopoly, as only one federation has been recognised, while new unions cannot obtain recognition unless they are affiliated to the single federation. The ruling party heavily interferes in the functioning of the single union federation. Most union leaders belong to the party.
Iran	There is only one authorised labour organisation, which is close to the political regime.
Israel	Union rights are adequately protected. Palestinian workers cannot create a union whose aim would be to represent solely their interests but can affiliate freely to any other type of union.
Jamaica	Requirements consistent with ILO Conventions.
Jordan	The only existing union federation is heavily dependent on government financing.
Kenya	There is only one main union federation, which is subject to government interference. The government can arbitrarily de-register a union.
Korea	The law permits only one union in each company. There are no complaints, however, that this requirement restricts freedom of association. Severe restrictions on the creation of federations and national confederations exist. Only one national confederation has been officially recognised so far.
Kuwait	There is only one union federation. Foreigners can only join a union after five years of residence, subject to presentation of a certificate of good conduct, and can neither vote nor be elected. Unions cannot engage in any political or religious activity.
Malaysia	Authorities can deny legal existence to a union if it might be used "for unlawful purposes or other reasons". Appeal to an independent court is not possible in case of dissolution of a union. A union can only represent workers for a particular industry or profession, as defined by the Register, so impeding the creation of nation-wide unions. As a matter of policy, the Register includes the electronics industry in the metal sector for the purposes of forming a union. This prevents the formation of a union in the electronics industry.

Table 3. Restrictions on the right to establish free unions *(cont.)*

Malta	Requirements consistent with ILO Conventions.
Mauritius	Authorities can arbitrarily de-register a union, and often do so in export-processing zones.
Morocco	Public authorities can limit union action because of political activity.
Niger	There is only one union federation, but others can be legally established. In practice the union federation is independent from political power. There are restrictions on the right to join unions for foreign workers.
Pakistan	Authorities can arbitrarily refuse registration of a union. Unions are banned in export-processing zones. The Essential Services Act restricts trade union activity in certain firms.
Panama	The minimum number of workers required by law to form a union is high. Authorities can inspect union activities. In export-processing zones there are practically no unions.
Papua New Guinea	Requirements consistent with ILO Conventions.
Peru	The minimum number of workers required by law to form a union is high (100 workers).
Philippines	For a union to be registered, its members must represent no less than a fifth of the workers of a bargaining unit. The law requires at least ten first-level unions to establish a federation.
Singapore	Union registration is hampered by certain restrictions. Authorities have discretionary power to refuse registration. Nearly all union members belong to the National Trade Union, but workers seem to be satisfied with this situation, as in practice no other organisation has applied for registration status.
South Africa	Requirements consistent with ILO Conventions.
Sri Lanka	Unions must submit reports to labour authorities, otherwise they are de-registered.
Surinam	Requirements consistent with ILO Conventions.
Swaziland	According to the ILO, authorities interfere in unions' activities.
Syria	There is only one union federation, which is closely linked to the ruling party.
Chinese Taipei	Authorities have discretionary power to certify a union. A non-certified union is disadvantaged in various ways (notably it cannot bargain collectively).
Tanzania	There is only one union federation, which is closely linked to the ruling party.
Thailand	Freedom of association is warranted in the private sector. In 1991, the government dissolved state-enterprise unions. In these enterprises, the government can limit the number of unions, dissolve them and prevent affiliation with private-sector unions. Most big companies belong to the state.

Table 3. Restrictions on the right to establish free unions *(cont.)*

Uruguay	Requirements consistent with ILO Conventions.
Venezuela	The minimum number of workers required by law to form a union is high (100 workers). According to the ILO, the list of attributions for workers' organisations is too detailed. Foreign workers are eligible as union officers after ten years of residence.
Zambia	Only one union per workplace is allowed.
Zimbabwe	Authorities can arbitrarily refuse registration and de-register existing unions.
OECD	
Australia	Requirements consistent with ILO Conventions.
Austria	Requirements consistent with ILO Conventions.
Belgium	Requirements consistent with ILO Conventions.
Canada	Requirements consistent with ILO Conventions.
Denmark	The law is in agreement with ILO Conventions. The law does not prohibit union security clauses.
Finland	Requirements consistent with ILO Conventions.
France	Requirements consistent with ILO Conventions.
Germany	Requirements consistent with ILO Conventions.
Greece	Requirements consistent with ILO Conventions.
Iceland	Requirements consistent with ILO Conventions.
Ireland	Requirements consistent with ILO Conventions.
Italy	Requirements consistent with ILO Conventions.
Japan	Requirements consistent with ILO Conventions.
Mexico	There are no legal impediments to the formation of a union and the Mexican authorities state that registration is denied only when workers' organisations do not fulfil the administrative and procedural requirements established in the law. However, registration requirements are reportedly used to deny recognition to certain workers' organisations (US NAO, submission 3, 1995). Most unions are affiliated to the Labour Congress (US Department of State, 1994). Only one union can be formed in each government agency or state enterprise (ILO, Report of the Committee of Experts, 1995).
Netherlands	Requirements consistent with ILO Conventions.
New Zealand	Requirements consistent with ILO Conventions.
Norway	Requirements consistent with ILO Conventions.
Portugal	Requirements consistent with ILO Conventions.

Table 3. Restrictions on the right to establish free unions *(cont.)*

Spain	Requirements consistent with ILO Conventions.
Sweden	Requirements consistent with ILO Conventions.
Switzerland	Requirements consistent with ILO Conventions.
Turkey	In the present Constitution, several limitations to the right of free association remain (ILO, 1994b). Government interferes in the functioning of unions, notably through the requirement that a government representative should attend unions' conventions [US Department of State, 1994).
United Kingdom	Requirements consistent with ILO Conventions.
United States	Requirements consistent with ILO Conventions.

Sources: ILO, various sources; US Department of State (1994); International Confederation of Free Trade Unions, *Annual Survey of Violations of Trade Union Rights*, various issues; and Blanpain (1991).

Table 4. Restrictions on the right to strike

Non-OECD	
Argentina	Organisations other than the one with representative status do not have the right to call a strike or intervene in disputes.
Bahamas	Prior administrative authorisation is needed for a strike to be legal.
Bangladesh	Strikes are banned in sectors believed to to be essential by the authorities.
Barbados	No noticeable restrictions.
Bolivia	General strikes and solidarity strikes are illegal.
Botswana	The right to strike is restricted by the imposition of compulsory arbitration.
Brazil	Arbitration is compulsory in certain sectors.
Chile	No noticeable restrictions.
China	The right to strike is not recognised.
Colombia	The right to strike is restricted by compulsory arbitration and the broad definition of essential services (where strikes are prohibited).
Ecuador	Compulsory arbitration is possible.
Egypt	Strikes are practically illegal.
Ethiopia	Strikes are restricted by compulsory arbitration and lengthy notice periods.
Fiji	Strikes are subject to serious limitations.
Guatemala	Cumbersome legal procedures make strikes difficult.
Haiti	The duration of strikes is limited.
Honduras	Strikes are subject to certain restrictions.
Hong Kong	Employment contracts can contain a clause whereby absences from work can lead to summary dismissal. Workers on strike can be dismissed under such a clause. Industrial actions are subject to legal intervention on criminal grounds, when action is believed to intimidate persons. These acts are punishable as criminal offences with fines or even imprisonment.
India	Strikes are legally protected. Some restrictions apply in several states: authorities can prohibit strikes in essential services, defined in a relatively wide sense; mediation and arbitration procedures can be made mandatory in "essential industries".
Indonesia	Mediation and prior notification to labour authorities is required for a strike to be declared legal. Because of difficulties in complying with these requirements, most strikes are illegal. Leaders of illegal strikes are often arrested.
Iran	Strikes are strictly controlled.
Israel	No noticeable restrictions.

Table 4. Restrictions on the right to strike *(cont.)*

Jamaica	Employers are allowed to dismiss strikers. Essential services, where strikes are subject to severe limitations, are broadly defined.
Jordan	Authorities can declare a strike illegal by asking for compulsory arbitration.
Kenya	Strikes are subject to lengthy notice periods and can be made illegal by the imposition of compulsory arbitration.
Korea	The law prohibits third-party intervention in labour disputes. In practice, independent unions (non-recognised) are often denied the right to intervene in disputes. In cases of non-respect, which occur frequently, strikers are laid off and union leaders arrested. The right to strike is subject to prior notification requirements and the imposition of ten-day "cooling-off" periods. In defence industries, the right to strike is prohibited.
Malaysia	The right to strike is severely restricted by the practice of compulsory arbitration. For a strike to be legal, prior notification that proves the existence of a dispute must be given, and labour authorities can bring the dispute to the court. In the latter case, strikes cannot take place (legally) before the dispute is settled by the court. There are restrictions in "essential services", which include a comprehensive range of sectors. Strikes that pursue political ends or are called in sympathy with other striking workers are illegal.
Malta	Compulsory arbitration is possible.
Mauritius	The right to strike is severely restricted by the imposition of long cooling-off periods. Compulsory arbitration is possible.
Morocco	Strikes based on extra-professional motives are illegal. Offence to the freedom to work can be condemned by employers or authorities. Most strikes do not comply with conciliation procedures (which are very long), causing mass lay-offs.
Niger	Conciliation is mandatory before strikes.
Pakistan	A strike believed to be against national interests can be prohibited and long cooling-off periods imposed.
Panama	No noticeable restrictions.
Papua New Guinea	No noticeable restrictions.
Peru	The government can suspend strikes.
Philippines	For a strike to be legal, a majority of workers have to approve it, prior notice must be given and a "cooling-off" period observed. Labour authorities can prohibit strikes in "strategic industries" (defined in a wide sense). Illegal strikes give rise to fines and legal prosecution.
Singapore	Most disputes are settled through consultation with labour authorities. Strikes, though permitted by the law, are unusual.
South Africa	A limit is imposed to the duration of strikes. Essential services are broadly defined.
Sri Lanka	Strikes in essential services, broadly defined, are illegal.
Surinam	No noticeable restrictions.

Table 4. Restrictions on the right to strike *(cont.)*

Swaziland	Strikes are subject to long mediation procedures.
Syria	There is no effective legal protection against anti-strike behaviour.
Chinese Taipei	To be legal, strikes have to be approved by a majority of unionised workers. Authorities may impose mediation or arbitration procedures, during which a strike is illegal.
Tanzania	Strikes are allowed only after complicated mediation and conciliation procedures.
Thailand	Authorities can prohibit a strike in the private sector. In state enterprises the right to strike is not legally recognised.
Uruguay	No noticeable restrictions.
Venezuela	No noticeable restrictions.
Zambia	Strikes are subject to long cooling-off and conciliation periods.
Zimbabwe	Strikes are subject to long cooling-off periods, and are forbidden in essential services, which are broadly defined.
OECD	
Australia	No noticeable restrictions.
Austria	No noticeable restrictions.
Belgium	No noticeable restrictions.
Canada	No noticeable restrictions
Denmark	No noticeable restrictions
Finland	No noticeable restrictions.
France	No noticeable restrictions.
Germany	No noticeable restrictions.
Greece	No noticeable restrictions.
Iceland	No noticeable restrictions.
Ireland	No noticeable restrictions.
Italy	No noticeable restrictions.
Japan	No noticeable restrictions.
Mexico	Conciliation by authorities is compulsory. Authorities consider this requirement guarantees the interests of workers. For a strike to be legal, certain conditions must be met. In particular, it must aim at harmonizing the rights of labour and capital, it must be approved by a majority of workers and written notice must be given to the employer and labour authorities.
Netherlands	No noticeable restrictions.

Table 4. Restrictions on the right to strike *(cont.)*

New Zealand	Strikes are legal only in the context of the negotiation of a collective employment contract or safety and health issues and when they are not related to freedom of association, personal grievances and other disputes defined as disputes of rights (ILO, CFA, case 1678).
Norway	Under certain circumstances, the government can invoke compulsory arbitration in labour disputes (ILO, CFA, case 1763 and cases therein).
Portugal	No noticeable restrictions.
Spain	No noticeable restrictions.
Sweden	No noticeable restrictions.
Switzerland	No noticeable restrictions.
Turkey	In mining, oil, defence and some other public services, workers do not have the right to strike. For a strike to be legal, prior collective bargaining and mediation is required. Authorities may suspend a strike for a 60-day period and ask for compulsory arbitration (ILO, Report of the Committee of Experts, 1994). Workers in export-processing zones do not have the right to strike for the first ten years of operation. During this period, disputes are settled by compulsory arbitration (US Department of State, 1994).
United Kingdom	Employers are allowed to dismiss strikers and selectively re-hire them after a period of three months (ILO, CFA, case 1540).
United States	During strikes, employers can hire workers in replacement of strikers (ILO, CFA, case 1543).

Source: see Table 3.

Table 5. Protection of union members and collective bargaining rights

Non-OECD	
Argentina	Protection is adequate.
Bahamas	Protection is adequate.
Bangladesh	Acts of anti-union discrimination are frequent and not adequately sanctioned. There is practically no collective bargaining in export-processing zones and outside the organised sectors.
Barbados	Protection is adequate.
Bolivia	Acts of anti-union discrimination are prohibited, but protection against such acts is inadequate owing to slow court proceedings.
Botswana	Protection is adequate.
Brazil	Anti-union legislation is not appropriately enforced. Unions estimate that cases of discrimination are seldom solved on time. Many of them take more than five years. Certain issues are excluded from collective bargaining.
Chile	Protection is adequate.
China	Collective bargaining is not possible in state-owned enterprises.
Colombia	There are ILO reports of grave acts of anti-union discrimination (see CFA, case 1686).
Ecuador	Protection is adequate.
Egypt	There is practically no collective bargaining, as government sets wages and working conditions by decree.
Ethiopia	Protection is adequate.
Fiji	Since 1992, free collective bargaining is permitted.
Guatemala	Employment of union officers is not adequately protected.
Haiti	Acts of anti-union discrimination have been numerous. There is virtually no collective bargaining.
Honduras	Acts of anti-union discrimination are not adequately sanctioned. Blacklisting practices are reported in export-processing zones.
Hong Kong	A fine may be imposed in case a worker is prevented from joining a union, but reinstatement in the enterprise is not required by the law. However, the workers' right to join unions is legally established.
India	Protection is adequate.
Indonesia	There is little effective protection against acts of anti-union discrimination.
Iran	Little information is available on the right to organise and collective bargaining.

Table 5. Protection of union members and collective bargaining rights *(cont.)*

Israel	Protection is adequate.
Jamaica	Though not prohibited, there are no unions in export-processing zones. Possible anti-union practices in these zones are facilitated by the lack of inspections.
Jordan	Protection against acts of anti-union discrimination exists but is not adequately enforced.
Kenya	Protection against acts of anti-union discrimination is reported to be inadequate.
Korea	Workers of unregistered federations and confederations do not have the right to intervene in company-level union activities, including collective bargaining (prohibition of third-party intervention). Certain members of unregistered unions have been subject to legal prosecution as a result of third-party intervention.
Kuwait	The situation is difficult to assess.
Malaysia	Anti-union discrimination is prohibited by law. But enforcement is weak due to long delays in court proceedings. Until 1993, collective bargaining rights were restricted in so-called pioneer industries.
Malta	Protection is adequate.
Mauritius	The government heavily interferes in collective bargaining.
Morocco	The ILO has registered complaints that certain union leaders have been arrested. Protection against acts of anti-union discrimination is inadequate. Authorities may extend to other employers and workers a collective agreement to whom it did not originally apply. The initiative of extension often comes from the Minister of Labour and not from unions.
Niger	Protection is adequate.
Pakistan	Acts of anti-union discrimination are not adequately sanctioned (see ILO, CFA, cases 1771 and 1726).
Panama	Employment security of union officers is not adequate, especially in export-processing zones.
Papua New Guinea	Authorities can arbitrarily cancel a collective agreement.
Peru	There are some limitations to collective bargaining.
Philippines	Anti-union practices exist despite the fact that protective legislation is in place.
Singapore	Annual wage supplements in new enterprises are limited. Promotion, dismissals, transfers and work organisation matters are excluded from the scope of collective bargaining. The court has discretionary powers to reject a collective agreement established in a new enterprise.
South Africa	Acts of anti-union discrimination are inadequately penalised in certain parts of the country.

Table 5. Protection of union members and collective bargaining rights *(cont.)*

Sri Lanka	Workers in export-processing zones cannot be represented by national unions.
Surinam	Protection is adequate.
Swaziland	The court may deny registration of a collective bargaining agreement if it does not comply with government directives.
Syria	There is practically no collective bargaining.
Chinese Taipei	Complicated mediation/arbitration procedures make collective bargaining difficult in small firms.
Tanzania	Collective agreements must be approved by the judiciary.
Thailand	Collective bargaining is severely restricted in state enterprises.
Uruguay	Protection is adequate.
Venezuela	Acts of anti-union discrimination are not adequately sanctioned (ILO, CFA, case 1739).
Zambia	Protection is adequate.
Zimbabwe	The situation is difficult to assess.
OECD	
Australia	Protection is adequate.
Austria	Protection is adequate.
Belgium	Protection is adequate.
Canada	Protection against acts of anti-union discrimination is adequate. According to ILO, restrictions apply in the public sector for certain provinces.
Denmark	Protection is adequate.
Finland	Protection is adequate.
France	Protection is adequate.
Germany	Protection is adequate.
Greece	Protection is adequate.
Iceland	Protection is adequate.
Ireland	Protection is adequate.
Italy	Protection is adequate.
Japan	Protection is adequate.
Mexico	The situation is difficult to assess.

Table 5. Protection of union members and collective bargaining rights *(cont.)*

Netherlands	Protection is adequate.
New Zealand	Protection against acts of anti-union discrimination is adequate. Legislation prohibits strikes designed to force an employer to enter multi-employer collective bargaining (ILO, CFA, case 1763).
Norway	Protection is adequate.
Portugal	Protection is adequate.
Spain	Protection is adequate.
Sweden	Protection is adequate.
Switzerland	Protection is adequate.
Turkey	To have bargaining power in a particular enterprise, a union must represent the majority of the workers of that enterprise and 10 per cent of the workers of the relevant industry (ILO, Report of the Committee of Experts, 1994).
United Kingdom	ILO experts have in the past raised questions on the adequacy of application procedures, but these have now been answered.
United States	Unions report that acts of anti-union discrimination are not adequately sanctioned. A complaint that procedures to obtain compensation for illegal dismissal for reason of union activity are too slow was presented to the ILO (CFA, case 1543).

Sources: see Table 3.

Table 6. Recent changes in freedom-of-association rights

Argentina	Following the end of the military regime in 1983, freedom-of-association rights were improved.
Brazil	The 1988 Constitution provides for better labour rights.
Dominican Republic	Freedom-of-association rights were improved in 1990.
Ecuador	Democracy was restored in 1979.
Fiji	Following the end of the military regime in 1992, labour rights were improved.
Guatemala	In 1992, the Labour Code was significantly amended, improving freedom-of-association rights.
Honduras	Since 1990, labour rights are better protected, following a period of political instability.
Korea	Freedom-of-association rights have been improved following the Declaration of Democracy in 1987.
Panama	Following the end of the authoritorian regime in 1989, freedom-of-association rights were improved.
Peru	Since 1990, following a period of political instability, labour rights are somewhat better enforced.
Philippines	Following the end of the military regime in 1987, labour rights were improved.
Surinam	The restoration of democracy in 1991 was accompanied by better enforcement of labour rights.
Chinese Taipei	The lifting of martial law in 1987 was accompanied by an improvement in the right to strike.
Thailand	Following the end of the military regime in 1992, labour rights were improved.
Turkey	In 1995, freedom-of-association rights were improved in the Constitution and in the Trade Union Law. Following the end of the military regime in 1986, labour rights were improved.
Uruguay	The restoration of democracy in 1985 was accompanied by an improvement in labour rights.
Venezuela	In 1990, a new Labour Code, providing for a higher degree of protection of basic labour rights, was adopted.

Source: see Table 3.

NOTES

1. The right to collective bargaining is closely related to workers' freedom of association. One main purpose of workers' organisations is to bargain collectively with employers; hence, a denial of collective bargaining rights would make the right to freedom of association practically meaningless.

2. See for example the International Agreement for the Suppression of White Slave Traffic of 1904, the International Convention for the Suppression of White Slave Traffic of 1910, the International Convention for the Suppression of the Traffic in Women and Children of 1921, and the International Convention for the Suppression of the Traffic of Women of Full Age of 1933.

3. The World Social Summit of Copenhagen was attended by 117 heads of state and of government. Its main purpose was to affirm countries' commitment to combat poverty, unemployment and social exclusion and to promote social development.

4. It is also interesting to note that, in January 1995, governments from non-aligned countries and other developing countries agreed on the so-called Delhi Declaration, whereby countries commit themselves to the promotion of working/living conditions of all people and to the provision of "better protection". The Delhi Declaration also calls for the elimination "of the practice of exploitative child labour and of gender discrimination in all economic activities".

5. Another source of international labour standards is embodied in the OECD Guidelines for Multinational Enterprises, which were adopted in 1976. According to the Guidelines, multinational enterprises (MNEs) are recommended to provide their employees with freedom of association and the right to collective bargaining. Also, workers' representatives should be given information on the performance of the enterprise. MNEs are asked to provide training, while also upgrading the skills of the local

labour force. Finally, the Guidelines call for a non-discriminatory implementation of MNEs' employment policies, including hiring/firing practices, wages, promotion and training. It is important to note that, according to the Guidelines, labour standards observed by MNEs must not be less favourable than those observed by comparable employers in the host country. (An overview of the functioning of the Guidelines is presented in Part III.).

6. As will be seen in Part III, peer pressure can be a powerful instrument to improve enforcement in certain cases.

7. More specifically, to the extent that the provisions of the Convention are not enforced by way of collective agreements, court decisions or any other practice, government action in the form of laws or regulations is called for.

8. Earlier child labour Conventions provided for a minimum age of 13. Even so, they still have legal force.

9. The important question of how labour standards might influence employment performance -- and the potential trade-offs at work -- is analysed in Part II.

10. The Employers' group of the ILO and several governments disagree with the interpretation of the Committee on Freedom of Association concerning the right to strike. They call for a stricter application of Conventions 87 and 98, which are silent on this issue.

11. The 176 Conventions have been ratified on average by slightly over 30 countries.

12 . It should also be noted that 84 more countries are bound by the provisions of one or more of the ten sectoral Conventions on minimum age (in industry, agriculture, non-industrial employment, underground work, etc.) that were adopted before Convention 138.

13. According to Convention 5, the minimum age for admission to employment should not be less than 14 years compared with 15 years in the case of Convention 138. Convention 5 applies to employment in industry, whereas Convention 138 refers to employment in all economic sectors. The two Conventions are mutually exclusive in that no country

can ratify both; ratification of Convention 138 implies the denunciation of Convention 5 and vice versa; if a country has ratified Convention 5 (without denouncing it), it cannot ratify Convention 138.

14. It should, however, be stressed that states can make reservations to UN Acts and Conventions, but not to ILO Conventions.

15. Information concerning the enforcement of ILO Conventions comes from different sources including ILO (1985); ILO (1994b); Blanpain (1991); International Confederation of Free Trade Unions (1994); and US Department of State (1994).

16. In general, only recognised unions have the legal capacity to represent workers and engage in collective bargaining.

17. The 1994 Conference Committee noted that protection against anti-union discrimination had strengthened.

18. UNESCO (1993).

19. See US Department of Labor (1995). This study gives evidence of child labour in a number of export-oriented industries around the world, including garments, footwear, carpets, furniture and mining.

PART II

POSSIBLE LINKS BETWEEN CORE LABOUR STANDARDS, TRADE, FOREIGN DIRECT INVESTMENT, ECONOMIC DEVELOPMENT AND EMPLOYMENT

PART II

POSSIBLE LINKS BETWEEN CORE LABOUR STANDARDS,

TRADE, FOREIGN DIRECT INVESTMENT,

ECONOMIC DEVELOPMENT AND EMPLOYMENT

This part focuses on possible economic outcomes of core labour standards. It does so by investigating the various possible economic impacts of core labour standards from both a theoretical and an empirical point of view. It also analyses the links between trade policy and core labour standards, including the important question of whether trade liberalisation precedes or follows changes in core labour standards. The final section summarises recent Secretariat research on the effects of trade between OECD and non-OECD countries on employment and relative wages.

Economic properties of core labour standards

The debate over possible links between labour standards and trade has been hampered by the lack of solid analytical underpinnings. Economic research in this area is practically non-existent. This section examines the roles core labour standards can perform in the economy (based in particular on an analytical framework developed in the Analytical Appendix) and then provides some empirical evidence.

The impact of core labour standards on economic efficiency

The first question that arises is whether the outcomes of free markets without any core standards are efficient. If the answer is that they are not, there is a *prima facie* case for considering whether government intervention can improve the situation; the issue then becomes one of whether core labour standards are an adequate policy response.

Are market outcomes efficient?

There are arguments for and against the view that markets lead to an efficient allocation of resources.

i)   Market outcomes are basically efficient

According to the neo-classical theory of perfectly competitive markets, relative prices reflect supply and demand conditions of all goods, services and factors traded in the economy. Under these circumstances, and assuming that a variety of other conditions are satisfied, economic efficiency will be achieved. For this result to hold, however, it is obvious that supply and demand forces must be allowed to operate freely. This will occur under several important conditions. First, economic agents must be free to choose, i.e. free to express their choices resulting from utility/profit maximisation decisions. Otherwise, supply and demand forces will be constrained, leading to inefficient outcomes. Second, an important characteristic of free markets is perfect competition. If certain agents have market power, they will shift the structure of relative prices in their favour. Third, market efficiency calls for perfect information, so that individual choices are made on the basis of accurate and complete information.

According to this theory, any government intervention, be it in the form of labour standards or other regulations, will impair the free functioning of markets, thus reducing efficiency. Market outcomes are *endogenous*, determined by the working of market forces. Proponents of this theory argue that the operation of the market can lead endogenously to an economically efficient degree of observance of core labour standards. For instance, compliance with the principle of freedom of association can be expected to improve as the level of income per capita rises, irrespective of whether legislation exists. Likewise, forced labour and child labour are likely to be more frequent in poor countries than in more developed ones. Even at similar levels of economic development, the particular manifestation of the freedom-of-association principle may vary across countries because the content of regulations, union structure, collective bargaining institutions and labour practices are (almost by definition) country-specific.

Overall, if conditions under which markets are efficient are in place, efforts to regulate them will cause inefficiencies. In this framework, for core labour standards to be consistent with free markets, they have to be both endogenous and country specific.

ii)   Market outcomes are not always efficient

Some or all of the conditions mentioned above may not hold in the real world. There may indeed be significant market distortions and failures, i.e. situations that are unlikely to be consistent with those that characterise a perfectly competitive equilibrium:

- The practice of forced labour represents a clear departure from the freedom-of-choice condition, for two different reasons. First, forced workers have little scope for utility maximisation, entailing a loss of welfare. Second, forced workers cannot move easily to other activities that match their skills and aspirations. As a result, the allocation of labour resources is distorted, thereby leading to a loss of economic efficiency (and output). Child exploitation constitutes another departure from the freedom-of-choice condition, for similar reasons. Finally, employment discrimination may also lead to a sub-optimal allocation of labour resources. For example, strict demarcation lines between male and female work are imposed in certain countries. This entails waste, as workers will not be employed in the sectors/occupations where they will be most productive. Also, when particular categories of the population are not allowed to work (for political, religious or other reasons), total output will be lower than otherwise. The (in)efficiency effects of these labour-market distortions are analysed in detail in the Analytical Appendix.

- Many product markets are characterised by imperfect competition. This, in the absence of measures that protect workers' rights, might aggravate imbalances of power in the labour market.

In addition to arguments about static efficiency, there might be instances where the market in and of itself does not provide sufficient incentives to maximise *dynamic* efficiency and/or help create positive market externalities:

- Workers may have practical views on how production in their firms can be made more efficient, but they may not be interested in sharing these views with management if they do not have incentives to do so. This is because individual workers may not perceive the benefits to themselves from suggestions they might make.

- There might be circumstances under which the labour market fails to provide individual employers with sufficient incentives to increase productivity[1].

- The market may fail to provide enough incentives to ensure an adequate level of investment in education and training. This is partly so because education and training are typically long-term investments, whereas the planning horizon of individual agents is often a short-term one. In addition, education and training can give rise to significant externalities for society as a whole, in terms of knowledge accumulation, research and development, etc. Since these benefits are not captured by private agents, the result is under-investment in education and training.

In this context the question arises as to how these market distortions and failures can be addressed. More specifically, is government action needed and, if so, under which form? Can the establishment of core labour standards go some way towards solving these problems? Alternatively, is there a danger that the imposition of core standards will worsen them, and what are the employment repercussions?

Can core labour standards improve the efficiency of market outcomes?

As shown in the Analytical Appendix, there are arguments that lend support to the view that core labour standards are a possible response to the various market distortions and failures mentioned above.

First, prohibition is the appropriate policy response to the existence of forced labour. This calls for ratification and enforcement of the relevant ILO Conventions, except perhaps in the case of prison labour (even when working for the private sector) as the latter may have social rehabilitation purposes.

Second, the elimination of *exploitative* forms of child labour would serve similar purposes. Besides, it would help preserve (if not improve) human capital, which is likely to depreciate rapidly when children work under unsafe or unhealthy conditions. It may be profitable for unscrupulous employers to exploit children, but certainly not for society as a whole[2].

Third, regulations on non-discrimination in employment, as provided by ILO Convention 111, can help reduce distortions to labour-market mobility across both occupations and sectors. At the same time, these regulations may stimulate the active labour-market participation of certain categories of workers, which again points to beneficial economic effects.

Fourth, freedom of association and collective bargaining may also produce positive efficiency effects:

– Freedom of association and collective bargaining rights are necessary instruments to counter-balance the market power of employers, where such power exists. The bargaining power of an individual worker may be very limited faced with a powerful employer or group of employers. In addition, when differences of interpretation of labour laws arise between a worker and his/her employer, legal protection can be expected to be stronger when the worker is supported by some collective organisation (union, workers' council, association). Such organisations typically offer legal advice and expertise so that individual workers can assert and defend their rights[3].

– Collective bargaining institutions can encourage workers to share their views with management about the running of the enterprise; the existence of such institutions provides some guarantees that higher productivity will bring benefits to all.

– Collective bargaining might also provide incentives for enterprise-based training.

The question arises, however, as to whether freedom of association and the right to collective bargaining are the most appropriate forms of intervention to deal with these problems:

– In some instances, imbalances of market power in labour markets may be best addressed by enhancing product-market competition, for example by way of trade liberalisation. Freedom of association and collective bargaining would be only a second-best solution.

– Even though it might well be true that freedom of association and collective bargaining can enhance labour market competition, the issue of what level of bargaining (centralised or decentralised) is likely to produce the best outcomes is still an important and complex one[4]. For example, it may well be the case that enterprise-based bargaining can counter-balance the market power of the employer, while avoiding the relative wage rigidity which is likely to be one of the outcomes of multi-employer bargaining conducted at the sectoral level. On the other hand, there is also evidence that centralised wage bargaining carried out at the national level can produce the same effects as decentralised bargaining.

– Some authors, while being in favour of world-wide promotion of core standards, including freedom of association, have highlighted possible distortions associated with certain expressions of the right to freedom of association[5]. One strand of the economic literature emphasizes the economic costs of unions. These costs arise when unions protect the rights of their members to the detriment of non-unionised workers and the unemployed. For example, there is strong empirical evidence that forming a union introduces a distortion between union and non-union workers in terms of a wage (and fringe benefits) premium (Freeman and Medoff, 1984). Also, unions might impose a high level of employment protection, thus creating a dual labour market. In this context, workers in unionised sectors (the so-called "insiders") are protected against wage competition from the unemployed (the "outsiders"). As a result, the latter cannot underbid unionised workers, making their re-employment difficult[6]. Wages of non-unionised workers may also be depressed as the supply of labour in that sector is raised. More generally, it is important from the economic point of view that union rights be exerted in such a way that they do not create a new source of distortions, with detrimental consequences for employment and economic efficiency. These arguments, however, relate to particular trade union practices and not to freedom of association as a principle.

In sum, prohibition of forced labour and of exploitative forms of child labour and regulations on non-discrimination in employment are likely to improve the efficiency of market outcomes. The efficiency effects of freedom of association and collective bargaining will depend on a variety of factors. First, freedom of association and policies that enhance product-market competition (such as trade liberalisation) can be regarded as complements. Second, freedom of association and collective bargaining can produce positive efficiency effects; for instance, they can counteract the market power of employers, while also improving worker-management co-operation and information sharing. Third, there are instances where the activities of unions can introduce distortions in the labour market, thus imposing costs on some parts of the workforce. The form of union and employer organisation that is conducive to the highest level of efficiency is likely to differ from country to country, as it depends on specific historical and cultural factors. Although freedom of association is a basic human right and may help reduce certain distortions in the economy, it is no less true that particular forms of union organisation and collective bargaining may introduce new ones.

Why are core labour standards not observed in certain parts of the world?

If core labour standards do enhance economic efficiency, the obvious question is: why are they not observed world-wide?

i)   The public good argument

One possible answer is that core labour standards are public goods, the optimal provision of which cannot be accomplished by market forces alone. According to Samuelson (1954), public goods can be consumed by all economic agents, while consumption by one agent does not reduce the amount of the public good available to others. Economic agents acting on their own would choose not to pay for a given public good because of the well-known free-rider problem: each individual consumer of the public good believes that this good will be produced, independently of whether he/she pays for it, because the cost will be borne by others. As a result, if all individual agents follow the same reasoning and behave as free riders, the good may not be produced at all. Some form of co-ordination is necessary in order to ensure an optimal level of production of the public good: this can take the form of government regulations (norms, standards, etc.) or the government can provide the public good directly.

Are core labour standards public goods? Freeman (1994) argues that some core labour standards might be appropriately conceptualised as private goods. If individuals are in fact concerned by and are willing to pay for the "social" content of the goods and services they consume (i.e. the extent to which the production of goods and services respects core labour standards), core labour standards are no longer a public good[7]. They then become one of the many *characteristics* of goods and services which influence consumers' preferences. In these circumstances, consumers will behave as in the case of (normal) private goods. In other words, they will buy the good which has the preferred characteristics, in terms of price, embodied labour standards and quality in general. Some consumers will be prepared to buy a product that is more expensive but is produced under conditions of "good" labour standards, others will prefer low-price, "bad-standards" products. There is no free-riding problem since no consumer will get a product embodying "good" labour standards without paying for them. This assumes, of course, that consumers are well informed about the "social content" of the physical goods and services they want to buy[8]. This is not the case at present.

Schoepfle and Swinnerton (1994), on the other hand, suggest that core standards may share some of the characteristics of a public good. According to them, union rights, prohibition of child labour and forced labour can be seen as a public good which they call "social moral consciousness". This good responds to a *universal* concern in the sense that "consumers" of this good are interested in the observance of core labour standards irrespective of whether the goods and services that are produced in the presence or absence of such standards are exported. For example, it might be argued that individuals in industrialised countries are concerned about exploitation of child labour in the rest of the world; this concern is equally strong whether children work in traded or in non-traded sectors. Social moral consciousness is a public good since individuals can "consume" it without reducing the amount available to others. A free-rider problem emerges because any given individual "consumer" (or country) may not be willing to pay for social moral consciousness; if others pay for it, he/she will benefit without paying any of the costs.

Finally, it could be asserted that core standards are an instrument that permits the provision of a public good. First, they can strengthen competition in the labour market. Competition, though beneficial for society as a whole, may entail costs for particular economic agents (e.g. those who benefit from forced labour, child exploitation, employment discrimination) who are able, in the absence of core standards, to maintain their rents. Second, the greater degree of participation and transparency between workers and employers to which freedom of association gives rise might also be regarded as a public good. Neither managers nor individual workers acting on their own have incentives to provide sufficient information. Finally, market forces alone are likely to lead to under-provision of education and training, hence the need for regulations in the form, for example, of prohibition of child exploitation and compulsory school attendance.

ii)   The blocking minority argument

Another possible explanation for the lack of observance of core standards is that, with the establishment of core labour standards in countries that are deprived of them, some individuals will be worse off, even if the society at large is better off. If some economic agents benefit by suppressing core labour standards and have the power to do so, it is in their interest to ensure that core standards are suppressed. The problem may well be that in certain countries the minority which benefits from forced labour, child exploitation and employment discrimination has more political power than the majority of the population. This suggests that denial of core labour rights is likely to be more frequent in non-democratic systems[9].

iii) The endogeneity argument

According to Bhagwati (1994) and Srinivasan (1994), core labour standards cannot be easily shaped by policies. Instead, they are market outcomes that will be influenced, *inter alia*, by economic growth. In the view of these authors, core standards are not international public goods: each country determines its own rules and regulations, including its labour-market regulations, according to its specific institutional and historical set-up, level of economic development, etc. Only the principles are internationally recognised, not the setting of standards, which is necessarily country-specific.

Several examples are worth mentioning here. Restrictions on freedom of association may be explained by a government's belief that particular forms of unionism produce detrimental economic effects. Thus, the limitations on the right to strike that prevail in many countries are often justified by governments on the grounds that unrestricted strikes will lead to social disorder and lower economic growth. Likewise, the ILO regularly issues complaints against the legal requirement that only one union can represent workers in each enterprise, because the form of association should be freely chosen. Enterprise-based union systems exist in many Latin American countries, probably for historical and cultural reasons. The system of enterprise-based unions is also rather common in Asia. To the extent that such a system has been democratically chosen, it can be viewed as a particular manifestation of freedom of association.

iv) The economic development argument

Finally, there are cases where non-observance of core standards is used as a tool to strengthen exports and foreign direct investment, especially in the case of export-processing zones. Unions are simply prohibited in the export-processing zones of Bangladesh and Pakistan (see Part I), while they are discouraged in Guatemala and Panama. A special legislation applies to the export-oriented electronics industry in Malaysia. These cases cannot be explained by differences in the approach to human rights (indeed, unions are allowed in the rest of the economy), nor by difficulties in implementation problems associated with a particular socio-cultural context. Instead, such regulations and practices seem to be part of a deliberate strategy to improve export performance. Whether they achieve this latter objective is, of course, another question.

Some empirical results

Empirical analysis can shed some light on the effects of core standards on certain observable economic indicators such as output, wages and productivity. On the other hand, workers' welfare is likely to be positively influenced by employers' degree of observance of their basic labour rights; but these welfare effects are not directly observable and cannot be estimated empirically. For this reason, the analysis in this section is limited to observable economic indicators. It is, however, important to stress the limitations of empirical work in this area. Information on the degree of enforcement of core standards is rather sparse, except in the case of freedom of association and collective bargaining. Moreover, empirical analysis has to focus on the possible relationship between economic indicators that can be easily quantified (such as output, wages and trade flows) and core standards, which are a qualitative variable in nature.

The effects of freedom of association and collective bargaining on wages and productivity can go in different directions. For example, as the analytical framework suggests, freedom of association can increase labour costs, but it can also raise productivity (and thus reduce unit labour costs). In one case, freedom of association might reduce economic efficiency, while in the other case it might foster growth and living standards. An empirical investigation of the economic effects of core standards has been carried out in the case of freedom of association, the only core standard for which information on the extent of implementation is available for all countries selected for the study.

Freedom of association and output

There appears to be a weak positive association between the level of per capita GDP and the degree of observance of freedom of association. Likewise, international comparisons of productivity growth show that countries belonging to group 1 have, on average, a better productivity performance than countries of groups 2 and 3. Certain countries where freedom of association is non-existent exhibit very rapid productivity growth, though from very low levels.

These weak associations imply nothing about the direction of causality. In order to have a better understanding of the relationship between economic development and the degree of observance of core standards -- and to assess whether one causes the other -- countries for which a significant change in freedom-of-association legislation and practice has been recorded are selected. In these countries (Table 6), there has been a clear-cut improvement in freedom of association over the past 15 years or so. In general, this reflects a more fundamental move towards democracy. GDP growth during the five years following the change is compared with GDP growth during the five years preceding the change. Interestingly, the (unweighted) average growth rates of GDP and manufacturing output are both higher after the improvement in freedom of association. However, no single pattern holds for all countries. In six countries (Argentina, Panama, Peru, the Philippines, Uruguay and Venezuela), GDP growth increased significantly after the improvement in freedom of association. On the other hand, in eight countries (Brazil, Ecuador, Fiji, Korea, Surinam, Chinese Taipei, Thailand and Turkey), GDP growth fell significantly after the improvement, while in the remaining countries (Dominican Republic, Guatemala and Honduras), no change was recorded. Not surprisingly, other factors (factor accumulation, technological change, oil price changes, debt crises, economic policies, etc.) play a much more important role than freedom of association in determining economic growth.

Freedom of association, wages and productivity

The wage and productivity effects of freedom of association and collective bargaining are difficult to gauge. *A priori*, the impact of union rights on wages and productivity is ambiguous (see the Analytical Appendix):

– The establishment of guarantees to union rights can lead to an improvement in working conditions through the collective bargaining process. This might happen even in the absence of legislation on these working conditions. For instance, unions may succeed in establishing a floor to wage levels through collective bargaining. Unions may also establish a premium in wages and fringe benefits for their members over the wages and benefits paid to non-union members. Both effects would tend to influence labour costs, and hence employment.

– Union rights and free collective bargaining might also influence the structure of labour costs (and the allocation of employment) across industrial sectors and skill groups. For example, in the absence of free bargaining rights, wages of some sectors might be maintained at artificially low levels compared with what market forces would justify[10]. The establishment of freedom of association and bargaining rights will therefore entail a shift in relative wages, inducing changes in the allocation of labour between firms and sectors.

– As discussed above, it is often argued that workers' representatives can shape management practices, thereby creating a favourable environment for improving productive efficiency. To the extent that these favourable effects occur, they would give rise to income effects which, in turn, would have repercussions on welfare and the demand for factors of production, including labour. But a favourable productivity effect would have to be traded off against the impact of a union in terms of generating a wage premium over non-union members, thereby leading to unemployment[11].

At the aggregate level, there appears to be no correlation between real wage growth and freedom of association (Chart 2). During the 1980s, countries belonging to group 1 have recorded rates of growth of real wages similar to those of countries belonging to groups 3 and 4. Even though freedom of association is not observed in countries such as Kuwait, Indonesia and China, real wages in these countries have grown faster than in most of the OECD area. The same conclusion holds when the growth in real wages is compared with productivity growth: for all four groups, real wages have grown less than productivity. In several countries where there is relatively little or no freedom of association (e.g. Kuwait, Malaysia, Singapore and Thailand), real wages have actually grown faster than productivity.

It is also interesting to note that in countries where core standards have improved, there is no evidence that real wages grew faster. This, taken together with the previous result, suggests that there is no empirical evidence that "low" core standards imply "low" real wage growth or that raising core standards would imply higher real wage growth.

Core labour standards and trade performance

This section looks at the implications for trade performance of different economic properties of core labour standards. It focuses on the issue of whether there is a relationship between core standards, however set, and trade. This issue can be looked at in three different ways. First, does trade between a high-standards' country and a low-standards country reduce real income and output in the former? Second, will a country that improves its observance of core standards suffer a loss of competitiveness and trade performance? Third, do core standards shape sectoral trade patterns?

Chart 2
Manufacturing employment, real wages, productivity and freedom of association

Employment
(average annual growth rate, 1973-92)

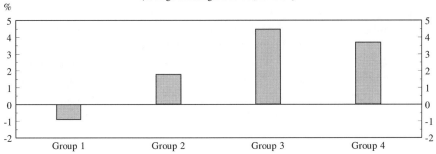

Real wages
(average annual growth rate, 1973-92)

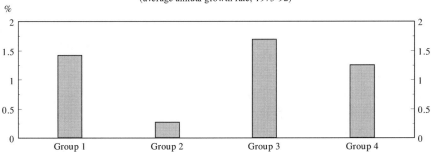

Productivity[a]
(average annual growth rate, 1973-92)

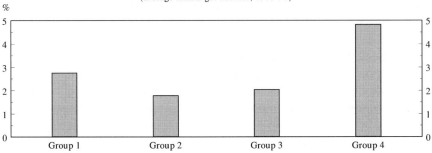

a) Manufacturing output per employee.

Sources: OECD, Analytical data bank; World Bank, *World Tables 1995;* and OECD estimates.

Trade performance of countries with different degrees of observance of core standards

As the analytical framework developed in the Analytical Appendix suggests, trade between countries with different degrees of observance of core standards is beneficial for all countries. The reason is that trade permits countries to exploit their comparative advantages, irrespective of the source of those advantages. There is, however, some concern that competition between countries with different levels of labour standards might trigger a "race to the bottom", especially in sectors where high-standards countries compete directly with low-standards countries. This view is based on the belief that "unduly low" labour standards can create a special competitive advantage, thereby stimulating exports and attracting inflows of foreign direct investment (FDI).

The purpose of this subsection is to present descriptive data on the trade performance of countries with different degrees of enforcement of core standards. The description is based on the CHELEM data base, which comprises trade statistics for the world as a whole, as well as for most individual countries. This data base is of special interest for this study as it is the only one that contains harmonized bilateral trade flows between all countries, including non-OECD trade. This subsection focuses on the countries selected in Part I of the study.

Before presenting the data, it is useful to elaborate on some data and methodological issues. First, the empirical work will mainly concentrate on freedom of association and collective bargaining[12]. Moreover, the potential trade implications of non-respect for child labour protection rules will be only addressed in the special case of exports of products for which blatant child labour exploitation seems to be a serious problem.

Second, in very general terms trade performance can be defined as the ability of an economy to adapt to ever-changing world market conditions. Trade performance can be positively influenced by a favourable level of cost competitiveness, but also by the intrinsic capacity of firms to adapt products (and production methods) to shifting tastes, trends in technology and other exogenous shocks. In this section, the export market share (the share of a country's exports in world trade) is taken as a proxy indicator of trade performance. A rise in the export market share is interpreted as an improvement in trade performance, and conversely a fall in export market shares suggests a deterioration in trade performance.

Third, when comparing trade performance, it is important to distinguish between manufactured products and raw materials (including oil products, commodities, non-ferrous metals, etc.). During the 1980s, the value (in US$) of world trade expanded by an average annual rate of 5 1/2 per cent. However, this masks a divergent trend between raw materials trade and manufacturing trade: the latter grew at an annual rate of 7 1/2 per cent while the former recorded a small decline. These opposite trends have to be borne in mind when comparing trade performance, as several of the countries examined here are major exporters of raw materials. Given the volatility of raw material prices, it seems appropriate to focus on manufacturing trade rather than total trade.

Fourth, the analysis attempts to explore the links between core labour standards and trade performance. Therefore, the empirical analysis reviews trade performance from 1980 to the early 1990s, the period for which data are readily available for all countries under study. For most countries, there were very few changes in core labour standards during this period. Notable exceptions are Argentina, Chile, Korea and perhaps Chinese Taipei, where core labour standards improved in the course of the 1980s. For the latter countries, an attempt will be made to assess trade performance before and after the changes in core labour standards.

Fifth, the extent to which core labour standards might explain trade performance depends on competing explanations. Over the medium and long run, trade performance is influenced by many factors[13]. In a nutshell, these factors can be grouped under two broad headings, namely market forces and government intervention, including the establishment of core labour standards. Market forces are likely to play a very important role; for example, according to the catch-up theory, less-developed countries will tend to exhibit a higher economic growth potential, thus permitting a relatively dynamic expansion of exports. In other words, the lower the level of economic development, the higher is the export potential of countries. In order to realise this export potential, however, market forces must be allowed to operate -- hence, the need to adopt market-oriented policies. Conversely, developed countries have by definition less room to catch up with the most advanced technologies. Their potential output (and export) growth will thus be more limited than in the case of developing countries.

Table 8 shows patterns of trade performance in OECD countries and selected non-OECD countries. Several countries have performed much better than others, especially the dynamic non-member economies (DNMEs) as well as several OECD countries. On the other hand, the majority of OECD countries have maintained their export shares in world markets, while some non-OECD countries have recorded sharp declines.

In order to understand better whether core standards might have accounted for these trends, Chart 3 shows trade performance for different groups of countries. Countries are classified according to the degree of compliance with freedom of association and the right to collective bargaining. If one focuses on either total trade or manufacturing trade, little relationship is found between changes in export market shares and these core standards. Therefore, it might be argued that low standards are not an important explanatory factor behind changes in trade performance.

Chart 4 suggests that market forces are likely to be a more important explanation of trade performance. The chart shows that there is some association between manufacturing trade performance and the level of per capita GDP: the lower the latter, the higher is the potential for exports. More specifically, during the 1980s, export market shares of the average high-income country declined; they rose by nearly half for the average medium-income country[14]. Most of the low- to medium-income countries reviewed here have exhibited export dynamism, irrespective of the levels of their core labour standards. For example, China, Portugal, Spain, Singapore, Chinese Taipei, Thailand and, especially, Turkey have all recorded impressive gains in export market shares[15].

It could be argued, however, that core standards influence export performance mainly via their possible impact on unit labour costs, which are a significant determinant of export performance; but, as shown above, there is empirical evidence that over the last decade, real wages have grown faster in low-standards countries than in high-standards ones. This finding is confirmed by a recent study (*International Economic Review*, 1995).

Changes in core labour standards and trade performance

Even though international differences in freedom of association and collective bargaining appear to have no detectable impact on cross-country trade performance, it is still possible that significant changes in a particular country's labour laws will have a measurable effect on the trade performance of that country. It is of interest to apply this type of analysis for a few countries under study, namely Argentina, Chile, Korea, Portugal, Spain and Chinese Taipei[16].

Chart 3

Freedom of association and export performance[a]

All industries

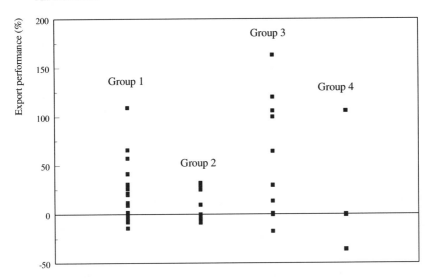

Manufacturing

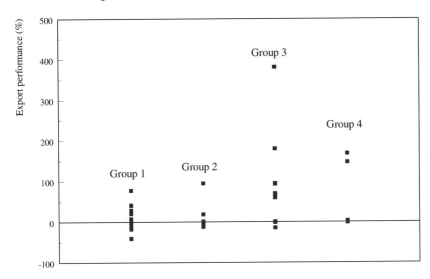

a) Export performance is measured as the change in percentage of the share of a country's exports in world markets over the period 1980-90.

Source: OECD.

Chart 4

Export performance and per capita GDP

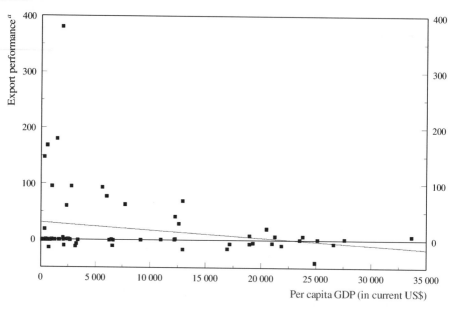

a) Export performance is measured as the change in percentage of the share of manufacturing
exports in world markets over the period 1980-90.

Source: OECD.

The recent history of these countries is characterised by important changes
in their political systems, entailing the creation of democratic institutions in
most of them. Reflecting political changes, freedom-of-association principles
have been strengthened in these countries. For instance, by the end of the
1970s, legislation and practice in the two Southern European countries was
made consistent with ILO Conventions. In Argentina, democracy was restored
in 1983, after seven years of military regime. Following the 1973-89 Pinochet
regime, democracy was restored in Chile. Finally, in 1987, labour relations in
Korea and Chinese Taipei shifted towards a more liberal stance following a
period characterised by martial law.

Chart 5 presents the evolution of export market shares during and after the
period of repressed labour rights in these countries. Except in the case of Chile,
trade performance was altered following the upgrading of core standards. In
Argentina, restoration of democratic institutions was followed by a worsening of

trade performance. However, this is likely to be the result of other factors, notably the build-up of a sizeable internal and external debt, rather than better freedom-of-association guarantees. Trade performance in Korea and Chinese Taipei also appears to have suffered after the improvement in core standards, but similarly the main causes lie elsewhere.

In Korea, a shift towards a democratic regime occurred in 1987 and various restrictions on trade union organisation and activity were consequently relaxed. As far as trade unions were concerned, before democratisation the emphasis was on enterprise-level organisation, in particular as stipulated in changes to labour law introduced in 1980. After the 1987 revisions to labour law, unions were allowed to organise at the level they chose, even if bargaining has tended to remain at the enterprise level. Several restrictions on freedom of association still remain, as noted in Part I[17].

Chart 5
**Export performance and changes in core labour standards
in selected countries**

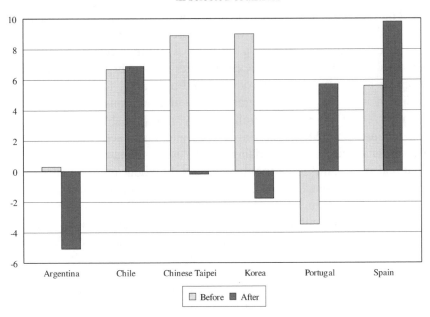

Note: The chart shows the average growth rate in the export market share for manufacturing products, before and after labour standards were improved.

Source: OECD.

According to Wilkinson (1994), who studied the inter-relationship between the state, employers and labour in the East Asian economies, a chronic labour shortage has developed since the late 1980s, and this has gone hand-in-hand with an improvement in working conditions. As a result, manufacturing labour costs were pushed up. After the democratisation process, Korean labour gained not only in terms of real wages but also in terms of improved working conditions. Between 1987 and 1990, nominal wages in the manufacturing sector, where trade unions are concentrated, increased faster than average, and this coincided with a loss of export competitiveness. In general, however, the deterioration of Korean trade performance is due to several factors, including the real appreciation of the won, which was part of the overall re-orientation of economic policies to stimulate domestic demand, and the relocation of many export firms abroad (OECD, 1994c).

Similar considerations apply to Chinese Taipei. Under martial law, which was lifted in 1987, strikes and collective bargaining were prohibited. Until 1987, trade union activities were not repressed but severely constrained by the ruling party. During the 1980s, as a consequence of international and domestic pressures, a number of changes intervened in labour laws. A Labour Standards Law was introduced in August 1984, which improved compulsory pension and severance benefits and established a 48-hour working week and minimum monthly wages. The major changes occurred after 1987, when better guarantees for freedom of association were introduced and a Council for Labour Affairs was established with the aim of upgrading labour conditions and maintaining social stability. As in Korea, union activity has probably contributed to increasing labour costs. Manufacturing wages and manufacturing unit labour costs in Chinese Taipei have been rising rapidly since the late 1980s. It can be argued that real wage gains are attributable to a tight labour market (since 1988, unemployment has remained below 2 per cent), and to trade union demands. In addition to the changes in labour law, in the late 1980s and early 1990s a number of factors have combined to constrain trade performance, including again a nominal appreciation of the currency which accompanied a deliberate policy shift to slow down the growth in the balance-of-payments surplus.

In sum, the relaxation of labour policies in Korea and Chinese Taipei in 1987, combined with the emergence of labour shortages, may have fuelled wage demands, entailing a temporary slowdown in exports. Over the longer run, however, no clear pattern emerges, perhaps because higher wages resulting from more liberal labour policies have been accompanied by better productivity. These conclusions lend support to the results presented in Table 7, which suggest that improved freedom of association is not associated with a significant change in the growth of total exports.

Core labour standards and sectoral trade performance

It has been argued that core labour standards might shape patterns of comparative advantage and thus sectoral trade patterns. This argument, if correct, would explain the perception among employers and workers in particular industries located in high-standards countries that trade practices in other parts of the world are "unfair".

Factor endowments and technology are key factors that shape comparative advantage. Thus, it can be expected that low-income countries will be specialised in low-technology/labour-intensive sectors. But it is well known that government policies can also modify comparative advantage. In particular, restrictive labour laws are sometimes part of a more general industrial policy, whereby governments favour particular sectors by way of subsidies, tax concessions and, perhaps, denial of core labour rights. It can thus be assumed that countries that restrict core labour standards in particular sectors will prolong or strengthen an existing comparative advantage, and, in some instances, create a new one. It is a fact that provisions on labour standards differ across sectors and industries (see below). Overall, the question that arises is: Can the pattern of comparative advantage that is justified on the basis of resource endowments and technology be altered by different degrees of enforcement of core labour standards?

Revealed comparative advantage

Table 9 provides an overview of comparative advantage patterns for several selected countries. It is based on an index of "revealed" comparative advantage, which takes into account the strengths and weaknesses of foreign trade at a very disaggregated level (71 products). In the table (column 2), the most competitive sectors in terms of the index of revealed comparative advantage are identified for each country. In the last column of the table, the main factors that create a comparative advantage in these sectors are identified[18]. For instance, differences in resource endowments explain why several countries at different levels of development display a comparative advantage in sectors with a high content of raw materials. This is the case for Australia (food products, metals), Canada and the Netherlands (gas sector), the United Kingdom (oil), New Zealand (agricultural products), Malaysia and Mexico (oil). This is not surprising since raw materials are abundant in these countries. Differences in technology also play a role: the higher the level of development, the higher the technological content of comparative advantages. For instance, comparative advantage in Germany (special machines) and Switzerland (pharmaceutical products) differs quite substantially from that in Morocco and China (textiles and clothing).

There is strong evidence of a technological catch-up: Korea has a comparative advantage in consumer electronics and Chinese Taipei in computer components. The main result that emerges is that patterns of specialisation are mainly governed by the relative abundance of factors of production and technology differences.

Are there cases where legislation on core labour standards interferes with specialisation? Analysis of compliance with the core standards on freedom of association and collective bargaining in specific export sectors based on reports of the ILO Committee on Freedom of Association suggests that in some cases these complaints have occurred in sectors where the examined countries have a comparative advantage. Most of these cases refer to a complaint against unlawful practices of employers. For example, in Morocco severe measures were taken against workers who had engaged in trade union activities in textiles and agriculture enterprises (case 1724, June 1994); in Korea, workers in the automobile industry and shipyard workers were pursued or arrested in connection with their union activities (case 1629, June 1994); and in the Philippines and India, cases of anti-union discrimination and interference in trade union activities were denounced by workers in the food sector (cases 1718 and 1651, November 1994). These complaints concern anti-union practices by specific employers which are not necessarily followed by other employers in the same sector. As mentioned above, these practices are mainly unlawful. Still, the possibility that some governments intentionally neglect to sanction employers for transgressing laws cannot be excluded.

By contrast, in Malaysia, a complaint concerning the inadequacy of sector-specific legislation with respect to national legislation (and international standards) has been filed with the ILO. Malaysia has a strong comparative advantage in electronic products, and special legal restrictions on freedom of association in this sector were noted in Part I. For example, electronics workers have faced intimidation aimed at eliminating the only in-house union in the industry (case 1552, November 1994). This restriction on freedom of association, since it is intended by government and applied to a specific sector, can be interpreted as a deliberate attempt to strengthen comparative advantage in the electronics industry. It is, however, difficult to assess whether such a restriction is a fundamental factor behind the comparative advantage.

A recent study provides some evidence that successful exporters of ten developing countries do not suppress core labour standards in order to reduce production costs (Aggarwal, 1995)[19]. On the basis of a review of labour regulations, it is argued that traditional exporting sectors in these countries have higher labour standards than non-exporting sectors. Also, within the export-oriented sectors, wages and working conditions are positively associated with firms' degree of involvement in exports.

Export-processing zones

Restrictions on labour rights in export-processing zones may also interfere with purely factor-based specialisation. The first export-processing zone (EPZ) was established in Ireland in 1959. By the 1970s, EPZs had begun to expand in East Asia as a way of attracting foreign investment and technology transfers to take advantage of the low labour costs in these countries and boost their exports of manufactures. Since then, EPZs have spread rapidly. Today it is estimated that there are over 500 zones world-wide located in 73 countries (Lloyd, 1995). It is still in Asia, however, that this form of export promotion is particularly important. Indeed, Asian EPZs account for much of the growth of this region's exports of manufactures and about 64 per cent of world-wide employment in EPZs, with over 50 per cent of the total in China alone. In absolute terms, other major EPZs exist in the Dominican Republic (150 000 employees), Brazil, Malaysia, Tunisia, Mauritius (about 100 000 each), Taiwan (70 000), Sri Lanka (70 000) and Guatemala (55 000) (UNCTAD, 1994)[20]. The types of activities in the zones have also expanded. Whereas industrialisation in EPZs used to be concentrated in textiles, garments and electronic products, diversification into high-tech industries and services is becoming commonplace today.

According to UNCTAD data for 1990, multinational enterprises (MNEs) employed nearly 4 million people in 200 EPZs, as compared with 10 million in total employment in foreign subsidiaries in developing countries -- a number that is estimated to have risen to 12 million in 1992 (UNCTAD, 1994). Moreover, MNEs appear to account for a very large share of investments and jobs in EPZs, with about two-thirds of such jobs held by women. For example, it is estimated that foreign-owned firms account for 30 per cent of all firms in EPZs in Mauritius, 63 per cent in the Philippines, 77 per cent in Korea, and over 80 per cent in the Dominican Republic, Sri Lanka, Jamaica and Mexico (*maquiladoras*) (ILO, 1993). In addition, many domestic firms established in EPZs often maintain close relations with MNEs.

The distinguishing feature of EPZs, as compared with other types of commercial zones, is the aim of attracting *export-oriented* enterprises or activities through the establishment of some sub-national customs area in which goods entering the area receive customs treatment that is different from, and more favourable than, that accorded to goods entering other parts of the same nation. Most EPZs also offer preferences or privileges with regard to other government policies. This definition is complicated, however, by the linking of zones across two or more countries, a pattern that has emerged lately as a new form of industrial co-operation. One consequence is that different geographic areas of one nation can be constituents of different zones.

According to the 1992 survey conducted on the basis of the ILO Tripartite Declaration, the majority of the governments which replied stated that the labour laws applicable in the EPZs did not differ from those applied elsewhere in the country. They also indicated that the special incentives offered to attract firms to invest in the EPZs did not affect basic human rights. Nevertheless, some governments felt that certain concessions in the social and labour fields had to be granted in order to attract FDI (ILO, 1993). According to the US Department of Labor, while many countries did not have special labour laws or regulations for EPZs, at least 14 countries did restrict labour rights in law and practice. For example, one or more restrictions on the right to form unions, to strike or to bargain collectively were found in Bangladesh, the Dominican Republic, Malaysia, Jamaica, India and Sri Lanka, among others.

Although there is no comprehensive study on this issue, only in six cases has it been demonstrated that the law is different in EPZs than in the rest of the country, indicating a deliberate government attempt to reduce core standards in these zones. In Bangladesh, professional and industry unions are simply prohibited in EPZs and this is presented as an inducement to attract foreign investors. Union officials do not have access to EPZs in Jamaica and Sri Lanka. In Pakistan, unions are banned in EPZs. In Panama, recent legislation restricts the right to strike in EPZs. Finally, in Turkey, workers do not have the right to strike for the first ten years of operation of EPZs.

It is a fact that governments in these six countries deliberately reduce core standards in EPZs compared with the rest of the country, and there is anecdotal evidence that governments of a few other countries do not sanction adequately cases on non-observance of the labour law in EPZs. However, it is difficult to assess whether such a policy will be successful for two main reasons. First, it is not at all certain that low core standards are a key factor in trade and investment decisions. As already discussed, there is indeed no evidence that low core standards are associated with low labour costs, an important determinant of trade and investment flows. Moreover, investors may prefer a stable social climate in their enterprise (which is likely to be associated with "good" standards), rather than a situation characterised by no or low core standards and social tension. Second, even if such practices do succeed in attracting certain foreign investors or in stimulating exports, the impact on the long-term growth of the country as a whole is very uncertain. Indeed, as discussed in the

Analytical Appendix, repression of basic labour rights may cause a misallocation of resources, impairing long-term economic prospects.

There is some evidence of a positive effect of EPZs on employment and wages. According to a recent study, between 1986 and 1990 employment in EPZs rose on average by 14 per cent annually (Starnberg Institute, 1991), that is, nearly five times more than the manufacturing average in developing countries. Moreover, ILO (1993) points out that wages in EPZs are higher than average wages in the rest of the economy.

Trade prices

More direct evidence of the sectoral trade effects of core standards can be found by looking at trade prices. Indeed, trade prices are one channel through which core standards may have an impact on export performance. One problem with this kind of analysis is that data on trade prices cannot be easily found. The only available source of information is the OECD Foreign Trade data base, which comprises data on trade values and volumes at a very detailed level of disaggregation. From this data base, one can construct measures of import (export) unit values, i.e. the ratio of import (export) values to import (export) volumes, which are used as a proxy for trade prices.

Using this data base, an attempt was made to assess the possible impact of freedom-of-association rights on US import prices of textiles. The analysis has focused on one country only (the United States), and not on the OECD area as a whole, in order to focus on the differences in trade prices by country of origin of the exports. Indeed, trade prices may also be influenced by differences in factors unrelated to the supply conditions in the country of origin, such as the structure of demand in the countries of destination. The textiles sector has been selected because it is often claimed that the effects of violations of core standards are especially acute in this sector.

It is important to bear in mind that international comparisons of import prices so calculated pose methodological problems. Even at a detailed level of disaggregation, products may indeed differ across countries because of different design or other qualitative characteristics. These differences may lead to differences in their price that are not attributable to cost conditions. It might even be claimed that these qualitative characteristics are so important that it is not legitimate to compare the prices of a product exported by different countries: the qualitative characteristics enable a differentiation of products. If this is the case, international comparisons of import prices would be irrelevant (just as it is irrelevant to compare the prices of different products), but then the issue of "unfair" competition (be it as a result of alleged differences in core standards, dumping, or other reasons) cannot be raised. Moreover, the structure of import prices by country of origin may be affected by differences in the trade regime applied to imports from each of these countries.

Bearing these problems in mind, prices of US imports of 39 textile products from 28 countries have been calculated. The 39 products correspond to the SITC international categories of textile products (four-digit level). Selected countries comprise four major OECD exporters of textiles for which freedom-of-association rights are fully enforced (France, Germany, Italy and Japan), as well as 24 developing countries. These countries, though having similar levels of economic development (per capita GDP of less than $1 600), have different records in terms of freedom-of-association rights. With this selection of countries, two questions can be addressed: To what extent are US imports from high-standards countries more expensive than other imports and have these countries been crowded out from the US market as a result? Do international differences in freedom-of-association rights among the selected developing countries translate into different import prices?

The results of this research are presented in Table 10. First, the prices of textile products imported from high-standards OECD countries are generally much higher than prices of products imported from the other selected countries. Even so, the share of these OECD countries in US markets for textiles is very high. This suggests that high-standards countries have successfully differentiated their products. Second, the prices of imports from developing countries shown in the table tend to be rather uniform, even though the degree of enforcement of freedom-of-association rights varies substantially among these countries. This result suggests that freedom of association *per se* plays little role in the determination of export prices. A similar conclusion can be drawn from Chart 6. There also seems to be some association between per capita GDP and export prices: the price level tends to rise with higher levels of per capita GDP.

Chart 6

Export price of textiles, per capita GDP and freedom of association

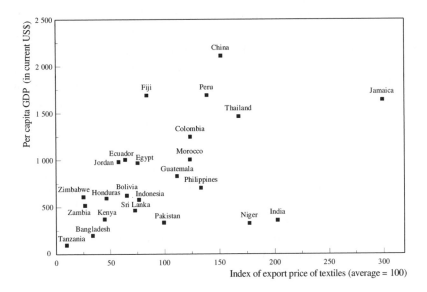

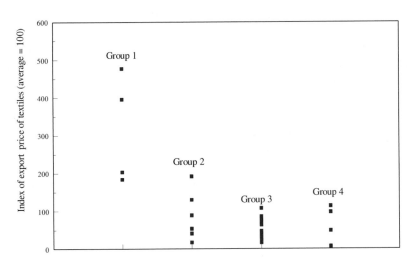

Source: OECD estimates.

Further empirical analysis of the possible relationship between core standards and sectoral trade patterns can be conducted by looking at the sectors where child labour exploitation is reportedly widespread. It could be argued that, because of child labour exploitation, export prices of the goods which embody this type of labour intensively are especially low. In order to assess the validity of such assertions, it is interesting to look at export prices of the carpet sector, where child labour exploitation is alleged to be widespread in several developing countries.

Table 11 presents data on export unit values (a proxy for export prices) for carpets for two groups of countries chosen among the largest world exporters of hand-made carpets. The export price of a hand-made carpet ranges from over US$40 in China to almost US$70 in Nepal, where child labour is reportedly pervasive (US Department of Labor, 1994). The use of child labour in the manufacture of hand-made carpets does not seem to have reduced the export prices of these carpets compared with other countries where the practice of child labour is not widespread. A similar estimate has been carried out for the export of carpets manufactured with artificial textiles. For this type of product, Belgium and the Netherlands have lower average export prices than Turkey, where there is some evidence of child labour, while the third developed country in the group, Denmark, has the highest average export price. Economies of scale are likely to be an important factor at work: the second column in Table 11 gives a measure of the volume of exports for each country.

The practice of exploitative child labour is morally reprehensible. Moreover, it appears to have an insignificant impact on the patterns of specialisation, even in the short run. This finding is consistent with evidence, cited in a recent ILO report, that in countries where child labour is used, the labour-cost savings realized through the employment of children are small (ILO, 1995).

Conclusions

It is difficult to carry out empirical analysis on the possible links between core standards and trade flows. The main problem encountered is that information on enforcement of core standards is sparse and incomplete, except in the case of freedom of association and collective bargaining. Any conclusions drawn relate mainly to these two core standards.

Within these limitations, empirical findings confirm the analytical results that core labour standards do not play a significant role in shaping trade performance. The view which argues that low-standards countries will enjoy gains in export market shares to the detriment of high-standards countries appears to lack solid empirical support. Countries can succeed in repressing real wages and working conditions only for a limited period of time. Thereafter, market forces will be such that wages will catch up, thus wiping out previous competitiveness gains. More generally, there is evidence that, as expected, low per capita income countries have recorded significant improvements in export market shares, suggesting that market forces work in the aggregate.

Moreover, the main result that emerges from a cross-country analysis of comparative advantage is that patterns of specialisation are mainly governed by the relative abundance of factors of production and technology differences. There is, however, some evidence that, in a few countries, the denial of core standards has been deliberately used by governments with the aim of improving the trade performance of certain sectors or of attracting investment to EPZs. Even though some economic gains might be obtained for these sectors, these gains are likely to prove short-lived; in the long term, the economic costs associated with low core standards are likely to outweigh any possible short-term gains.

These findings also imply that any fear on the part of developing countries that better core standards would negatively affect either their economic performance or their competitive position in world markets has no economic rationale. On the contrary, it is conceivable that the observance of core standards would strengthen the long-term economic performance of all countries.

Core labour standards and trade liberalisation

Possible links between the level of core labour standards in a given country and the openness of its trade regime are also important to consider. Questions about such links concern not only the direction of causation but also the nature of the relationship, whether it is mutually supportive or conflicting. More specifically:

– Does trade liberalisation have an effect on the level of core labour standards in a liberalising country?

– Does better enforcement of core standards in a newly liberalising country make trade reform more successful by increasing the actual and potential gains from trade, or does it constrain trade reform by slowing down the ability of firms to adjust to international competition?

Because the links between core standards and comparative advantage patterns have proved to be tenuous, the emphasis in this section is placed on the dynamic adjustment process that takes place in an economy over time when more liberal trade policies are being credibly pursued. The two questions set out above are considered in turn. In the first subsection, the decisions of firms and governments about the level of core standards during periods of continuing structural adjustment are considered. In the second, some empirical evidence regarding freedom of association and collective bargaining rights is presented.

Possible relationships between core standards and trade liberalisation

Can trade liberalisation affect core standards?

i)   Firms and adjustment pressures

Trade liberalisation can create sizeable and lasting increases in an economy's real income and welfare, but it can give rise to severe adjustment pressures, especially for particular firms and their employees and in certain geographical locations (Richardson, 1989; Venables, 1995). Although the burden of adjustment is likely to diminish over time, especially if pro-competitive social policies are implemented (Burniaux and Woelbroeck, 1996), it can be particularly severe at the start of reforms, leading many firms to change outputs and activities and workers to change industries and jobs.

The decisions that firms make with regard to core labour standards will be related to the effects they perceive standards to have on their ability to adjust. Based on the analysis in the first section of Part II, to the extent that low (or non-existent) core standards are a cause of resource misallocation or a constraint on innovation, and are perceived by managers as such, trade liberalisation can, over time, impel higher standards. However, when markets function less than perfectly, managers may not perceive any link between the new incentives and the need for higher standards. Or, when core standards have significant public-good attributes, managers may perceive the link, but still be unwilling to improve core standards on their own because their personal gains are relatively greater under the *status quo*. This will be especially true in concentrated industries or in enterprises that have been protected for a long time, particularly by non-tariff barriers (Gaston and Trefler, 1995).

ii)   International convergence

Illustrative evidence on a closely related set of issues indicates that for countries that are linked together by international trade, not only do their growth rates tend to converge (Larre and Torres, 1991; Williamson, 1995) but so do their institutional systems (Sachs and Warner, 1995), with the poorer countries catching up to the richer ones. Most programmes of economic reform now under way in the developing and transition economies have as their strategic aim the integration of the national economy with the world economy. Integration means not only increased market-based trade and financial flows but also institutional harmonization with the OECD economies with regard to trade policy, legal codes, tax systems, ownership patterns and other regulatory arrangements.

Can core labour standards make trade reforms more successful?

Experiences in liberalising countries over the past two decades have shown that for trade reforms to be successful, they need to be sustained over a considerable length of time, and not reversed. One of the requirements for a durable reform process has proved to be a widespread coalition in support of freer trade. In other words, the more numerous the individuals in a society are with an "encompassing interest" in that society, the more likely that the liberalisation process can be successfully sustained.

According to Olson (1982), an encompassing interest gives an individual an incentive to care about the productivity of the society and to attempt to increase it. His/her interests are served not only by obtaining a larger share of the social output, but also by increasing the total output of the society. By contrast, an individual with a "narrow" interest has only an incentive to strive to obtain a larger share of the society's output through distributional struggle, even if this distributional struggle reduces the national income by much more than the narrow interest obtains.   The evidence suggests that societies lacking encompassing interests have not been able to carry out a well-planned trade liberalisation programme over an extended period (Thomas and Nash, 1991).

Can core labour standards foster the prevalence of encompassing interests in a society? Two opposing arguments are reviewed, assuming different economic properties of core standards.

i)   Core standards and enforceable contracts

When core standards are guaranteed, their effects can be equivalent to those of enforceable contracts. For example, whether considered as the framework conditions for other labour standards or separately, core standards can provide a reliable and impartial mechanism to enforce needed contracts in the work place. In securing the credibility of such negotiated contracts, core standards can free the individuals concerned from many of the constraints that keep their interests narrow. For the first time, they will be able to enter into certain kinds of transactions that take place over a long period of time, or involve many parties; such transactions are not feasible when there is no such mechanism to enforce work-related contracts. In these circumstances, core standards can enable encompassing interests to become more prominent in society as a whole.

The interaction between advancing trade reforms and better core standards in this case will be mutually reinforcing. Freer trade will increase the potential returns from complex transactions. At the same time, rising core standards will permit a growing number of individuals to undertake such transactions and to benefit from their returns.

ii)   Core standards and dual labour markets

When the form in which core standards are exercised in practice results in the protection of an exclusive group of workers, the effects of core standards will tend to reinforce the narrow interests of both the protected and unprotected individuals. As pointed out earlier, this could be the case when unions protect the rights of their members to the detriment of the non-unionised workers and the unemployed. In these circumstances, neither of the groups of workers nor individuals among the unemployed will have an incentive to care about the productivity of society at large.

The interaction between the trade liberalisation process and core standards in this case may be ambiguous. On the one hand, to the extent that core standards create distortions in the labour market, this can clearly constrain the dynamic adjustment of the economy towards the international prices and best practices that it is being exposed to by the trade policy measures. On the other hand, the discipline imposed by markets on such distortions should increase over time as international competition is progressively introduced by the trade reforms. In an open and competitive economy, the costs of collective bargaining agreements will fall mainly on the firm and the unionised workers, deterring them from reaching unrealistic agreements (World Bank, 1995).

Some empirical results

This subsection attempts to evaluate the relationships discussed above on the basis of some empirical evidence gathered for a sample of countries. It is reasoned that if trade liberalisation is an effective policy instrument for raising core standards, then trade liberalisation episodes should precede improvements in core labour standards. Similarly, if core standards can make trade reforms more successful, then better standards should precede the final phase of a trade liberalisation episode. The possibility of a mutually supportive or incompatible relationship is also tested.

The approach adopted is to track the sequencing patterns observed between trade liberalisation episodes and improvements in freedom-of-association and collective bargaining standards, proxied by progress in compliance with ILO Conventions 87 and 98. Comparable data for the other core standards were not available at the time of this writing so any conclusions drawn from this analysis relate only to freedom-of-association and collective bargaining rights.

The concepts of "trade liberalisation" and "improving compliance with freedom-of-association standards", as they are used here, are closely related to the data sources used to measure changes over time in the openness of trade regimes and in the extent to which association rights are respected. Thus, trade liberalisation is evaluated on the basis of the coverage and intensity of quantitative restrictions and the average level of (all-inclusive) statutory tariffs according to a method developed by the IMF to monitor trade reforms in Fund-supported programmes (IMF, 1995). Improving compliance with freedom of association and collective bargaining is evaluated on the basis of a method developed by the Secretariat. It consists of computing an index for individual countries of their compliance with ILO Conventions 87 and 98, and of measuring changes in the degree of compliance over time. Observations made by the ILO Committee of Experts and the Conference Committee in their annual country reviews are weighted according to the category of observation and the severity of the Committees' evaluations. It must be stressed that the resulting index values embody an element of judgement on the part of the Secretariat. Moreover, the empirical results emphasize changes in individual countries' practices over time rather than cross-country comparisons. There are two reasons for this. First, countries interpret these two ILO Conventions in different ways. Second, the ILO takes no position in the rating of countries as compared with one another.

The time period covered is 1980-94. It was determined by the availability of consistent data series as well as the fact that trade liberalisation episodes in most low-standards countries have been concentrated in this period. Details of the IMF and Secretariat methodologies are presented in the Annex.

Does trade liberalisation precede freer association rights?

The first step was to identify those initially low-standards countries which put in place a major trade-reform programme during 1980-94. This resulted in a selection of 44 countries which are grouped in Table 12 according to the estimated restrictiveness of their trade regime in 1994. Next, progress in complying with ILO Conventions 87 and 98 was estimated for each of the countries over the same time period. In this case, progress reflects both improvements in a country's legislation governing freedom-of-association and collective bargaining rights as well as improvements in implementing the laws as verified by the ILO Committee of Experts and Conference Committee.

To gauge the sequencing between trade liberalisation and better compliance with Conventions 87 and 98, an attempt has been made to pinpoint the respective time periods when each process began. Though the intensity of the reforms differs across countries, the focus here is on the timing of the starting points.

The patterns of sequencing that emerge for the sample countries are presented in Table 13. No single pattern is dominant. First, free association rights tended to improve at least three years after the start of trade reforms in 15 countries (Bangladesh, Bolivia, Chile, Colombia, Costa Rica, Ghana, Korea, Malaysia, Mexico, Morocco, the Philippines, Chinese Taipei, Thailand, Tunisia and Turkey). Second, better association rights preceded the trade reforms by at least three years in nine countries (Argentina, Brazil, Ecuador, Honduras, India, Jamaica, Kenya, Pakistan and Zimbabwe). Third, the two processes began at about the same time in eight countries (Algeria, Ethiopia, Guatemala, Mali, Peru, Sri Lanka, Uruguay and Venezuela). Fourth, trade reforms were pursued in six countries without any observable improvement in association rights (Cameroon, China, Egypt, Indonesia, Nigeria and Tanzania). Finally, there was insufficient information reported to the ILO on association rights to evaluate any possible change in six countries (Benin, Burundi, Côte d'Ivoire, El Salvador, Malawi and Nepal).

The question of whether freer trade, through its effects on institutional as well as economic systems, can foster better association rights appears to be answered affirmatively for the 15 countries where trade reforms came first. However, in the 17 countries where freer association came first or occurred at about the same time as the trade reforms, there appears to be a positive two-way relationship between these processes. Indeed, comprehensive policy and institutional reforms have been implemented simultaneously in most of the liberalising countries.

Do freer association rights precede successful trade reforms?

The second test is to find out whether improved compliance with Conventions 87 and 98 can lead to more successful trade reforms in newly liberalising countries. This is attempted by categorising the sample countries in two ways (Table 14). First, countries are grouped according to the estimated restrictiveness of their trade regime in 1994, the most recent year for which comparable information is available (from Table 12). It is reasoned that the more open the trade regime, the more successful the trade reform, even though in some countries the process has taken a much longer time than in others.

Second, within the trade-restrictiveness categories, countries are grouped according to the extent to which they have been found to comply with the ILO's freedom-of-association and collective bargaining requirements in 1994. It is recalled that four groups were defined in Part I: group 1, where freedom of association is by and large guaranteed in law and practice; group 2, where some significant restrictions still persist; group 3, where restrictions severely hamper freedom of association; and group 4, where freedom of association is practically non-existent. Since the analysis in this section is concerned with relatively low-standards countries, all of the sample countries fall within groups 2, 3 or 4; none is included in group 1. A final grouping in Table 14 includes countries for which information on association rights is lacking. Such a striking absence of information is interpreted in itself as disrespect for freedom-of-association norms.

The results reveal a relatively clear pattern. The more successful the trade reform in terms of the degree of trade liberalisation achieved, the greater is the respect of association rights in the country. Conversely, the more restrictive the trade regime, the worse is the country's compliance with the ILO Conventions in question.

For example, the 12 countries with relatively open trade regimes also display the best record in terms of association rights. Seven belong to group 2 and five others to group 3, while none is included in group 4 or lacks sufficient information. Next, for the 21 countries with moderately restrictive trade regimes, four are included in group 2, 12 in group 3, one in group 4, and four others lack adequate information. Finally, the 11 countries which have restrictive trade regimes appear to have the worst performance as a group with regard to compliance with freedom-of-association norms. That is, only one country is in group 2, just three in group 3, five in group 4, and two lack information.

Conclusions

The empirical results presented for the sample of 44 countries do not provide unambiguous support for one pattern of sequencing over the other as to whether trade liberalisation or freer association rights come first. Rather, the clearest and most reliable finding is in favour of a mutually supportive relationship between successfully sustained trade reforms and improvements in association and bargaining rights. This positive two-way relationship appears to be strongest after trade reforms have been in place for several years. Excluding the countries with insufficient information, there was notably no case where the trade reforms were followed by a worsening of association rights. Similarly, there was no case where promoting freedom-of-association and bargaining rights impeded trade liberalisation. This means, at least for these countries, that fears that freer trade could lead to an erosion of these standards, or that improved compliance with them could jeopardise trade reforms, are unfounded.

Core labour standards and foreign direct investment

In order to improve the understanding of the economic links between FDI and core labour standards, this part of the study addresses two key questions:

- Do core labour standards influence the decisions of MNEs on where to invest?

- Do MNEs have an impact on core labour standards in the country of operations and/or in the home country of the investor? Can they improve respect for core labour standards?

Core labour standards and investment decisions[*]

Conceptual issues

The relevance of core labour standards to investment decisions could be analysed at both the aggregate and the microeconomic levels. In the first case, the analysis would have to examine whether or not a relationship between labour standards in individual countries and the direction of FDI flows could be established. This link has been addressed to a certain extent in a previous analysis of FDI, trade and employment carried out by the Committee on International Investment and Multinational Enterprises (CIME) in 1994 (OECD, 1995a).

The second approach could explore the role of core labour standards in the investment decisions of enterprises. Labour standards could influence the decision on the *location* of the investment -- in which country to invest and where in the country. They could also impact on the internal organisation of MNEs, especially with respect to subcontracting as part of the corporate strategy. Finally, core labour standards may influence the management of human resources.

In both cases, the economic relevance of core labour standards arises from their link to labour costs -- either directly, where, for example, prohibition of forced labour or child labour translates into higher labour costs; or indirectly, where freedom of association and collective bargaining provide employees with the opportunity to negotiate wages and working conditions. In this sense, labour standards could be a variable in the decision of investors trying to minimise labour costs. The importance of this variable would tend to be greater, the more the production is labour-intensive. Nevertheless, cost considerations are only one among a whole range of factors that determine the investment decisions of MNEs.

While in a static view lower standards may in fact translate into lower labour costs, the relationship could be reversed in a dynamic perspective. As noted above, higher standards may very well work as an incentive to raise productivity through investment in both human and physical capital, thus contributing in the longer run to greater cost competitiveness of companies.

---

[*] This section is based on a contribution by the Committee on International Investment and Multinational Enterprises.

An important conceptual issue arises from the fact that the economic importance of the individual core standards is not identical. If freedom of association attracts primary attention among investors in OECD and non-OECD countries, it is because this standard could influence other labour standards including wage levels and working conditions. In the absence of freedom-of-association rights, it may be difficult to protect other labour standards. Where unions exist, salary levels may be higher than without them, though there is no necessary correlation between respect of freedom-of-association rights and wage growth. Unionisation and a more stable industrial relations environment may, however, also be associated with productivity gains and lower unit labour costs.

The importance of the right of association is reflected in the OECD Guidelines for Multinational Enterprises, where the chapter on industrial relations deals prominently with the right of employees to be represented by trade unions and other *bona fide* organisations of employees. Moreover, among the 30 cases of alleged violations brought to the CIME for clarification, the majority have touched upon trade union recognition, provision of adequate information, production and staff transfer across borders and access to the real decision makers during negotiations or collective bargaining (see Part III).

A final issue concerns the existence of corporate employment policies. To the extent they govern globally the operations of MNEs, their relationship with national labour standards set by the government of host countries would need to be examined. In principle, two cases have to be distinguished. Corporate employment policies could provide better conditions for employees in host countries than those set by the government, or they may strictly follow the labour-market provisions of the host country which may or may not include the respect and enforcement of core labour standards.

Empirical evidence

The bulk of FDI -- 73 per cent in 1993 -- is directed to OECD countries where compliance with core labour standards is by and large guaranteed in law and practice. The overwhelming importance of OECD destinations for OECD outflows is confirmed when stock figures for FDI are examined. The ten largest outward investor countries hold on average only 17 per cent of their assets in non-OECD countries.

FDI outflows to non-OECD countries exhibit some cyclical fluctuations. Their share fell from 32 per cent in 1985 to a low of 16 per cent in 1989, before increasing again to 27 per cent in 1993 (Chart 7). There are indications that the trend may have levelled off in 1994. "Rather than a structural shift away from

OECD countries, the rising non-OECD share in the early 1990s was at least partly the result of the recession in major OECD countries and the combined effect of economic growth and policy reform outside of the OECD area" (OECD, 1995c). The most recent projections by UNCTAD of an increase of FDI flows in 1995 to developing countries, in both absolute and relative terms, do not necessarily question this assessment. UNCTAD does not differentiate between the sources of the flows to non-OECD countries. It seems likely that the increase is attributable not to a rise in outflows from the industrialised world, but rather to greater foreign investment activities of non-OECD countries. Taking some of the most active outward investor countries, their outflows may have reached about US$30 billion in 1993. Recent estimates for the countries of the Asia-Pacific Economic Co-operation forum indicate that the newly industrialising countries are especially dynamic investors among themselves, but are also increasingly significant investors outside the region.

Among the non-OECD destinations, the dynamic Asian economies (Chinese Taipei, Hong Kong, Korea, Malaysia, Singapore, Thailand) have attracted most of the OECD's outward investment over the past decade, accounting for about 26 per cent in 1993. "Other Asia" (China, India, Indonesia, the Philippines) and Latin America (Argentina, Brazil, Chile, Colombia, Venezuela) also have registered a strong expansion of OECD inflows since the early 1990s, in the latter case after a period of substantial decline. Accounting for about 13 per cent of outflows to non-OECD destinations in 1993, Central and Eastern Europe has managed to come close to the share of "other Asia" (Chart 8).

Much of the non-OECD investment is directed to a handful of countries, including in 1993 Brazil (12 per cent), Singapore (10 per cent), Hong Kong (10 per cent) and China (7 per cent).

It may be surprising that data for OECD Member countries do not support the wide perception of China as the most rapidly expanding location for FDI. Apart from the fact that the data situation on OECD outflows may not be satisfactory, much of the investment in China originates from non-OECD countries. No reliable data are available, for example, for Hong Kong which is considered a major source of investment in China.

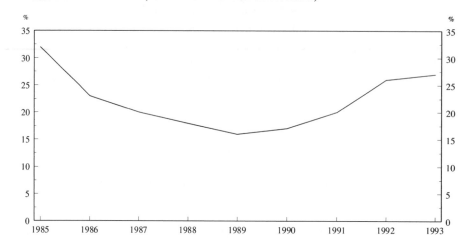

Chart 7
OECD investment outflows to non-OECD countries
(share of total OECD investment)

Source: OECD, *International Direct Investment Statistics Yearbook 1995.*

Chart 8
OECD investment outflows to non-OECD region
(US$ million)

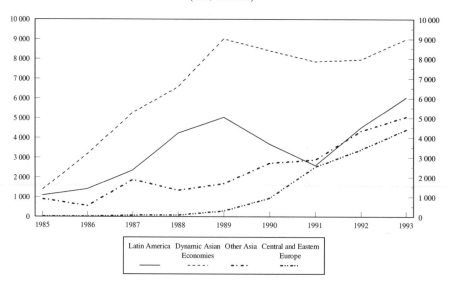

Source: OECD, *International Direct Investment Statistics Yearbook 1995.*

116

In sectoral terms, FDI in services has reinforced its dominant role over manufacturing in the recent past (Chart 9). In 1993, OECD outward investment in services was twice as high as investment in manufacturing. Within manufacturing, there are wide differences. Investments in textiles and clothing -- a sector that is frequently considered a prime activity for delocalisation -- amounted to just about US$1 billion out of a total of US$54 billion. Except for a few individual countries, OECD-wide data on sectoral flows by host-country destination are not yet available, impeding a more detailed analysis of investment flows.

Chart 9
OECD investment outflows by sector
(US$ million)

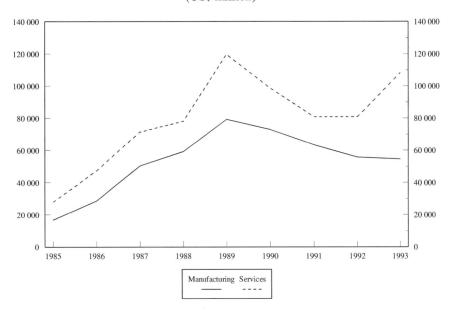

Source: OECD, *International Direct Investment Statistics Yearbook 1995.*

Examining the FDI pattern from an employment perspective, the previous picture is largely confirmed. The vast majority of MNE employment is located in the industrialised world, both in the parent company at home and in affiliates in developed countries. Some 16 per cent of total MNE employment (including home countries and foreign affiliates) is estimated to be located in developing countries (Table 15). However, 41 per cent of MNE employment in foreign affiliates is located in developing countries. Indications are, however, that employment creation has been more dynamic in the recent past in developing

117

countries and in particular in EPZs. Five million out of eight million jobs created by MNEs between 1985 and 1992 are located in developing countries (Parisotto, 1995).

What do the data on FDI and MNE employment imply for the relevance of core labour standards as a determinant of investment flows? The vast majority of OECD investments are directed to other OECD countries where core labour standards are generally respected. In order to address the question in the context of flows into non-OECD countries, the issue of the determinants of FDI needs to be revisited.

Over the years there have been many efforts to explain why firms engage in FDI (see Graham, 1995, for a recent overview). While the preconditions for corporate investment centre on political and economic stability, analysts have largely looked to the internal characteristics of MNEs, identified economies of scale, special management skills, and new product technology as determinants of both international trade and foreign investment. Theories not related to the organisational theory of firms are based on the dynamics of oligopoly and on new theories of economic geography. Other factors examined in this context are output and market size, product cycles, capital-market relationships, exchange rate risks, infrastructure etc.

Reflecting the variety of approaches, "at present there is no unique widely accepted theory of FDI. Instead there are various hypotheses emphasising different microeconomic and macroeconomic factors that are likely to affect it. While most of those hypotheses have some empirical support, no single hypothesis is sufficiently supported to cause the others to be rejected" (Lizondo, 1991).

This lack of theoretical and empirical consensus on the determinants of FDI is a severe constraint for empirical analysis. It is, however, not only the multitude of factors that determine investment flows and the lack of data which render it difficult to isolate the relevance of core labour standards. The variety of countries, their investment conditions and the legal and practical situation regarding core labour standards in these countries also prevent clear-cut answers to the question. Country case studies and analyses of conditions in EPZs can contribute to an informed discussion of policy recommendations, though drawing general conclusions may remain difficult.

In a number of non-member countries which are among the primary destinations for OECD investment, the record of compliance with core labour standards is tarnished, particularly with respect to freedom-of-association rights, although to different degrees. In China and Indonesia, freedom of association is practically non-existent, while in Malaysia, Thailand and Singapore significant restrictions persist. In Brazil and Hong Kong, some restrictions exist, but it is possible to establish independent workers' organisations and union confederations. However, there is no definitive evidence on the extent to which FDI responds to the level of core labour standards.

In a recent survey of MNEs on their investment behaviour in transition economies in Central and Eastern Europe, the key attractions for foreign investors were the size of the market and the opportunities and growth potential that it offers. "The often-quoted 'traditional' advantages of the region, such as low labour costs, cheap resources and investment incentives, though considered in the investment process, do not appear as prime motivators and are perceived instead as potential short-term benefits which, though attractive, should not form the main basis for long-term investment decisions" (OECD, 1994d). This result is confirmed by a survey of corporate investment intentions according to which companies' main reason for investing abroad for the rest of this decade will be to improve access to foreign markets, not to cut production costs[21].

While participants at a recent Business and Industry Advisory Committee (BIAC) workshop in OECD questioned the relevance of any general approach to investment criteria, some precision was provided with respect to labour-market considerations. "Where they do play a major role, it is usually a question of the availability of skills, education levels or productivity levels rather than a question of cost" (OECD, 1995d). There may, nevertheless, be greater importance attached to cost considerations for labour-intensive, low-skill production activities. This, however, would favour investment in developing countries only if wage differentials are not compensated by productivity differentials.

The difficulty of defining the role core labour standards play in the investment decisions of MNEs also applies with respect to EPZs. EPZs in many developing countries offering favourable investment conditions, including in the area of employment, are increasingly under scrutiny, particularly where they appear to aim at attracting "delocalising" MNEs from industrialised countries.

In addressing the issue of core labour standards in EPZs, their promotional character should be taken into account. EPZs offer a package of investment incentives and subsidies that are all geared towards inducing a positive investment decision by MNEs. While isolating the effects of individual elements of the package may be difficult, there is evidence that some governments felt that restricting certain core labour standards would help to attract inward FDI (see above).

In evaluating the non-respect of labour standards from an FDI perspective, it has been argued that labour repression has more to do with local politics than with the need to create or maintain international competitiveness or to attract foreign capital. Moreover, low or non-existent labour standards may have a detrimental effect on FDI decisions. They indicate a risk of future social discontent and unrest, and include the risk of consumer boycotts. For example, business representatives claim that it is despite -- not because of -- the existence of forced labour that MNEs have invested extensively in China. On the other hand, it is readily admitted that expectations of high profitability due to the economic environment provided in host countries may be able to outweigh some of the concerns of foreign investors about low levels of observance of core labour standards by the host government.

Regarding the impact of corporate employment policies, there seems not to be enough empirical evidence to draw definite conclusions on the actual behaviour of MNEs. Many companies have developed principles on employment to be applied in all their subsidiaries. However, the subsidiaries are often left with the primary responsibility for the day-to-day implementation of these principles. "It is clear from various ILO studies that there are considerable differences between the working conditions and practices of MNE affiliates across national boundaries" (Dunning, 1993). The decentralised approach offers flexibility for the local management to adjust employment policies to the circumstances of the host countries. For example, laws and regulations of the host country have, of course, to be respected independent from the recommendations included in corporate policies -- a principle that can be found also in the OECD Guidelines which encourage MNEs to respect freedom of association and the right to collective bargaining. Working conditions provided by MNEs will usually be fairly close to the norm for the particular country or industry.

The issue of external flexibility of MNEs -- although only indirectly related to the behaviour of foreign investors -- is attracting much attention in the discussion of core labour standards. In the wake of internationalisation of costs, many businesses are moving their software and programming services to countries such as India and the Philippines. Air carriers, such as Cathay Pacific or Lufthansa, employ a small number of experts in India to process flight tickets, the aircraft maintenance is carried out in Ireland and China, and a fixed percentage of flight personnel is hired abroad at local conditions. These changes in the internal organisation of MNEs underline the importance of cost considerations.

A more contentious aspect of external flexibility is the practice of subcontracting by MNEs in countries where, for example, child labour exploitation is a well-known phenomenon, particularly in the textile industries and carpet production. It is extremely difficult to provide an accurate assessment of the situation due to the lack of data, the complex arrangements of subcontracting, chains of production across borders, etc. While MNEs seem in some cases to have tolerated the non-respect of core standards by their suppliers, other MNEs require their subcontractors to respect their own standards, partially driven by the fear of consumer boycotts. A recent initiative by three textile companies in France, for example, aims at reassuring potential consumers that "social criteria" are used in selecting their suppliers. Admittedly, however, their enforcement is not always guaranteed.

The impact of MNEs on core labour standards

Conceptual issues

Foreign investment is generally a corner-stone of globalisation, competitiveness and development, since it brings technology, management techniques and market access -- in addition to access to additional capital. Does the role model function that associates MNEs with new ways of thinking, knowledge, technological and managerial methods also apply with respect to business ethics and core labour standards?

Two categories of potential influence may need to be distinguished: i) the direct and indirect impact of FDI and MNEs on core labour standards, including the practice of core labour standards; and ii) the direction of the impact, i.e. to lower or raise the situation in a host country for FDI as far as core labour standards are concerned. Frequently, the latter aspect is also discussed in the framework of a "global convergence" of standards as a consequence of the globalising economy.

Among the direct beneficiaries of MNEs could be their employees. Where home-country corporate employment policies apply, employees of MNEs could benefit from standards which are superior to legal minimum requirements in the host countries. Direct beneficiaries could also include employees of domestic suppliers if MNEs require that the same standards apply as in their own production.

Conceptually, direct links between the presence of MNEs and changes in the legal obligations for labour standards cannot be excluded. For example, MNEs may engage in efforts to lobby governments to change labour legislation to a more "investor-friendly" environment. However, there is no published evidence on this matter.

Where MNEs entertain good industrial relations with their employees, their presence could set an example to be followed by domestic companies as well. Indirect effects also include, of course, also the impact of FDI and MNEs on the prospects for growth of the domestic economy, which has often been an important ingredient for countries to raise labour standards. In this respect, a recent analysis concluded that "FDI and MNEs can have both positive and negative economic effects on host countries. Overall, the evidence seems to support those who maintain that foreign direct investment tends to have net positive effects on host nation economies" (Graham, 1995). Regarding the employment effects of FDI, MNEs increase the demand for labour in those countries where they establish greenfield operations, but labour-market implications change as the conditions and modalities of FDI change (OECD, 1995a).

Empirical evidence

There is little evidence that foreign investors from OECD countries employ child labour or are guilty of exploiting child labour; similarly, violations of standards for forced labour and discrimination have not been documented. However, there have been a number of published accounts of MNE subcontractor violations, particularly with respect to child labour.

Regarding the impact of MNEs on freedom-of-association rights in OECD countries, a rough proxy measure could be provided through the degree of unionisation. Data on the relative performance of foreign subsidiaries in a few OECD countries indicate that unionisation seems to be higher in foreign-controlled enterprises than in domestic ones; this stands in sharp contrast with the claim that foreign investors have a preference for union-free locations. In the United States, the level of unionisation has been found to be nearly twice as high in foreign subsidiaries as it is in American enterprises, but it should be noted that the comparison might be regarded as problematic on methodological grounds and, as a result, unionisation rates are likely overstated. An anti-union attitude can also be rejected for MNEs operating in the United Kingdom. The degree of unionisation of outward investment by Japanese firms generally follows the attitude in host regions, but also reflects Japanese attitudes. In the case of Japanese subsidiaries in Europe, union presence depends on the size of the subsidiary, the date of its establishment and the way it was set up. In the case of acquisitions, Japanese investors go along with union pluralism but adjust their attitudes to the specific circumstances.

The results seem to be different in the case of MNEs in non-OECD destinations. The radically lower degree of unionisation in EPZs in comparison with the domestic economy as a whole could suggest that MNEs do not contribute to the improvement of the practical situation of unions.

Regarding the issue of a global convergence of labour standards, some are of the view that an increase in the potential for downward pressures may be expected in response to growing competition from investors from non-OECD countries, where core labour standards are not (fully) respected. Investors from Korea and Chinese Taipei, in particular, have been identified as responsible for violations of freedom-of-association rights in EPZs in Central America and in Asia. According to this view, other foreign investors may feel greater pressure to relax their observance of core labour standards in order to stay competitive, taking into account the rapid expansion of outward investment from non-OECD countries.

Conclusions

The debate on labour standards deals primarily with the economic and social implications of trade between countries with different levels of labour standards. However, reflecting the rapid expansion of international investment flows, in particular to the developing world, links between FDI and labour standards are attracting separate attention. While there seems to be agreement on the net positive impact of FDI on the prospects for economic growth in host economies, which provides the conditions for an improvement in labour standards, views differ on the direct relationship between FDI and core labour standards.

Empirical evidence on the direct relationship between FDI and core labour standards is scarce and remains open to different interpretations. While core labour standards may not be systematically absent from investment decisions of OECD investors in favour of non-OECD destinations, aggregate FDI data suggest that core labour standards are not primary factors in the majority of investment decisions of OECD companies. Nonetheless, some governments in non-OECD countries have restricted labour rights (especially in EPZs) in the belief that doing so would help attract inward FDI from both OECD and non-OECD investors. Inward FDI from non-OECD countries, some of which have had problematic records of respecting core labour standards, has also increased. According to reports by MNEs from OECD countries, core labour standards are not considered a factor in assessing investment opportunities in a potential host country.

In these circumstances, host countries may be able to enforce core labour standards without risking negative repercussions on FDI flows. Enforcement may work as an incentive to raise productivity through investment in human and physical capital and may help maintain a level playing-field for OECD investors in the non-OECD area, where the role of non-OECD investors is increasing significantly.

Trade, employment and wages

Introduction

Although the world-wide increase in international trade after the second world war is generally regarded as having made a major contribution to economic growth, trade, especially with low-wage developing countries, has more recently been identified by some observers as contributing to higher unemployment and/or lower wages in OECD countries, especially for the low-skilled. It is also sometimes argued that certain low-wage developing countries derive their comparative advantage from their failure to observe or enforce core labour standards. In the second section of Part II, the possible links between comparative advantages and certain core standards were explored and little evidence of such a relationship was found. However, even assuming that core standards do shape wages and comparative advantage, it is still of interest to assess the recent evidence in support of the basic proposition that trade with developing countries is a significant cause of higher unemployment and/or lower wages in OECD countries.

Summary of empirical work

In recent years, there have been several empirical analyses of the impact of changing trade patterns on employment, including two conducted by the OECD Secretariat and reported on below. There have also been many studies which examine the links between trade and the growth in wage inequality which has been observed in a number of OECD countries over the past decade. Most studies have tended to concentrate on US experience, since the United States has witnessed a substantial increase in its openness and major changes in the geographical distribution of its main trading partners at the same time as a sustained and large widening in earnings inequality. The swing into a large trade deficit during the 1980s was one impetus to analysis, as were the potential impacts of NAFTA and rising trade with low-wage Asian countries on production, employment and relative wage patterns in the United States. Some of the work is summarised in Baldwin (1995) and Richardson (1995), and there have been a number of recent Working Papers published by the National Bureau for Economic Research (NBER) in the context of its research programme on trade and resource allocation. More recently, some studies have focused on the European experience (Dewatripont *et al.*, 1995; Courakis, Maskus and Webster, 1995; Hine and Wright, 1995; Cortes *et al.*, 1995).

Typically, analysts find that the impact of trade on employment and wage relativities has been significant in specific sectors. They also find that the measurable negative impact arising through increased import penetration is highest in sectors that employ relatively large numbers of low-skilled workers. Almost all studies find that the impact of trade on employment is small relative to changes in employment overall.

Until recently, empirical research has followed mainly two methodologies: factor-content analysis of import and export industries, and the analysis of goods prices. The factor-content method estimates the amount of employment used in the production of a particular country's exports, and the amount of employment that would have been used to produce the country's imports. The difference between the employment content of exports and the employment content of imports is interpreted as the net impact of trade on the demand for labour. On the basis of this methodology, Sachs and Shatz (1994) and Lawrence (1995), as well as other researchers, find that this impact is small. Wood (1991, 1994), on the other hand, argues that the conventional factor-content method of measuring the employment content of imports from developing countries seriously understates their true impact on demand for low-skilled labour in OECD countries[22]. When he makes various adjustments to the factor-content calculations in order to correct for this alleged bias, his estimates suggest that trade with the South has had a significant impact on demand for labour in the North.

The factor-content method in general and Wood's methodology in particular have been criticised. It is argued, for example, that the factor-content analysis, by ignoring the crucial transmission role of relative goods prices, misinterprets the possible impact of imports from developing countries on the demand for labour in OECD countries. Indeed, the proposition that trade with the South has led to a relative (and possibly absolute) fall in real wages for unskilled labour in the United States (or lower unskilled employment in Europe) is based on the Stolper-Samuelson theorem. For this proposition to hold, the theorem requires that the relative price of the goods intensive in unskilled labour should have fallen in the first place.

Recent empirical studies find somewhat conflicting evidence on such relative price changes:

- Lawrence and Slaughter (1993) analyse the behaviour of US prices of manufacturing industries over the 1980s and find no significant relationship between relative price changes and relative factor intensity. They also find that during the 1980s, relative trade prices of unskilled-labour intensive goods increased slightly (computer prices are included in the sample). It has been argued that this result (i.e. the lack of a statistical relationship between trade prices and relative factor intensities) is explained by the fact that the price of computers is included in the sample; since the price of computers (which are skilled-labour intensive) has recorded a massive fall, their inclusion in the analysis might distort the picture. In another study (Sachs and Shatz, 1994), computer prices are excluded from the sample and a modest relationship between trade prices and relative factor intensity is found: relative prices of goods produced in industries relatively intensive in unskilled labour have declined somewhat. Lawrence's latest work also shows that the picture does not greatly change even when computers are excluded (Lawrence, 1996)[23].

- Krueger (1995) obtains different results. He finds evidence that relative prices of unskilled-labour intensive goods in the United States declined during the 1989-95 period, but he recognises that these changes are consistent with different explanations including trade, as well as technological and institutional changes[24].

- Sachs and Shatz (1995) have further investigated the link between trade with developing countries and relative wage changes in the United States. Reviewing existing research, they object to previous results on both theoretical and empirical grounds[25]. Sachs and Shatz argue that, because of the factor-price magnification effect, even small price changes may significantly affect wages. The authors find evidence of a fall in relative prices of unskilled-labour intensive goods and conclude that the link between trade and wages is probably more significant than they previously estimated it to be.

126

– In another study of US price data over the period 1970-90, Leamer (1996) finds that the effects of trade on income inequality are more important than the technological effects.

Several recent surveys of this literature (Lawrence, 1995; Freeman, 1995; Richardson, 1995; Burtless, 1995, on US data), conclude that trade with low-wage countries is not a major explanatory factor behind the observed trend in wages employment of unskilled workers in OECD countries. Instead, they tend to accord a modest role to such trade in accounting for observed trends in unemployment and wage inequality. The use of technologies biased against unskilled labour is often considered a more plausible explanation even though direct evidence in support of this hypothesis is difficult to find. However, it seems clear that the issue of the relative importance of trade versus competing explanations for growing wage inequality and/or high unemployment of the unskilled is not settled yet.

Evidence from the Jobs Study

In Chapter 3 of the *OECD Jobs Study: Evidence and Explanations*, the relation between changes in trade patterns and employment patterns was analysed for a large number of OECD countries. Two pieces of analysis were reported, one using an econometric approach, the other input/output (IO) analysis[26]. The econometric work concentrated on changes in relative employment and relative wages in the tradeables sector, and specifically the manufacturing sector, as non-availability of data severely restricts any analysis of the service sector. The IO analysis, on the other hand, covered services as well as manufacturing industries.

By and large, as regards total trade, the findings of the OECD's econometric analysis were similar to those of previous studies, even though the number of countries in the OECD sample was considerably larger than in previous studies, and the data were more recent. Changes in trade intensities were found to be associated with changes in employment in particular sectors as resources are reallocated in response to underlying cost and price changes. The changes were usually in the expected direction, i.e. a rise in import penetration was associated with a fall in employment and a rise in export intensity with an increase in employment (the export-employment link is strongly positive only in the long term). However, insofar as the empirical analysis could determine, the employment changes associated with changes in trade intensities were small relative to changes induced by other factors (above and beyond the long-term trend changes in employment in the sectors and countries concerned). There was no evidence that trade-related employment effects were any stronger or weaker in European countries, where the ratio of trade to GDP is relatively high, than in the United States or Japan, where this ratio is much lower.

Chapter 3 of the *Jobs Study* also reported on work carried out by the Directorate for Science, Technology and Industry. This analysis was based on a sectorally disaggregated IO approach covering eight OECD countries during the period 1971 to 1986 (few IO matrices are available after this date). The aim was to decompose changes in employment in major economic sectors by major proximate causes: economic growth, labour productivity, changes in industrial structure, net trade. The IO approach differs from the regression analysis described above in that more sectors were analysed, and the change in employment was broken down exhaustively (in an accounting sense) into its various components. The analysis showed that trade-related changes in employment were small relative to employment changes related to other influences, and that the net effect was broadly positive, especially in the service sectors. As with other studies of this nature, the IO approach found that in an accounting sense, the largest positive trade-related employment gains for particular countries were during periods when external balances in goods and services were moving into substantial surplus, and vice versa. The conclusions of this analysis were thus very similar to those of earlier studies using similar methods (see references in Baldwin, 1995).

The two studies thus confirm the results of previous work (usually on individual countries) that changes in trade intensities as such have negligible influence on employment (although changes in trade imbalances will usually be associated with significant employment shifts in the tradeables sector), but that there are changes in relative employment by sector. Even there, though, the changes are generally small relative to those caused by other factors.

Trade with low-wage countries

Even though it is possible to demonstrate that trade-related employment shifts broadly net out at the aggregate level, absent large changes in trade balances, there could be a significant net impact on the employment of different *types* of labour, if labour is not homogeneous.

Chapter 3 of the *Jobs Study* attempted to quantify to what extent trade between OECD and developing countries has been associated with falls in employment and/or falls in relative wages for the low-skilled. As in the case of total trade, the approaches used included regression and IO analysis. Although trade between the OECD area and the sample of developing countries involved

(China plus the dynamic Asian economies, which together account for nearly half of OECD imports from developing countries) has grown in recent decades, it is still quite small, around 2 per cent of OECD GDP, and close to balance[27]. It was therefore not expected that the analysis would detect a major impact of such trade on OECD employment, either in total or by type of labour, nor did it. The IO analysis implied an employment gain between the early 1970s and the mid-1980s of about 0.75 million jobs in Japan and losses in other countries (except France) which ranged from about 1 million persons in the United States to a few tens of thousands in the smaller countries and Germany. Of the countries in the sample, only the United States and the United Kingdom registered net job losses associated with their total trade: in the case of the United States, losses associated with trade with developing countries were greater than gains on trade with other OECD countries. In the case of the United Kingdom, employment losses were associated with both kinds of trade, but especially trade with other OECD countries.

The regression analysis of the *Jobs Study* confirmed and extended these results, showing the existence of significant negative employment effects related to trade between the OECD and developing countries. The effects were confined to a small number of industries, especially textiles, clothing, footwear and electronic goods. The actual measured impact was small, because the trade involved is small. Interestingly, and unexpectedly, it was found that on balance, negative employment effects were most marked in industries employing (in OECD countries) a high proportion of skilled workers. Because of data limitations, it was not possible to investigate the impact of OECD/developing country trade on relative wages for skilled and unskilled workers.

Conclusions

Theory suggests that any shift in total employment associated with changes in trade patterns is likely to be small, provided that the external trade balance remains broadly unchanged at the macro level. Empirical analysis, including that carried out by the OECD Secretariat in the course of the *Jobs Study*, bears out this theoretical conclusion. Theory also suggests, and the analysis confirms, that there will nevertheless be shifts in employment between sectors as trade patterns change in response to cost and price pressures. However, there is no agreement among researchers on the size of the trade impact on sectoral employment patterns relative to the impacts of other forces, e.g. technological progress and institutional changes.

There is a similar lack of consensus on the size of the impact of shifts in trade patterns on wage inequality. While the majority view is that shifts in trade

Table 7. Economic performance before and after improved freedom of association[a]

(average growth rate in per cent)

	GDP		Manufacturing output		Real exports of goods and services	
	before[b]	after[c]	before[b]	after[c]	before[b]	after[c]
Argentina (1983)	-0.2	1.0	-0.5	0.0	0.6	2.8
Brazil (1988)	5.3	0.9	4.5	-2.2	9.5	4.8
Dominican Republic (1990)	4.4	4.5	1.7	4.2	9.1	5.6
Ecuador (1979)	7.1	1.3	11.6	2.1	0.4	2.3
Fiji (1987)	9.8	5.8	4.2	-0.6	14.3	6.7
Guatemala (1992)	4.1	4.1	n.a.	n.a.	5.6	8.6
Honduras (1990)	3.0	3.3	4.0	3.8	1.9	1.8
Korea (1987)	10.7	8.6	15.7	8.3	15.6	6.9
Panama (1989)	-0.5	10.5	-2.5	8.9	0.2	8.9
Peru (1990)	-0.9	1.8	n.a.	n.a.	-3.8	-23.2
Philippines (1987)	-1.3	4.0	-2.4	3.1	2.4	7.2
Suriname (1991)	1.7	0.6	-3.2	-2.4	n.a.	n.a.
Chinese Taipei (1987)	9.6	6.9	n.a.	n.a.	n.a.	n.a.
Thailand (1992)	10.7	8.2	14.7	11.5	17.3	13.2
Turkey (1986)	6.1	2.7	7.9	5.7	16.1	8.1
Uruguay (1985)	-7.6	4.4	-5.4	3.7	2.7	6.8
Venezuela (1990)	2.7	5.2	-3.3	4.5	6.8	3.6
Average of above countries	3.8	4.4	2.4	3.6	6.6	4.3

a) In parenthesis, the year when freedom-of-association laws were improved.

b) Average growth rate during the five-year period preceding improved freedom of association.

c) Average growth rate during the five-year period (or less if data are not available) following improved freedom of association.

Source: World Bank, *World Tables 1995.*

Table 8. Export performance[a]

	Group	Total 1990	Total 1990/1980	Manufacturing 1990	Manufacturing 1990/1980	Raw materials 1990	Raw materials 1990/1980
Argentina	2	0.4	-8.5	0.3	-7.4	0.7	21.7
Australia	1	1.1	-5.2	0.7	-6.9	2.9	48.6
Austria	1	1.3	41.5	1.5	20.1	0.4	56.6
Bahamas	1	0.0	-0.9	0.0	0.7	0.1	-0.9
Bangladesh	3	0.0	0.1	0.0	0.0	0.0	0.6
Barbados	1	0.0	-0.2	0.0	-0.5	0.0	42.8
Belg-Luxembourg	1	3.6	9.0	4.0	-5.3	1.4	10.4
Bolivia	3	0.0	-0.5	0.0	0.0	0.2	-0.1
Brazil	2	1.0	-4.7	0.9	-12.0	1.4	30.0
Canada	1	3.6	11.9	3.3	6.8	4.9	42.4
Chile	2	0.2	9.8	0.2	-10.7	0.5	103.5
China	4	1.7	105.9	1.6	147.3	2.2	82.8
Colombia	3	0.2	0.0	0.1	-0.5	0.6	-0.8
Denmark	1	1.0	21.7	1.1	0.9	0.6	94.1
Ecuador	2	0.1	-0.3	0.1	-0.2	0.3	-0.9
Egypt	4	0.1	-0.5	0.1	-0.2	0.6	-0.8
Ethiopia	2	0.0	-0.6	0.0	-0.7	0.0	0.0
Fiji	2	0.0	-0.2	0.0	-0.3	0.0	-0.3
Finland	1	0.8	11.6	0.9	1.6	0.3	-11.3
France	1	6.3	11.7	6.9	-6.1	3.5	60.9
Germany	1	11.8	20.0	14.0	0.1	2.1	29.8
Greece	1	0.2	-7.8	0.2	-11.2	0.4	18.4
Guatemala	3	0.0	-0.5	0.0	-0.5	0.0	-0.6
Haiti	3	0.0	-0.6	0.0	-0.7	0.0	-0.2
Honduras	3	0.0	0.6	0.0	-0.6	0.0	-0.4
Hong Kong	2	0.9	25.4	1.0	1.3	0.3	158.1
India	2	0.5	29.3	0.5	18.8	0.8	79.3
Indonesia	4	0.8	-35.9	0.4	168.4	2.6	-25.0
Iran	4	0.5	-0.3	0.0	-0.4	3.2	0.3
Ireland	1	0.7	65.8	0.8	41.2	0.2	79.1
Israel	1	0.4	0.3	0.2	0.1	0.0	-1.0
Italy	1	5.0	26.3	5.8	7.6	1.3	24.5
Jamaica	2	0.0	-0.3	0.0	-0.3	0.0	-0.3
Japan	1	8.6	30.8	10.5	6.8	0.3	80.1
Jordan	3	0.0	0.4	0.0	0.3	0.1	1.3
Kenya	3	0.0	-0.5	0.0	-0.5	0.1	-0.6
Korea	3	2.0	120.1	2.3	93.4	0.3	3.1
Kuwait	4	0.2	-0.8	0.1	-0.7	1.2	-0.7
Malaysia	3	0.9	29.7	0.7	60.0	1.8	52.8

Table 8. Export performance[a] *(cont.)*

	Group	Total 1990	Total 1990/1980	Manufacturing 1990	Manufacturing 1990/1980	Raw materials 1990	Raw materials 1990/1980
Malta	1	0.0	0.4	0.0	0.2	0.0	0.5
Mexico	2	1.2	32.2	1.0	95.2	2.1	23.6
Morocco	3	0.2	13.6	0.1	95.0	0.2	-14.1
Netherlands	1	4.2	-0.4	4.2	-7.1	4.2	16.2
New Zealand	1	0.3	1.7	0.2	-17.1	0.4	88.1
Niger	2	0.0	-0.7	0.0	-0.8	0.1	-0.4
Norway	1	1.0	-14.1	0.7	-40.4	2.6	100.2
Pakistan	3	0.2	0.2	0.2	0.1	0.0	-1.0
Panama	3	0.0	-0.4	0.0	-0.4	0.0	-0.8
Papua New Guinea	2	0.0	-0.4	0.0	-0.5	0.2	0.1
Peru	2	0.1	-0.5	0.0	-0.5	0.4	-0.9
Philippines	3	0.3	-17.5	0.3	-14.3	0.2	-24.7
Portugal	1	0.5	109.3	0.6	77.6	0.2	172.2
Singapore	3	1.1	64.5	1.0	69.6	1.6	93.4
South Africa	2	0.4	-0.4	0.2	-0.5	1.1	-0.6
Spain	1	1.7	57.4	1.8	29.0	1.3	180.6
Sri Lanka	3	0.1	0.1	0.1	0.3	0.0	-0.5
Surinam	1	0.0	-0.5	0.0	-0.5	0.1	0.1
Sweden	1	1.7	9.7	1.9	-7.1	0.8	45.2
Switzerland	1	2.0	30.3	2.4	6.7	0.1	60.5
Syria	4	0.1	0.2	0.1	3.3	0.5	0.3
Taiwan	3	2.0	99.7	2.4	62.8	0.2	241.6
Tanzania	4	0.0	-0.5	0.0	-0.6	0.0	-0.2
Thailand	3	0.6	106.0	0.6	180.3	0.6	37.1
Turkey	3	0.4	163.0	0.4	380.8	0.5	73.2
United Kingdom	1	5.6	-4.1	6.1	-15.9	3.1	7.6
United States	1	11.1	-1.4	11.7	-9.7	8.5	7.4
Uruguay	1	0.1	-0.1	0.1	-0.2	0.1	0.8
Venezuela	2	0.5	-0.5	0.1	0.9	3.1	0.0
Zambia	2	0.0	-0.5	0.0	-0.6	0.3	0.0
Zimbabwe	3	0.0	-0.4	0.0	-0.4	0.2	0.2
Group 1		72.6	15.7	79.7	2.6	39.8	46.4
Group 2		5.4	4.9	4.4	5.1	11.3	25.8
Group 3		8.2	27.5	8.4	44.1	6.5	24.2
Group 4		3.5	9.7	2.2	45.3	10.3	8.1

a) Exports as a share of world exports in 1990 and changes in the share with respect to 1980
(percentage of world exports and percentage change respectively).

Source: CHELEM.

Table 9. Comparative advantage patterns

Countries[a]	Sectors with a comparative advantage[b]	Factors which affect competitiveness[c]
High-income countries		
Australia (1)	Processed food, metals, steel	RI, SI
Austria (1)	Engines, paper, iron	SS, SI
Belgium-Lux. (1)	Iron & steel, cars, plastic articles	SI
Canada (1)	Paper, cereals, metals, gas, cars	SI, RI
Denmark (1)	Meat, furniture, engines, pharmaceutical	RI, SS, SB
Finland (1)	Paper, food, iron & steel	SI, RI
France (1)	Processed food, cars, aeronautics	RI, SI, SB
Germany (1)	Special machines, cars, engines	SS, SI
Israel (1)	Processed food, chemicals, electronics	RI, SI
Italy (1)	Leather, hardware, clothing, machines	LI, SS, SB
Japan (1)	Cars, engines, electric and electronic goods	SI, SS
Netherlands (1)	Gas, processed food, chemicals	RI, SB
Norway (1)	Oil, gas, metals, meat	RI
Sweden (1)	Paper, iron & steel, equipment, engines	SI
Switzerland (1)	Clocks, special machines, pharmaceutical	SS, SB
United Kingdom (1)	Oil, engines, aeronautics	RI, SS, SB
United States (1)	Cereals, aeronautics, engines	RI, SB, SS
Medium-income countries		
Greece (1)	Food, knitwear, cement	RI, LI
Hong Kong (2)	Clothing, knitwear, clocks, computers	LI, SB
Ireland (1)	Meat, computer equipment, chemicals	RI, SI
Korea (3)	Textiles, consumer electronics, ships, cars	LI,SI
New Zealand (1)	Agricultural products, metals, paper	RI, SI
Portugal (1)	Textiles, clothing, leather, wood articles	LI, RI
Singapore (3)	Petroleum products, computer equipement, consumer electronics	RI, SI
Spain (1)	Food, petroleum products, cars, iron & steel	RI, SI

134

Table 9. Comparative advantage patterns *(cont.)*

Chinese Taipei (3)	Textiles, leather, computer components	LI
Low-income countries		
Argentina (2)	Unprocessed food, leather	RI, LI
Brazil (2)	Iron ores, steel, unprocessed food	RI
Chile (2)	Metals, unprocessed food	RI
China (4)	Clothing, oil, carpets, leather	LI, RI
Colombia (3)	Oil, unprocessed food, textiles	RI, LI
Ecuador (2)	Oil, processed food, meat	RI
Egypt (4)	Oil, textiles, clothing	RI, LI
India (2)	Food, clothing, textiles, leather, carpets	LI, RI
Indonesia (4)	Oil, wood, unprocessed food, textiles	RI, LI
Malaysia (3)	Oil, fats, consumer electronics	RI, SB
Mexico (2)	Oil, unprocessed food, cars	RI, SI
Morocco (3)	Textiles, fertilisers	LI, SI
Pakistan (3)	Textiles, processed food, carpets, leather, clothing	LI, RI
Peru (2)	Metals, processed food, petroleum products, textiles	RI, LI
Philippines (3)	Unprocessed food, clothing, textiles	RI, LI
South Africa (2)	Metals, iron & steel, minerals	RI, SI
Thailand (3)	Unprocessed food, clothing, leather	RI, LI
Turkey (3)	Unprocessed food, iron, textiles	RI, LI
Venezuela (2)	Oil, petroleum products, iron ores	RI

a) The number in parenthesis indicates the group to which a country belongs. Group 1 comprises countries which fully observe freedom of association. Group 4 comprises countries where observance is weakest. For further details of the country grouping, see Part I, under "Observance of core labour standards in selected countries".

b) This is based on an index for comparative advantages calculated for 71 sectors, on the basis of foreign trade performance of each sector. For more details on how the index is calculated, see text.

c) Industrial sectors are classified according to the main factors believed to affect competitiveness. RI, LI, SI, SS and SB denote, respectively, resource-intensive, labour-intensive, scale-intensive, specialised-supplier and science-based sectors.

Source: OECD Secretariat, based on CHELEM data base.

Table 10. US imports of textile products by group of countries[1]

| Products | Average price[2] (US$ per ton) | | | |
	Group 1	Group 2	Group 3	Group 4
Silk yarn and yarn spun from noil	39.0	..	28.9	18.7
Yarn of wool or animal hair	16.0	5.1	..	60.5
Cotton yarn	20.4	3.9	3.0	3.2
Yarn with over 85% of synthetic fibres	4.8	2.0	4.3	3.7
Yarn of discontinuous synthetic fibres (less than 85%)	17.7	..	4.2	4.7
Yarn of regenerated fibres, not for retail sale	13.7	3.6	3.1	4.2
Yarn of textile fibres n.e.s. (incl. yarn of glass fibres)	3.6	1.0	1.1	2.5
Cotton fabrics, woven, unbleached, not mercerised	11.2	3.0	3.9	3.3
Other cotton fabrics	13.7	8.6	5.9	8.8
Fabrics, woven of continuous synthetic textile	18.5	8.9	9.1	7.6
Fabrics, woven with over 85% of discont. synth. text. mater.	20.4	4.3	12.7	3.4
Fabrics, woven of discont. synth. text. mater.	22.9	8.7	8.7	4.3
Fabrics, woven of continuous regenerated textile	33.3	21.1	15.8	7.5
Fabrics, woven with over 85% of discontinuous regenerated textile	23.9	11.4	9.1	6.1
Fabrics, woven (less than 85% of discontinous regenerated textile)	25.7	14.5	11.2	5.9
Pile and chenille fabrics, woven of man-made fibres	55.3	18.3	..	23.6
Fabrics, woven, of silk, of noil or other waste silk	171.3	35.3	101.2	44.0
Fabrics, woven, with over 85% of wool/fine animal hair	50.0	22.6	29.3	20.4
Fabrics, woven, of wool/fine animal hair n.e.s.	46.1	..	..	18.9
Fabrics, woven, of flax or of ramie	29.2	3.0	11.8	8.7
Fabrics, woven, of jute or of other textile bast fibres	12.2	0.7	0.7	4.6
Fabrics, woven, n.e.s.	40.6	44.0	..	6.2
Knitted/crocheted fabrics of synthetic material	28.9	5.8	10.2	4.5
Knitted/crocheted fabrics of fibres other than synthetic	29.1	4.2	4.8	4.0
Tulle, lace, embroidery, ribbons and other small ware	28.1	37.9	21.2	23.0
Coated/impregnated textile fabrics and products	13.6	2.4	6.5	6.1
Twine, cordage, ropes and cables	10.2	1.7	1.7	2.1
Wadding textile fabrics for use in machinery	43.4	9.6	1.8	6.9
Special products of textile materials	26.8	2.9	..	4.3
Sacks and bags of textile materials	13.8	2.1	2.0	1.9
Tarpaulines, sails, awnings, sunblinds, tents	12.9	..	10.1	7.9
Travelling rugs and blankets	15.9	7.1	16.5	4.0
Bed linen, table linen, toilet and kitchen linen	24.9	10.3	7.9	8.2
Other made-up articles of textile materials	14.3	11.3	7.2	4.3
Carpets, carpeting and rugs, knotted	41.8	13.8	26.9	27.3
Kelem, schumacks and karamanie rugs and the like	30.4	3.8	24.1	13.7
Carpets and rugs of wool and fine animal hair	19.2	7.2	18.5	8.7
Carpets and rugs of man-made textile materials	17.8	8.6	6.0	8.9
Carpets and rugs of other textile materials	18.8	59.2	11.5	8.0
Number of products for which a group's exports to the US are the cheapest	*0*	*13*	*9*	*17*

Table 10. US imports of textile products by group of countries[1] *(cont.)*

Products	Market share[3] Group 1	Group 2	Group 3	Group 4
Silk yarn and yarn spun from noil	23.0	..	5.2	46.1
Yarn of wool or animal hair	33.1	3.2	..	0.2
Cotton yarn	18.7	4.2	15.4	21.1
Yarn with over 85% of synthetic fibres	28.1	0.0	1.1	1.6
Yarn of discontinuous synthetic fibres (less than 85%)	7.3	..	30.6	4.6
Yarn of regenerated fibres, not for retail sale	36.8	0.1	1.1	0.6
Yarn of textile fibres n.e.s. (incl. yarn of glass fibres)	37.9	2.5	5.7	0.8
Cotton fabrics, woven, unbleached, not mercerised	1.0	11.2	16.8	29.9
Other cotton fabrics	29.2	8.3	5.8	8.4
Fabrics, woven of continuous synthetic textile	..	..	..	..
Fabrics, woven with over 85% of discont. synth. text. mater.	22.2	0.6	0.5	5.8
Fabrics, woven of discont. synth. text. mater.	21.9	0.3	22.8	15.1
Fabrics, woven of continuous regenerated textile	60.0	1.0	3.8	5.8
Fabrics, woven with over 85% of discontinuous regenerated textile	58.8	0.3	11.0	5.8
Fabrics, woven (less than 85% of discontinous regenerated textile)	34.5	0.0	6.8	0.9
Pile and chenille fabrics, woven of man-made fibres	10.9	0.2	..	6.7
Fabrics, woven, of silk, of noil or other waste silk	50.8	8.6	2.3	9.5
Fabrics, woven, with over 85% of wool/fine animal hair	34.6	2.5	0.1	4.5
Fabrics, woven, of wool/fine animal hair n.e.s.	46.0	..	..	0.4
Fabrics, woven, of flax or of ramie	27.3	0.1	0.2	17.3
Fabrics, woven, of jute or of other textile bast fibres	1.1	52.3	45.9	0.1
Fabrics, woven, n.e.s.	45.0	4.4	..	28.7
Knitted/crocheted fabrics of synthetic material	7.8	0.0	1.3	2.6
Knitted/crocheted fabrics of fibres other than synthetic	15.7	1.2	28.7	0.8
Tulle, lace, embroidery, ribbons and other small ware	22.2	2.1	4.4	9.3
Coated/impregnated textile fabrics and products	34.6	0.0	2.8	0.6
Twine, cordage, ropes and cables	8.3	0.6	13.3	6.2
Wadding textile fabrics for use in machinery	42.2	0.0	0.1	0.5
Special products of textile materials	38.4	0.6	..	0.3
Sacks and bags of textile materials	1.3	16.2	27.7	13.2
Tarpaulines, sails, awnings, sunblinds, tents	0.7	..	7.3	30.6
Travelling rugs and blankets	8.9	1.3	1.8	11.3
Bed linen, table linen, toilet and kitchen linen	2.9	10.4	15.8	31.7
Other made-up articles of textile materials	3.3	2.3	10.4	32.4
Carpets, carpeting and rugs, knotted	0.2	36.5	17.4	35.9
Kelem, schumacks and karamanie rugs and the like	2.4	28.1	14.6	17.4
Carpets and rugs of wool and fine animal hair	3.3	10.3	4.1	30.6
Carpets and rugs of man-made textile materials	5.1	0.1	0.7	7.7
Carpets and rugs of other textile materials	5.0	61.4	1.6	7.0
Average market share of the group	*21.9*	*8.0*	*9.9*	*11.9*

1. Countries are grouped according to the degree of observance of freedom-of-association rights. Group 1 includes France, Germany, Italy and Japan. Group 2 includes Ecuador, Fiji, Jamaica, Peru and Zambia. Group 3 includes Bangladesh, Bolivia, Colombia, Guatemala, Honduras, Jordan, Kenya, Morocco, Pakistan, Philippines, Sri Lanka, Thailand, Zimbabwe. Group 4 includes China, Egypt, Indonesia, Niger, Tanzania.

2. The average price is calculated as the ratio of import values to import volumes.

3. The market share is the ratio of US imports of a particular product from a given group of countries to total US imports of the product.

Source : NEXT data base.

Table 11. Export prices and receipts of carpets (1992)[a]

	Average unit value of an exported carpet (US$)[b]	Export receipts of carpets (US$ million)
Hand-made carpets		
China (2)	43.8	423
India (3)	54.9	173
Nepal (3)	67.7	78
Pakistan (3)	67.5	204
Carpets manufactured with artificial textiles		
Belgium (1)	3.7	1 743
Denmark (1)	4.9	97
Netherlands (1)	3.3	458
Turkey (2)	4.0	54

a) The table provides figures for exports of hand-made carpets (SITC 6592) and carpets manufactured with artificial textiles (SITC 6595).
b) For hand-made carpets, figures refer to unit export values per square meter. For carpets manufactured with artificial textiles, figures refer to unit export values per metric ton.

(1) Country for which there is no evidence of child labour.
(2) Country for which there is some evidence of child labour.
(3) Country where child labour is pervasive in the carpet industry.

Source: United Nations, *International Trade Statistics*, 1993; and OECD estimates.

**Table 12. Recent trade liberalisation episodes in 44
initially low-standards countries
(1980-94)**

Trade regime status in 1994	Year began	Number of years sustained to date
Relatively open		
Argentina	1987	8
Bolivia	1985	10
Chile	1985	10
Costa Rica	1985	10
Ghana	1986	9
Korea	1984	11
Malaysia	1986	9
Mexico	1985	10
Peru	1990	5
Uruguay	1985	10
Venezuela	1989	6
Chinese Taipei	1985	10
Moderately restrictive		
Benin	1993	2
Burundi	1991	4
Brazil	1991	4
Côte d'Ivoire	1984	11
Colombia	1985	10
Ecuador	1985	10
El Salvador	1992	3
Ethiopia	1992	3
Guatemala	1992	3
Honduras	1992	3
Indonesia	1985	10
Jamaica	1991	4
Kenya	1988	7
Mali	1992	3
Morocco	1983	12
Philippines	1985	10
Sri Lanka	1987	8
Thailand	1982	13
Tunisia	1987	8
Turkey	1980	5
Zimbabwe	1992	3

Table 12. Recent trade liberalisation episodes in 44 initially low-standards countries *(cont.)* (1980-94)

Trade regime status in 1994	Year began	Number of year sustained to date
Restrictive		
Algeria	1991	4
Bangladesh	1985	10
Cameroon	1991	4
China	1978	17
Egypt	1991	4
India	1988	7
Malawi	1988	7
Nepal	1986	9
Nigeria	1986	9
Pakistan	1989	6
Tanzania	1988	7

Sources: IMF (1992, 1995); WTO/GATT, Trade Policy Reviews.

Table 13. Better association rights before/after trade liberalisation?

Before	After	Together	Rights virtually non-existent	Rights uncertain
Argentina	Bangladesh*	Algeria*	Cameroon	Benin
Brazil	Bolivia*	Ethiopia	China	Burundi
Ecuador	Chile	Guatemala*	Egypt	Côte d'Ivoire
Honduras*	Colombia*	Mali*	Indonesia	El Salvador
India	Costa Rica	Peru	Nigeria	Malawi
Jamaica	Ghana*	Sri Lanka*	Tanzania	Nepal
Kenya*	Korea*	Uruguay		
Pakistan*	Malaysia*	Venezuela		
Zimbabwe*	Mexico*			
	Morocco*			
	Philippines*			
	Chinese Taipei*			
	Thailand*			
	Tunisia*			
	Turkey*			

* Weak improvement in association rights.

Sources: Association rights: Tables 3-5 and ILOLEX (1995). Trade liberalisation: IMF (1992, 1995); WTO/GATT Trade Policy Reviews.

Table 14. Association rights and successful trade reforms, status in 1994

Relatively open trade regime			
Some restrictions persist	*Significantly restricted association rights*	*Association rights virtually non-existent*	*Information lacking*
(Group 2)	*(Group 3)*	*(Group 4)*	
Argentina Chile Costa Rica Mexico Peru Uruguay Venezuela	Bolivia Ghana Korea Malaysia Chinese Taipei		
Moderately restrictive trade regime			
Some restrictions persist	*Significantly restricted association rights*	*Association rights virtually non-existent*	*Information lacking*
(Group 2)	(Group 3)	(Group 4)	
Brazil Ecuador Ethiopia Jamaica	Colombia Guatemala Honduras Kenya Mali Morocco Philippines Sri Lanka Thailand Tunisia Turkey Zimbabwe	Indonesia	Benin Burundi Côte d'Ivoire El Salvador

Table 14. Association rights and successful trade reforms, status in 1994 *(cont.)*

Restrictive trade regime			
Some restrictions persist	*Significantly restricted association rights*	*Association rights virtually non-existent*	*Information lacking*
(Group 2)	(Group 3)	(Group 4)	
India	Algeria	Cameroon	Malawi
	Bangladesh	China	Nepal
	Pakistan	Egypt	
	Nigeria		
	Tanzania		

Sources: Tables 3-5, 12 and 13.

Table 15. Employment by multinational enterprises, 1990 or latest year available

	Employment (millions)	Share of total MNE employment
Total MNE employment		
Home-country employment in parent company	44	60.3%
Employment in foreign affiliates	29	39.7%
Total MNE employment, all countries	73	100.0%
Foreign affiliate employment		
Developed countries	17	23.3%
China	6	8.2%
Other developing countries	6	8.2%
Employment in foreign affiliates	29	39.7%
Employment in export-processing zones		
China	2	2.7%
Other developing countries	2	2.7%
Total MNE employment in EPZs	4	5.4%

Source: UNCTAD, *World Investment Report 1994.*

NOTES

1. In his study of the so-called sweat-shop, Piore (1994) provides an interesting illustration of the positive effects of core labour standards. According to Piore, the sweat-shop capitalism prevailing in the United States in the 19th century was based on "worker exploitation", i.e. poor labour standards. Piore mentions the particular case of the textile industry where, owing to the lack of labour standards, employers paid little attention to human capital and management issues. By the end of the century, the federal government introduced labour standards, including health and safety regulations. This forced employers to look for new strategies to improve competitiveness. It followed a period of organisational and technical innovation, permitting an unprecedented increase in productivity levels in the textile industry. Higher productivity levels in the textile industry, in turn, freed up resources which could be used more productively in other sectors. For a more recent discussion of these issues, see also Swinnerton (1995).

2. As mentioned earlier, there is no ILO Convention which is specifically devoted to the elimination of child labour exploitation.

3. Work by Freeman and Medoff (1984) lends support to this interpretation. There is an interesting parallel with competition legislation. The latter is designed to prevent practices that distort the free working of product markets. In particular, competition legislation seeks to provide consumers and producers with protection against abuses of dominant positions. Similarly, there might be cases where employers enjoy a dominant position in the labour market, with detrimental repercussions on the structure of wages across sectors and/or professional categories.

4. For a thorough review of the literature, see Calmfors (1993).

5. For example, see Freeman (1994).

6. Evidence that high dismissal costs and other provisions of employment protection legislation inhibit job creation provides some support to this argument (OECD, 1993).

7. In reality, these individuals may also be concerned by social moral consciousness. But they may think this issue is of special importance when they buy goods. An example of this is when consumers select environmentally friendly goods, as designated by special eco-labelling.

8. For a discussion on how consumers might be informed about the social content of their purchases, see Freeman (1994).

9. For two recent studies on the links between civil rights and economic growth, see Bhalla (1994) and Sachs and Warner (1995).

10. An example might be restrictions on collective bargaining in the electronics industry in Malaysia, which are designed to maintain wages in this industry at below-market rates.

11. The empirical literature on this issue has been reviewed by Freeman and Medoff (1984). Even if favourable productivity effects are present, as Freeman and Medoff claim, the issue is whether they offset the substitution effects on labour demand arising from union wage premia.

12. The issues of forced labour and non-discrimination will be ignored, owing to the lack of reliable information on these standards in the countries selected here.

13. In the short run, relative cyclical positions play a key role in export determination.

14. In low per capita income countries, GDP per capita (in current US$) is less than $5 000. In medium per capita income countries it ranges from $5 000 to $15 000. GDP per capita (in current US$) in the remaining countries exceeds $15 000.

15. Particularly impressive is the export performance of Turkey, which appears as an outlier in the chart.

16. Turkey would also provide a good example. However, labour law changes have occurred relatively recently (in most cases in 1991), making

it difficult to assess subsequent trade effects. It should be stressed that CHELEM contains complete data only up to 1992.

17. Even after 1987, many labour leaders and trade unionists have been prosecuted for activities considered illegal (Wilkinson, 1994).

18. This is based on a classification of industries according to the primary factors that are believed to affect competitiveness (see OECD, 1992a).

19. The ten countries examined in the study are China, Hong Kong, India, Indonesia, Korea, Malaysia, Mexico, the Philippines, Singapore and Thailand.

20. It is important to note, however, that data on EPZs differ widely depending on the sources. The lack of accurate empirical evidence hampers the analysis and particularly comparisons over time.

21. "Flow of foreign funds to China jumps 12 per cent" and "Asia set up to become top investment target", *Financial Times,* 6 February 1996.

22. The reason put forward by Wood is that developing countries typically export goods no longer produced in OECD countries. According to Wood, the conventional factor-content method is based on domestic labour coefficients, which refer to the production of goods that are skilled-labour intensive, whereas imports are unskilled-labour intensive. It follows that the conventional methodology underestimates the number of unskilled workers who would be needed (in the absence of trade) to produce the goods that are now imported from developing countries. Instead, Wood begins with the labour coefficients used in developing countries to produce their exports and then makes a number of adjustments to correct for relative factor price differentials between developing and developed countries. The resulting "counter-factual coefficients" are then used to estimate the factor content of developed countries' imports from developing countries. For a critique of Wood's method, see Baldwin (1995); Wood (1995) sets out his response to the critiques of his method.

23. It has also been pointed out, however, that even if such a relationship were stronger, the conclusion that the result would be a fall in the real wages of the unskilled (or a rise in unskilled labour unemployment) is

based on several strong assumptions that may or may not hold true (Bhagwati, 1995).

24. In fact, in the case of complete specialisation (all the more relevant when examining the impact of trade with countries that produce goods no longer manufactured in OECD countries) and in the presence of scale economies, real wages of both skilled and unskilled workers can well rise as a result of trade with non-OECD countries.

25. Sachs and Shatz agree that the standard model of international trade emphasizes the transmission role of relative prices. But they argue that according to other models, trade may affect relative wages through other routes, which do not involve price changes of low-skilled goods.

26. The detailed econometric analysis was published separately in Larre (1995). For further in-depth analysis of trade and wage issues, see Oliveira-Martins (1994).

27. This is true for the OECD area as a whole. Japan runs a substantial surplus *vis-à-vis* these countries, the United States a large deficit and Europe a somewhat smaller one, relative to their respective GDPs.

PART III

MECHANISMS TO PROMOTE CORE LABOUR STANDARDS WORLD-WIDE

PART III

MECHANISMS TO PROMOTE

CORE LABOUR STANDARDS WORLD-WIDE

This part of the study sets out to review and evaluate different types of mechanisms to promote, directly or indirectly, core labour standards. Some of these mechanisms are already operational, some have been adopted but are not yet functioning, while others have merely been suggested. Further, while some deal only with one core labour standard (e.g. child labour exploitation), others seek to address a broader set of human rights.

In Part I, core labour standards are defined as fundamental human rights, providing framework conditions for the exercise of other working rights. These core labour standards are embodied, albeit imperfectly, in a number of ILO Conventions, and they also are enumerated in the United Nations Covenants on Human Rights, including the Convention on the Rights of the Child. Since these instruments have been ratified by a large number of countries, it can be argued that the principle of a set of core labour standards, representing basic human rights, receives near-universal acceptance. Nevertheless, Part I also shows that the existence of national norms on basic labour rights or ratification of the relevant ILO Conventions does not necessarily imply universal respect of these norms. The lack of observance of these basic norms thus constitutes the major problem.

Some advocate letting market forces, fostered by trade liberalisation, "do the job", and indeed the evidence in Part II points to the existence of a positive relationship between sustained trade liberalisation programmes and improvements in core labour standards. However, there are reasons to doubt that trade liberalisation alone will automatically lead to an improvement in core labour standards, as acknowledged by the ILO Working Party on the Social Dimensions of the Liberalisation of International Trade (ILO, GB.264/WP/SDL/1, November 1995). First, the existence and direction of a causality link cannot be inferred from the fact that trade liberalisation and improvements in core labour standards are positively correlated. The relationship between trade liberalisation and social development is part of a broader set of interactions including economic growth and the build-up of democratic institutions. Trade liberalisation can thus be seen as providing basic conditions that are important, but not sufficient, for higher levels of core labour standards in a country. In this perspective, it does not seem appropriate to consider it, strictly speaking, as a promotion mechanism in the same vein as the ones surveyed below.

When discussing each of these mechanisms, it may be useful to have in mind the following questions as a framework for their evaluation:

− Is it an effective means of promoting core labour standards worldwide? That is:

   • *Is the mechanism directed at the source of low core labour standards?*

Three distinct causes of low standards can be identified, although in general these causes will vary depending on the standards and the countries concerned. First, in a few countries, national legislation does not embody core standards. Denial of core standards is part of the political system. Though the countries in this situation are few in number, one of them, China, accounts for a large share of world population and a significant and increasing proportion of the world economy. Second, in a few countries there is a deliberate policy to reduce core standards in certain parts of the economy, such as EPZs, but not across the board. Third, there are cases of non-enforcement of national legislation on core standards by certain employers; in these cases the policy is to enforce core standards, but some individuals or employers do not respect the law. These cases are likely to occur more often in poor countries, where governments lack the means to enforce the law, than in developed countries. In addition, non-enforcement of core labour standards may be a result of poverty, under-development and cultural factors, notably in the case of exploitative child labour.

   • *Does it refer to internationally defined core labour standards (as in the relevant ILO and UN Conventions), or to specific national labour legislation?*

   • *Does it have universal or partial coverage in terms of states and/or private agents?*

   • *Is it politically acceptable for all concerned countries?*

– What is its likely economic impact, notably on trade and/or investment flows?

It is extremely difficult to assess with very much precision the economic impact of the various mechanisms, especially when they have been recently adopted or have only been proposed. The evaluation here will thus be very much qualitative, trying in most cases only to identify the type of economic effect (if any) of the mechanism in question. In the case of existing mechanisms, an attempt will be made to assess their impact on the core labour standard(s) targeted.

This review is organised according to whether, for each mechanism, the channelling of incentives (or disincentives) is accomplished through: (i) government decisions at the multilateral, bilateral or unilateral level; or (ii) private actions. If, as mentioned in Part II, core labour standards share some of the characteristics of public goods, then there is scope for welfare-enhancing government intervention. Alternatively, in situations where core labour standards are more adequately viewed as private goods, then consumer demand can lead to an efficient market outcome. This will be the case if consumers derive utility from purchasing goods produced under conditions where core labour standards are respected. Through market forces, economic benefits derived from the suppression of core labour standards will tend to disappear.

The ILO supervisory mechanism is reviewed first, along with current proposals to improve and strengthen it. The second section looks at the positive role of development co-operation programmes, focusing on the process of economic development. The third deals with other proposed mechanisms at the multilateral level. In particular, it examines suggestions which have been made to introduce core labour standards in the WTO. Suggestions to link labour standards with multilateral financial assistance are also reviewed. Regional and unilateral government actions are examined in the fourth section, while the fifth focuses on the role of voluntary codes of conduct for MNEs. Finally, mechanisms based on private actions such as labelling schemes and investment programmes are considered in the last section.

An overview of the ILO monitoring system

Since its creation in 1919, the ILO has established an all-embracing set of Conventions on social, labour and workers' rights (see Part I). Once set, the Conventions are subject to an elaborate review process for those countries that have chosen to ratify them. Another important role of the ILO is to monitor closely the application of certain obligations arising from membership of the Organisation. This section presents an overview of the ILO's supervisory system and a brief assessment of the effectiveness of its functioning.

The ILO supervisory system

The ILO has at its disposal a variety of methods which aim to ensure application of the existing Conventions.

Regular supervisory system

The aim of the regular supervisory system is to ensure compliance with Conventions for countries that have ratified them. The first stage of the procedure is the provision of a report by governments which have ratified a particular Convention. Countries submit these reports every two or five years, depending on the Convention; they can sometimes be requested to submit reports more frequently. Copies of these reports are sent to the most representative employers' and workers' organisations in the country under examination. These organisations are invited to comment on the report and, if necessary, to contradict it or provide additional information concerning the application of the Convention in question.

The report, together with any comments from employers' and workers' organisations, is then submitted by the Secretariat of the ILO to the independent Committee of Experts on the Application of Conventions and Recommendations, which meets annually. This Committee comprises 20 independent legal experts, appointed by the Governing Body of the ILO, acting upon proposals of the Director-General. The Committee examines compliance. It can ask for additional information and, if necessary, call for changes in law and practice in order to ensure compliance with the Convention.

The Committee of Experts, in turn, submits a report to the tripartite Conference Committee on the Application of Conventions and Recommendations. This report, produced annually, contains a general overview of the main trends and problems, a review of the implementation of obligations by particular countries and a summary of national laws and practices based on reports submitted by member states. In the light of the report, the tripartite of Conference Committee may invite governments to appear for further discussion. In particular, it may ask governments to explain intended measures to fulfil their obligations. A final report is then discussed at the plenary session of the International Labour Conference.

Procedure based on complaints

Two complaint procedures for violations of ILO standards are provided for in the ILO Constitution:

– Representations may be made by any employers' or workers' organisations alleging non-observance by a government of a Convention that the country in question has ratified. Representations are examined by a special tripartite committee designated by the Governing Body. The committee can request information from the government which is examined. If necessary, the Governing Body can also publish the representations. So far, very few (only 59) representations have been presented, but it is interesting to note that this procedure appears to be increasingly used, as attested by the fact that in 1994 alone 13 representations were made.

– Complaints against a government that has ratified a particular Convention may be presented by another government that has ratified the same Convention, by a delegate to the International Labour Conference, or by the Governing Body of the ILO. These complaints are examined by an independent Commission of Inquiry, set up by the Governing Body. The Commission can issue recommendations. The government concerned then informs the ILO whether it accepts the recommendations of the Commission or proposes to bring the complaint to the International Court of Justice. A decision of the latter in regard to a complaint is considered final. Few complaints have been made so far (only 23 in number) and there is no sign that this procedure is being used more frequently. One reason for this may be the fact that this procedure is both slow and expensive.

Special procedure on freedom of association

Established in 1951 as a tripartite body comprising nine members of the Governing Body, and chaired since 1978 by an independent personality, the

Committee on Freedom of Association examines complaints containing allegations of infringements of the principle of freedom of association, regardless of whether the countries concerned have ratified the freedom-of-association Conventions. The consent of the governments concerned is not necessary in order for these complaints to be examined: the legal basis for this concept resides in the Constitution of the ILO and the Declaration of Philadelphia. This Declaration, which has been part of the ILO Constitution since 1944, mentions freedom of association as one of the building principles of the ILO; it also insists on the role of the ILO in implementing the necessary programmes with a view to ensuring the effective application of the right to collective bargaining. Accordingly, member states, by virtue of their membership in the Organisation, are bound to respect the fundamental principles contained in its Constitution, particularly those concerning freedom of association and collective bargaining, even though they may not have ratified the Conventions on this subject.

Complaints can emanate from organisations of workers and employers of the country concerned, from international organisations of workers and employers when one of their members is directly concerned with the complaint, or from international organisations of employers and workers with consultative status at the ILO. The Committee on Freedom of Association systematically examines the substance of the cases submitted to it and presents conclusions to the Governing Body, recommending, where appropriate, that it draw the attention of the governments concerned to any principles called into question, and in particular to any recommendations made with a view to settling the difficulties raised in the complaint. When the case concerns a country that has ratified one of the relevant Conventions (notably 87 and 98), the conclusions and recommendations of the Committee are brought to the attention of the Committee of Experts on the Application of Conventions. Otherwise, when the case concerns a country that has not ratified the relevant Conventions, the Committee on Freedom of Association can request this country to provide information on the measures taken to follow up its recommendations and ask the Director-General of the ILO to discuss the issue with the government of the country concerned.

The Committee meets three times a year, thus facilitating the establishment of a continuous dialogue. The system also enables the presentation of complaints quickly after the alleged case occurs. Not surprisingly, the Committee on Freedom of Association is very busy: since its creation, it has examined some 1 800 cases concerning 135 countries. It has established a series of principles which constitute a unique body of jurisprudence on freedom of association.

Direct contacts and technical assistance

The ILO also establishes dialogue with member countries. First, missions and direct contacts are carried out with the aim of examining particular issues raised by the Committee of Experts on the Application of Conventions. Obviously, the nature of these contacts depends on the political will of the government concerned. Among recent direct contacts, it is worth mentioning those with Thailand concerning the application of Convention 29 on forced labour, and those with Costa Rica, Indonesia, Pakistan and Malaysia concerning freedom of association.

In order to facilitate compliance with ILO Conventions, the ILO also proposes technical assistance programmes to its member countries. These programmes can take the form of legal advice when a review of national legislation is needed, but they can also be more focused on implementation issues, especially in the area of child labour. In 1993, technical assistance was granted to about 50 countries.

Outcomes of the ILO supervisory system

The ILO has recently undertaken an evaluation of its supervisory procedures, and it is beyond the scope of this study to make a definitive assessment of the effectiveness of those procedures. The aim of this section is simply to make some remarks on the functioning of the ILO system, with particular focus on how ILO Conventions on core labour standards, as defined in Part I, are monitored.

Freedom of association and collective bargaining

There appears to be some agreement that one of the most important procedures of the ILO is that of the Committee on Freedom of Association. Because of its tripartite composition and the frequency of its meetings, the Committee has examined numerous cases. Also, procedural rules are rather flexible, thereby facilitating inspections and inquiries. The role of the Committee is particularly effective in cases of blatant violations of freedom of association, in particular concerning acts of anti-union discrimination. These cases can often be readily proven, and international public opinion appears to be rather sensitive to them. On the other hand, cases of restrictions on the freedom to form unions, collective bargaining and the right to strike are much less spectacular. The procedure can also take a long time, as it deals with areas which are very complex from the legal point of view. Finally, certain restrictions are deeply embedded in the industrial relations systems of particular countries, and it is not easy to modify them without undertaking a complete overhaul of the system.

According to the ILO, the role of the Committee has been particularly useful in countries which recently acceded to democracy (Eastern Europe, Chile, etc.). For example, in Poland the ILO has maintained close links with unions that were unofficial at the time of the communist regime.

More generally, most governments appear to be extremely sensitive to freedom-of-association issues. They are reluctant to see any complaints on this issue appearing in the media. This is one reason why nearly all countries examined under the Committee's procedure respond to the complaints, often indicating that action will be taken to solve the issue.

In general terms, a trend towards an improvement in the situation regarding freedom-of-association rights can be discerned. Thus, the 1994 report of the Committee of Experts mentions two interesting figures:

- Since 1964, the Committee of Experts has expressed satisfaction in 2 070 cases, where progress towards resolution of the complaints had been made as a result of ILO monitoring.

- In 1995, the Committee of Experts highlights progress in 36 cases, concerning 22 countries. A large number of these cases relate to core labour standards: seven concern Conventions 87 and 98, one concerns forced labour, and seven non-discrimination in employment.

It is, however, difficult to gauge the extent to which this progress is due to the effectiveness of ILO procedures or whether it reflects instead a more general tendency towards the establishment of democratic institutions observed, in particular, since the end of the Cold War.

Despite these encouraging trends, the activity of the Committee on Freedom of Association has been criticised on several grounds. First, it is sometimes argued that its recommendations are not given enough publicity. Giving greater publicity in the international media to the most important cases might encourage more countries to comply with their obligations. Second, the recommendations of the Committee are often very legalistic. Thus, there is a risk that the Committee devotes as much attention to relatively minor differences with respect to the Conventions as to more fundamental violations of labour rights. Finally, the special procedure functions on the basis of complaints which often originate from national unions. As a result, countries where unions are relatively free are subject to more numerous complaints compared with countries where unions are either repressed or under close political control.

Forced labour and non-discrimination

Forced labour and non-discrimination in employment are monitored mainly through the regular procedure. In 1994, the regular procedure on forced labour led to observations concerning 49 countries. Some of those observations apply to OECD countries, but the most blatant violations of the ILO Conventions in this area concern Thailand, Bangladesh, Brazil, Haiti, India, Pakistan, Sudan and Peru. Most cases relate to prison labour, compulsory labour, bonded labour (including children) and slavery. Complaints procedures have been used recently in the cases of Brazil, Guatemala, Myanmar and Thailand.

The ILO made 22 observations concerning cases of discrimination in employment in 1994 (43 observations in 1993), 5 of which concerned OECD countries (11 in 1993).

There are various problems with the regular procedure, making its effectiveness problematic. First, the procedure only applies to countries that have ratified the Conventions. Second, it is meaningful only if and when governments submit a report to the Committee of Experts at the date requested. Only 16.4 per cent of the reports on ratified Conventions had been submitted at the requested date for the 1995 examination by the Committee of Experts, which has expressed great concern about this issue[1]. Many reports are submitted after the requested date: 68 per cent of the reports were submitted by the end of the 1995 session of the Committee of Experts. However, some of these reports are submitted so late that the Committee does not have the time to examine them in detail. According to the Committee, a number of these reports are incomplete and do not enable it to reach conclusions regarding the application of the Conventions. Third, the regular procedure is more limited in its application than the Committee on Freedom of Association.

Measures to strengthen the ILO supervisory system

Given the importance of ILO Conventions on freedom of association and collective bargaining, forced labour and non-discrimination in employment, the Director-General of the ILO recently proposed measures to strengthen the supervisory system of these Conventions[2]. The intention of these proposals was to promote application of the principles of prohibition of forced labour and non-discrimination in employment in all member states, irrespective of their ratification of the corresponding Conventions. This could be achieved, *inter alia*, through i) the extension of the freedom-of-association procedure; or ii) the application of Article 19 of the ILO Constitution whereby member states may be requested to report on a regular basis on obstacles to ratification and application of an ILO instrument. The latter procedure already exists for Convention 111 and the Director-General has proposed to extend it to other fundamental Conventions.

Discussion of these proposals took place during the November 1995 and March 1996 sessions of the ILO Governing Body. The proposal to extend the special procedure for freedom of association to the forced labour and non-discrimination standards met with considerable opposition. The other proposal was accepted. There will be further discussion of the strengthening of the ILO supervisory system at the November 1996 session of the ILO Governing Body. Several ILO member countries believe that the priority is to improve the efficiency and effectiveness of existing supervisory procedures.

Concluding remarks

The ILO has established a well-developed system for monitoring the application of its Conventions. The special procedure on freedom of association appears to be relatively effective: there is some evidence that most governments respond to complaints presented under this procedure. But it functions on the basis of complaints, so that governments from countries where union rights are best protected are likely to be more often criticised than other governments less concerned with union rights. Its effectiveness could perhaps be increased if important recommendations formulated by the Committee were given more publicity, since most governments are very sensitive to the issue of freedom of association.

Monitoring of the application of Conventions related to forced labour and non-discrimination is more problematic. First, according to the regular procedure, only countries that have ratified these Conventions are examined. The ILO Secretariat has suggested the use of a procedure already applied to Convention 111 to inquire about reasons for non-ratification of key Conventions, with the aim of promoting ratification. Second, such examinations may not be frequent enough; they depend on the examining government's sending a report to the ILO, on the availability of relevant information as well as on the submission of comments by workers' or employers' organisations. Other existing procedures are used infrequently. The

ILO Secretariat is therefore proposing other avenues, including the possibility of examining cases of forced labour and discrimination in employment irrespective of whether the relevant Conventions have been ratified. Some of these proposals, notably the creation of a special procedure (similar to that on freedom of association) to deal with other core labour standards, have met with opposition on the part of some governments, but discussions in the ILO will continue. Whatever the agreement, monitoring and enforcement could be further strengthened if the procedures focused on serious violations of labour rights, leaving aside relatively minor inconsistencies between the Conventions and national practices.

More generally, the ILO has an important role as a focal organisation where universal agreement on core labour standards can be reached. It can also persuade countries that it is in their own interest to promote basic labour rights and to avoid exploitation of workers, while also informing the international community on cases of non-respect of core labour standards. In poor countries, ILO technical assistance may also contribute to the eradication of child labour exploitation.

The contribution of development co-operation programmes

This subsection reviews the contribution of development co-operation programmes in promoting some core labour standards, particularly the reduction of child labour and the respect of trade union rights and freedoms. Donor support is provided in a wide range of relevant areas such as for equitable and sustainable economic growth; poverty alleviation; good governance and human rights; capacity building for improving legislation and enforcement; assistance in the areas of health, education and nutrition; gender equality; advocacy and awareness raising.

The reduction of child labour

Basic conventions

The long-term objectives of improving the lives and development of children are set out in a range of international instruments. As discussed in Part I, the ILO Minimum Age Convention (No. 138) of 1973, along with its companion Recommendation No. 146, has as objective the abolition of child labour (Preamble and Article 1). The ILO doctrine reflects the conviction that below a certain age children should not have to engage in an economic activity and that childhood is a period in life that should be devoted not to work but to education and training. The elimination of some of the most dangerous forms of child labour is covered in part by the Forced Labour Convention (No. 29) of 1930. There is, however, no similar instrument that outlaws other intolerable forms of exploitation such as the traffic or sale of children for employment or prostitution and other contemporary forms of slavery.

The UN Convention on the Rights of the Child of 1989, which has now been ratified by nearly every developing country (with 167 states parties, as of October 1994[3]), is the most comprehensive legal instrument available for the protection of children, and extends far beyond issues of child labour. It incorporates standards laid down in ILO Conventions and Recommendations. The UN Convention states that children have the right to survival, protection, care, development and participation. It sets forth in Article 32 that children shall be protected from economic exploitation and from performing any work likely to be hazardous to or interfere with a child's education or be harmful to a child's health. The UN Committee for the Rights of the Child is monitoring its implementation.

The Plan of Action adopted at the World Summit for Children in New York in 1990 specifies goals to be achieved by the year 2000, especially with respect to reduction of child mortality (by one-third) and malnutrition (by one-half), access to basic education, drinking water and sanitation.

Development co-operation programmes

As much as these international acts reflect a commitment to reduce child labour, they must be underpinned by multifaceted development strategies which put a strong emphasis on human development and offer viable economic alternatives to the vast majority of poor families who depend on the important contribution of child labour for their very survival.

The 1995 DAC Policy Statement on Development Partnerships in the New Global Context sets out, in its "integrated strategies" approach, some of the most effective means to reduce child labour: an overriding focus on poverty alleviation; strong investment in education; enhanced participation of women in all aspects of development; generation of income through many types of private-sector development; and greater involvement of civil society and local government.

While poverty is a fundamental reason for children working, it is not necessarily always the deciding one. Social conditioning and political will are among other important factors. Donors have concluded from experience that in some cases of extreme poverty (e.g. single-parent households), child labour can be effectively eliminated only if the family's poverty is also addressed. However, poverty alleviation efforts will always have to be part of an integrated set of measures in order to combat child labour effectively.

Investments in primary education which contribute to freeing children from work and, not least, yield major economic, social and political returns need to be increased substantially to fulfil the stated goals of education for all[4]. Although primary schooling for children is compulsory in most countries, some 128 million children, or 20 per cent of the school-age population, were excluded from primary education in 1990[5]. Most of these children live in remote rural areas or in urban slums and belong to marginalised population groups. Three-quarters of the out-of-school children live in South Asia and in sub-Saharan Africa. Given the economics of poverty and the high opportunity cost of education from the family's perspective, especially for girls, specific policies have been identified to remove impediments to the enrolment of children, for instance, by bringing schools closer to home, improving the relevance of curricula, reducing direct costs, promoting the recruitment of female teachers and engaging in informal education activities.

Creating new employment opportunities for adults is also key to reducing the pressures on children to work in order to supplement the family income. Micro-enterprise development and private-sector development generally may, with targeted donor assistance, contribute to providing such opportunities for poor families[6]. In addition, projects to provide basic services, such as access to clean water, fuelwood and small farming technology, can make an important contribution by relieving children from domestic chores.

Central to the success of these development activities are approaches that focus on enabling the full participation of women and on removing the obstacles impeding their access to resources and services. In most developing countries women are the main food producers, providers of water and firewood, and they have a major responsibility for health care, nutrition and hygiene in the family and the community. They exert a critical influence on family size and the education of children. They also play a predominant role as entrepreneurs in the informal sector and are often primary income-earners, as a large number of households are headed by women. However, women face unique constraints. Social values and legal systems are often biased against them and impede their access to key resources and services such as land, credit, education and technology. Programmes to promote more active participation of women in the process of development, therefore, have far-reaching implications for the economy, improved family welfare and social standards[7].

Complementing these programmes, donors support a wide range of small projects targeted at children and child labour, which would need to be multiplied and further replicated to have a broader impact. These are generally carried out by non-governemental organisations (NGOs), which are particularly well suited to reach children and their families in poor communities through community-based projects[8]. Such approaches are based on local initiatives and carried out in partnership with governments and civil society, involving a whole range of actors such as social workers, teachers, the police, the judiciary, churches, employers, unions and the media. In India, the Philippines, Brazil and Bangladesh, wider efforts are being made to combat child labour at its cultural roots, including sustained campaigns to break the climate of indifference over the issue and to enlist the understanding and participation of society as a whole.

International organisations and their work on child labour

International organisations, particularly the ILO and UNICEF, have also developed programmes specifically aimed at reducing child labour. As noted above, the ILO provides technical assistance to help countries develop policies on child labour, and sponsors development programmes to combat child labour. It is currently running the most important international programme in this field, the International Programme on the Elimination of Child Labour (IPEC). This global offensive against child labour was launched in 1991 with donor assistance and is currently implemented in a dozen countries[9]. IPEC is an innovative and flexible programme which relies on a substantial role for NGOs in project delivery. As broad social support is essential for carrying out measures which aim at preventing child labour, key aspects in implementing ILO-IPEC's strategies are to raise awareness and to seek the involvement and commitment of individual governments to address child labour in co-operation with a wide variety of public and private groups. Some components of the programme, therefore, include training of government and private organisations, strengthening of national capacities to address child labour problems and participation by unions and employers' organisations. In working towards the progressive elimination of child labour, IPEC lays special emphasis on protecting children from the worst exploitation by targeting the most vulnerable groups such as bonded child labourers; children working in hazardous occupations and under abusive conditions; very young children, below 12 years of age; and working girls. The objective is to remove these children from work and send them to school, provide alternatives or improve working conditions as a transitional measure towards the ultimate elimination of child labour[10].

UNICEF addresses the problems of child labour within the framework of its programme on Children in Especially Difficult Circumstances. This programme, however, covers only partially the child labour question. It includes children in circumstances of armed conflict and other disasters (UNICEF's oldest mission), children in circumstances of exploitation, and children in circumstances of abuse and neglect. UNICEF has identified a number of strategic priorities in fighting child labour: eradicate the most exploitative forms of child labour; improve the working conditions of children; provide universal primary education; make better use of existing legal instruments to combat child labour; encourage co-operation between government, industry, unions and NGOs; and improve assistance to developing countries.

The UN Commission on Human Rights adopted in 1993 a "Programme of Action for the Elimination of the Exploitation of Child Labour". Activity under this programme is in an early stage. So far, the main outcome has been the provision of information by a number of governments on the situation of child labour in their countries. Child labour has also received attention by the "expert-level" Sub-commission on Prevention of Discrimination and Protection of Minorities, a subordinate body to the Commission on Human Rights, as well as by the Sub-commission Working Group on Contemporary Forms of Slavery. Finally, the UN Commission on Human Rights has established an Office of Special Rapporteur to consider matters relating to the sale of children, child prostitution and pornography. The Special Rapporteur reports each year to the Commission.

Minimum-age laws, compulsory education and labour-law enforcement have been milestones in the economic and social history of developed countries. While achieving these goals in developing countries will require a long-haul effort at the fundamental level of grassroots economic and social change, development co-operation can make a positive contribution in these areas. Indeed, one of the main challenges in the years to come will be to support efforts to enact national legislation, including labour laws in conformity with human rights standards, and to promote their enforcement. Some workers' organisations have begun to disseminate information to working children on their legal rights. Initiatives also exist to provide children with legal aid, but a great deal more experience is needed on how to involve the judiciary actively, streamline legislation, set up networks of paralegal extension staff to disseminate information to the target groups and further enforce the application of existing legislation. As enforcement capacity is still limited, initial efforts might concentrate on the most intolerable cases, such as bonded child labour. There is a need to look further into the possibilities for increasing the potential for development co-operation to promote these efforts.

More evaluation is now needed of the impact of targeted programmes aimed at combatting child labour and of the progress made in reducing the incidence of child labour through broader development programmes. There is a need to devise relevant indicators and to carry out objective assessments of development co-operation effectiveness in this area.

Policy dialogue

It is generally agreed that a positive approach to assisting and encouraging adherence to international labour standards in developing countries is the most effective and efficient approach. The solution rests, ultimately, in the hands of societies and their national authorities. Development co-operation can provide a channel through which OECD countries can help developing countries improve their labour standards through constructive policy dialogue, technical assistance and financial support.

As part of their development co-operation efforts, a number of OECD countries pursue the issue of exploitative child labour through human rights fora, policy dialogue and awareness raising. DAC Members have been active, for instance, in raising the profile of child labour as an international human rights issue at the UN Commission on Human Rights. They raise their concerns and encourage the application of international legal obligations in bilateral consultations with recipient countries and in multilateral fora; publish annual human and labour rights reports; and co-finance the advocacy activities of NGOs.

Promotion of freedom of association and the right of collective bargaining

The current thrust of OECD Members' programmes on good governance, participatory development and the protection of human rights opens a window of opportunity for enhanced co-operation in the field of labour standards[11]. OECD Members work for the promotion of human rights both at the policy level, where they pursue these issues in their policy dialogue with recipient countries, and at the operational level through special projects and integration into broader development co-operation.

Policy dialogue in a multilateral setting

In the 1990s, the promotion of human rights has become an accepted issue in the multilateral policy dialogue conducted in the framework of Consultative Group and Round Table meetings. A more open attitude of many developing countries at these meetings has contributed to establishing a constructive dialogue on the broad issues of fundamental political and civil rights, good governance and respect for the rule of law. It is noteworthy that, in particular, those developing countries which have recently engaged in a process of democratisation have demonstrated a growing understanding of the need for this dialogue to touch upon areas considered until recently as highly sensitive and impinging on national sovereignty.

Dialogue on these kinds of issues may lead in different directions. The issue of labour rights, for example, was raised by the donor community at the Consultative Group meeting for Indonesia in July 1994. For many years, the Indonesian government had been urged by some OECD countries to improve its labour legislation and practices concerning trade union rights. When legislative changes introduced in early 1994 to repeal a law authorising military interference in labour disputes and to allow collective bargaining were not followed in practice, donors took the opportunity of the Consultative Group meeting to express their concern over the government's repressive policy in labour disputes. Since then, international pressure has continued to intensify, including the possibility of exclusion from the US Generalized System of Preferences (see below).

While human rights issues are gaining prominence in multilateral fora, policy dialogue also continues to have a special place and role in bilateral development assistance programmes, especially where a genuine national will to act can be encouraged by a genuine willingness to help. Policy dialogue can help establish an appropriate policy climate for successful programme and project development and implementation, and thus maximise the effects of assistance targeted to support policy change.

Development co-operation programmes to promote freedom of association and the right of collective bargaining

All over the world, labour organisations have frequently played a key historical role in furthering workers' rights, improving social conditions and promoting respect for human rights and democratisation. The freedom of trade unions to assemble, speak out and take actions including strikes is generally linked to respect for a broader range of human rights and the growth of a healthy civil society which is strongly correlated with development progress. For these reasons, support for trade unions, professional associations, farmers' unions, rural workers' organisations and independent co-operatives forms a key part of donors' efforts in assisting the development of a genuinely participatory and equitable economic culture, and the institutions and practices of a strong civil society.

Many assistance programmes in the area of human and labour rights are initiated and implemented by NGOs with the financial support of bilateral donors. NGOs have long played a significant and pioneering role in the observance and promotion of human rights, especially where it was considered difficult for outside governments to intervene directly.

In particular, NGOs, including labour unions, are active in monitoring government observance of relevant international labour standards and of national labour legislation[12]. They play a critically important role through monitoring, research, analysis of laws, advice, training, publications, dissemination of findings and advice through the media and audio-visual means, especially in local languages. Efforts are also made to provide organisational support, advisory services and leadership training for workers in the formal and informal sectors of rural and urban areas. Over the past decade, trade union confederations in OECD Member countries have increased and diversified their activities in support of developing countries. Their programmes not only assist trade unions in developing countries to develop and organise themselves, but also focus on the economic and social context in which the workers of these countries live.

The contribution of labour organisations to the development and the emergence of a strong civil society could be further strengthened and expanded, particularly as regards their monitoring and advocacy roles. In many developing countries, however, professional associations and trade unions are weak and threatened by outright persecution, restrictive legislation and other obstacles such as slow registration, hindrance in dissemination of their views and obstructions to receiving external aid. Assistance programmes to strengthen good governance, accountability and the rule of law should therefore address these problems.

Many developing countries lack the institutional and technical capacity to develop and enforce comprehensive labour legislation, including labour standards. There is scope in this area for expanding donor co-operation bilaterally and multilaterally, particularly through the activities of the ILO, the

World Bank and other UN bodies. As part of efforts to reinforce the rule of law and to secure an independent judiciary, attention is increasingly paid to strengthening the legal process which allows citizens and workers to seek enforcement of their rights.

Proposed mechanisms in international organisations

Labour standards and WTO disciplines

Introduction

The debate about linkages between trade disciplines and labour standards is not new. Indeed, Article 7 of the Havana Charter, which was meant to establish an International Trade Organisation (ITO), referred to the importance of satisfactory social conditions for the smooth operation of the trading system and invited Members to work for the establishment of such conditions within their territory. However, this article was among the provisions of the Charter that never entered into force [13].

Suggestions have been made recently to establish closer links between trade and core labour standards, in particular as regards the operation of the GATT/WTO system of multilateral rules and disciplines for international trade. For instance, in 1983, the European Parliament called for the negotiation of a GATT provision on labour standards engaging all GATT Members to respect ILO Conventions on freedom of association, collective bargaining, forced labour and non-discrimination [14]. In 1986 and in 1994, the United States suggested, without success, to add worker's rights to the Uruguay Round and to the WTO agenda [15]. In 1994, the European Parliament further suggested that GATT Article XX(e) on prison labour be amended to include forced and child labour, as well as violations of the principle of freedom of association and collective bargaining [16]. Some have suggested making use of the WTO Trade Policy Review Mechanism (TPRM). There have been other proposals (e.g. by TUAC) for the introduction of a "social clause" into the WTO, with the aim in particular of strengthening the enforcement of "basic" labour standards.

Discussions have also taken place within the ILO. The objective was to ensure that the gradual liberalisation of markets be accompanied by improvements in conditions of work, or at least by the elimination of the most flagrant abuses and forms of exploitation [17]. The ILO Secretariat discussed the applicability of ᴉsing anti-dumping and countervailing duties provisions, general exceptions provisions, or nullification and impairment provisions for that purpose.

Subsequent debate on these ideas within the ILO Working Party on the Social Dimension of the Liberalisation of World Trade underlined their controversial nature. Many participants, in particular among the employers and the developing countries, were opposed to the implementation of a "social clause" in the WTO. In fact, the consensus that emerged at an important session of the ILO Working Party was that it "should not pursue the question of trade sanctions and that any discussion of the link between international trade and social standards, through a sanction-based social clause, should be suspended" (GB.264/WP/SDL/1, para. 13). Instead, the Working Party will look at ways to promote core labour standards through encouragement, support and assistance and at the means to strengthen ILO's effectiveness in achieving this task.

Whether to introduce additional objectives, to negotiate new provisions and mechanisms or to interpret existing WTO provisions would imply the existence of sufficient political will among WTO Members, and would be a matter for their consideration and decision. Accordingly, the comments below simply draw attention to certain key elements that would need to be addressed satisfactorily in relation to specific proposals to establish links between WTO disciplines and core standards. Certain OECD governments, while proposing that the trade and labour standards issues be discussed among WTO Members, have not presented precise suggestions so far on how the existing WTO system of rules and disciplines might be adapted. The debate on the possible "introduction of a social clause in the WTO" thus remains speculative, in the absence of agreement to consider the issue in the WTO and of detailed proposals regarding its scope and implementation mechanisms. As such, it is not discussed here.

Elements of proposals concerning the use of WTO provisions

"Social dumping"

Low levels of labour standards applied by exporting firms are considered by some as a form of "social dumping" which unfairly affects firms in countries adopting more advanced standards. It has been proposed that there be application of anti-dumping duties against so-called "social dumping".

As currently formulated in the WTO Agreement on Implementation of Article VI of GATT 1994, a product is considered as being dumped when it is introduced into the commerce of another country at less than its normal value. This occurs if the export price is less than the comparable price in the ordinary course of trade for the like product when destined for consumption in the exporting country. When there are no sales, or when, because of insufficient sales volume or a particular market situation, such sales do not permit a proper comparison, the margin of dumping is to be determined on the basis of either a comparable price of the like product exported to a third country or on the basis of constructed value. Investigating authorities must, therefore, base their determination either on actual price discrimination or on an actual comparison of production costs to export price as set forth in the Agreement. It is to be noted also that anti-dumping duties can be levied in respect of an imported product determined to have been dumped, only if that product is causing or threatening to cause material injury to the domestic producers of the like product in the importing country; and also, that the anti-dumping duty shall not exceed the margin of dumping.

All of these, and other requirements, must be met if a WTO Member is to act in a manner consistent with its WTO obligations. Thus, to the extent that application by an investigating authority of anti-dumping duties rested on any other separate or distinct criterion in its own right, such as "violation of core labour standards" *per se*, this would not be compatible with the existing provisions of the Agreement. These provisions do not allow for the determination of a margin of dumping on the basis of non-enforcement of core standards. Moreover, if determination of a dumping margin involves an assessment of costs of production, these must be actual, and not notional or hypothetical costs.

"Social subsidies"

The concern has been expressed that governments may, in effect, assist production and/or exports by enforcing either low labour standards, or labour standards that deviate from those that are generally applicable at the national level, for example by instituting "union-free" export-processing zones within a country that otherwise permits the establishment of independent unions. This action is characterised by some as a subsidy, or as an indirect export subsidy. In this context it has been proposed that countervailing duties be applied against exports from such countries. Although the analysis in Part II indicates that the suppression of core standards is not an effective "social subsidy" and that there is little evidence that core standards influence trade patterns in practice, the discussion below deals with the problems in applying remedial actions in any case.

First, it would depend on whether "abnormally" low labour conditions represent a form of subsidy within the meaning of GATT Article XVI and the definition of the WTO Agreement on Subsidies and Countervailing Measures. The definition of a subsidy in the WTO Agreement includes a number of situations in which a benefit is conferred either by a financial contribution granted by the government or public bodies[18], or by "any income or price support in the sense of Article XVI of the GATT 1994". Violation of core standards does not involve any financial contribution by the government, as defined under the existing WTO Agreement. There remains a question of whether it could be deemed to meet the latter criteria relating to income or price support. It is unclear how any measure to *reduce* core labour standards could constitute *income* "support". It is also difficult to envisage how the criterion of "price support" could be satisfied, given that non-enforcement of core standards is not a governmental measure that supplies assistance to firms or producers through regulation of prices.

Even if a measure is deemed to satisfy the criteria for definition as a "subsidy" within the terms of the Agreement, action against it can only be taken if it is also "specific" within the meaning of the Agreement. There are a number of tests which apply; *inter alia,* the "granting authority" must limit access to a subsidy to "certain enterprises". A subsidy which is "limited to certain enterprises located within a designated geographical region" shall be determined to be specific.

This would seem to suggest, for instance, that a country-wide, objective implementation of labour standards, albeit at a low level, would be unlikely to meet the specificity test in any case, as it would appear to be generally applicable by definition.

The more limited case of lower core standards in export-processing zones would, to the extent that these satisfied the criteria for determination of the existence of a subsidy, need to be evaluated precisely against the criteria related to specificity, as well as the other relevant provisions of the Agreement.

Furthermore, the primary means for taking "remedial" action against any subsidy that satisfies the specificity test are countervailing actions (often called "Track one") or recourse to the procedures for dispute resolution in relation to nullification and impairment or serious prejudice (often called "Track two").

Recourse to either of these tracks gives rise to a further set of requirements. In the case of any measures that satisfied the criteria for countervailability, it would be necessary, *inter alia,* to satisfy all the requirements for a determination of injury to the domestic producers of the subsidised product. It should be noted that in the absence of such injury or threat of injury, it is not permissible to apply countervailing measures. It would also be necessary to be consistent with the requirements for the calculation of the amount of a subsidy, in particular the requirement that the countervailing duty should not exceed the level of subsidisation. This would be vital if it was in principle possible to quantify any specific benefit arising from non-observation/non-enforcement of core labour standards.

General exceptions provisions

GATT 1994 provides for certain general exceptions, such as Article XX(a) on public morals, Article XX(b) on human life or health and Article XX(e) on products of prison labour. As exceptions to other provisions of the Agreement, any party seeking to invoke these provisions would bear the burden of demonstrating that it satisfied the relevant criteria, including those specified in the "chapeau" to Article XX, viz. that "measures are not applied in a manner which would constitute a means of arbitrary or unjustifiable discrimination between countries where the same conditions prevail; or a disguised restriction on international trade". Article XXI provides also for certain security exceptions.

Subject to the above-mentioned "chapeau" requirements, a WTO Member may, under Article XX(e), restrict imports of goods made with prison labour. Other provisions under the General Exceptions Article include Article XX(d) and Article XX(h). The idea of using Article XX(d) (on measures necessary to secure compliance with laws or regulations not inconsistent with the GATT) in relation to labour standards was envisaged and abandoned during the negotiations on the Havana Charter. The Sub-committee which considered the general exceptions to Chapter IV noted that "in discussing an amendment to [Article XX(d)], designed to exempt measures against so-called 'social dumping' from the provisions of Chapter IV, the Sub-committee expressed the view that this objective was covered for short-term purposes by paragraph 1 of Article 40 [Article XIX] and for long-term purposes by Article 7 [on worker rights] in combination with Articles 93, 94 and 95 [on dispute settlement]". The text of Article 7 was not, of course, included, in the GATT.

Article XX(h) allows GATT Members to adopt measures "undertaken in pursuance of obligations under any inter-governmental commodity agreement which conforms to criteria submitted to the CONTRACTING PARTIES and not disapproved by them or which is itself so submitted and not so disapproved". Within the framework of the Integrated Programme for Commodities of the

UNCTAD, a number of international commodity agreements contain provisions on "fair labour standards"[19]. These provisions, however, seem to be more declarations of intent than precise contractual undertakings; they are limited to a general reference to fair working conditions without quoting any concrete provisions referring to existing international agreements. Special sanctions or control mechanisms are not provided for, and their effects in practice depend largely on the leverage which concerned countries can exert in securing compliance with such clauses. None of the commodity agreements, nor criteria with respect to commodity agreements, have ever been formally submitted to the GATT Members.

Nullification and impairment provisions

It has been suggested by some that the dispute-settlement provision of the WTO might offer a means to address enforcement of core labour standards in certain circumstances. Under Article XXIII, 1(b) or (c), and Article 26 of the Understanding on Rules and Procedures Governing the Settlement of Disputes, a Member may bring an action if it believes that any benefit accruing to it under the Agreement is being nullified or impaired, or that the attainment of any objective of the Agreement is being impeded, as a result of *inter alia* "the application by another of any measure, whether or not it conflicts with the provisions of the Agreement" or the "existence of any other situation". Paragraph 2 of that Article also refers to the scope for CONTRACTING PARTIES to consult with other inter-governmental organisations. Under the terms of Article 26, the complainant shall present a detailed justification of any complaint relating to Article XXIII, 1(b). There is no obligation to withdraw the measure if a panel or Appelate Body rules that it did nullify or impair benefits. The panel or Appelate Body shall recommend that the Member concerned make "a mutually satisfactory adjustment". There is no case law on complaints of the type described in Article XXIII, 1(c) of GATT 1994.

The original Article 7 of the Havana Charter would have involved incorporating worker's rights provisions in the Agreement as a potential basis for any invocation of nullification and impairment provisions. With respect to all such matters referred to dispute-settlement procedures, co-operation was to be instituted between the ITO and the ILO. In 1953, when a US proposal to re-insert the provision in the GATT was rejected, the United States declared that, taking into account the distortions likely to be created by unfair labour conditions, considered the possibility of invoking nullification or impairment in terms of Article XXIII as existing already under the current provisions[20]. No action was ever taken in this direction, although the United States indicates that it still considers it has reserved its right to do so.

"Opt-out" provisions

It has been argued that GATT Article XXXV presented an opportunity for contracting parties to exercise a *de facto* labour rights exception to GATT rules. This was the so-called "opt-out" clause, under which a contracting party had the right upon the accession of a new CONTRACTING PARTY (or upon its own accession to GATT) to declare that it will not apply GATT in its trade relations with a specific CONTRACTING PARTY. There were no limitations placed on a country's decision to exercise this option, apart from the requirements that it be invoked only at the time of accession, and that it could not be invoked if tariff negotiations had taken place between the two parties in the course of GATT-accession negotiations. This provision of the GATT first emerged in response to India's concerns over the accession of South Africa in 1948. To the extent that one considers the specific opposition to apartheid to have been, *inter alia*, a labour rights issue, those countries that invoked Article XXXV against South Africa employed this provision as a labour-related political exception. Of the 12 invocations of the Article that were still in effect as of 1990, four related to South Africa. The issue has since been rendered moot by the abolition of apartheid and the establishment of the WTO, although it remains an option for any WTO Member to take recourse to the provision of Article XIII regarding future new WTO Members for whatever reason[21]. There are, however, good reasons to consider such an approach as rather unflexible and probably disproportionate in regard to most of the labour standards issues presently under consideration.

Labour standards in the Trade Policy Review Mechanism (TPRM)

It has also been suggested that policies that deliberately attempt to reduce core labour standards in certain export sectors or export-processing zones be included and discussed in the country reviews undertaken in the framework for the Trade Policy Review Mechanism on the grounds that the publicity and peer pressure involved in this exercise might eventually improve the situation of core labour standards in some countries. It has been proposed that the ILO might play an active part in such a procedure, first by defining the set of core labour standards and then by participating in the elaboration of that part of the WTO Secretariat report dealing with labour policies. This TPRM option would provide a peer review process that would not be substantially different from the existing procedures in the ILO.

The TPRM focuses on trade and trade policies. Export-processing zones *per se* can be the subject of TPRM discussions. Any proposals to deal with core labour standards issues would need to be consistent with, *inter alia*, Articles A(i) and (ii) of the TPRM annex, whereby the subject matter of review is to be a background for better understanding and assessment of the country's trade policies and practices, and cannot in any case be used as a basis either for dispute-settlement procedures or for imposing new policy commitments on Members. It should be noted that all proposals to include labour policies in trade policy reviews undertaken in the past have encountered strong opposition from developing countries.

Concluding remarks

Applying the proposals reviewed in this section would pose, in the first place, a number of questions concerning the appropriateness and the effectiveness of various WTO mechanisms which, in their present forms, are directed towards the enforcement of trade policies and practices. A second observation is that the use of various WTO articles or procedures would, in all appearance, require amendments, reinterpretations or common understandings. These remain, ultimately, a matter for WTO members themselves to determine. It is, however, apparent that there is presently a lack of consensus within WTO to move in such a direction.

From a broader perspective, considering the criteria mentioned at the beginning of Part III, the use of trade measures to promote core labour standards would raise the following questions. First, since the analysis in Part II does not point to the existence of a significant relationship between trade performance and the degree of enforcement of core labour standards, there is a major question of the suitability of trade measures as an appropriate instrument. Second, with respect to their function as an enforcement mechanism, since they would fall more heavily on more open economies, and mainly affect the traded goods sectors, the question arises of whether and how they could be uniformly targeted at the source of low standards. In addition, within the export sector, firms with adequate levels of core labour standards would be sanctioned as well. Third, would the application of trade measures be mainly driven by the seriousness of the human rights abuse or by the alleged impact on domestic interests? Fourth, trade sanctions would cause political frictions between the countries involved and might even lead to retaliatory trade restrictions.

Conditional lending by international financial institutions

Another proposed way of promoting core labor standards would be to make international financial assistance conditional on the respect of basic labour rights by borrowing countries. Such suggestions may have been inspired by a recent US legislative action to encourage the multilateral financial institutions (i.e. the International Monetary Fund, the World Bank and the regional multilateral development banks) to promote core labour standards. In August 1994, the US Congress passed a law requiring the Secretary of the Treasury to instruct the US directors of international financial institutions to "use the voice and vote of the United States to urge the respective institution... to adopt policies to encourage borrowing countries to guarantee internationally recognised worker rights and to include the status of such rights as an integral part of the institution's policy dialogue with each borrowing country"[22]. To define these "internationally recognised worker rights", the law explicitly cites the relevant ILO Conventions on, *inter alia*, the core labour standards defined in the present study.

The law also requires that the Treasury Department report annually to the US Congress on progress made in international financial institutions towards the above-mentioned goals. The first such report (for the year 1995) concludes that "international financial institutions have not specifically integrated ILO worker rights standards into their operational procedures"[23]. One exception is the European Bank for Reconstruction and Development, which includes in its Articles of Agreement a provision requiring that it assess progress in the area of worker's rights. However, the existence of substantial lending activities aiming to improve the functioning of labour markets as well as workers' education and productivity was also noted. In addition, operations involving financing of labour code revisions have been conducted by international financial institutions.

Therefore, while international financial institutions already play a role in the policy dialogue on labour issues, and thus have an indirect impact on the level of core labour standards in recipient countries, it seems that the idea of a more direct involvement through the screening of project lending for worker's rights would raise a number of important questions. First, there is a question of consistency and coherence: would it be able to target all systematic denials of basic labour rights, when it can reach only those countries which are applying for multilateral loans? Second, can it be reconciled with the principles for well-designed conditions laid out by the World Bank, in particular that conditionality should concentrate on the programme's critical goals, and that it should be within the borrower's implementation capacity? With respect to the latter principle, it must be remembered that when violations of workers' rights occur in the informal sector of the economy, it may be difficult for the government to find rapid and effective remedies. Finally, limiting some countries' access to international financing may hamper their economic development and thus run ultimately against the stated policy objective of improving core labour standards.

Regional and unilateral government actions

The North American Agreement on Labor Cooperation

The North American Agreement on Labor Cooperation (NAALC) -- more commonly known as the labour supplemental agreement to the NAFTA -- links each of the North American countries' labour laws to the regional trade agreement. Both agreements entered into force on 1 January 1994. The NAALC promotes mutually recognised labour principles including core labour standards and other standards such as the occupational health and safety of workers and the protection of migrant workers (NAALC, Art. 1, Art. 3, Art. 49; *NAALC: A Guide*, 1995)[24].

The main objective of the NAALC is to improve working conditions and living standards in the United States, Mexico and Canada. The emphasis of the agreement is on encouraging transparent and effective enforcement of the existing labour laws in each country through co-operation and the exchange of information. The agreement also provides for consultations between the National Administrative Offices (NAOs) or at the Ministerial level, as well as comparative assessments among the three countries. Should these steps fail to solve a matter in dispute, a dispute-resolution process can be invoked. This process may ultimately result in fines (monetary enforcement assessments) backed by trade sanctions in the event that Mexico or the United States does not observe and enforce its own labour laws, but it must be noted that trade sanctions are not available against Canada (NAALC, Part 4 and Part 5)[25]. Complaints or petitions can be submitted by any person with a legally recognised interest under the law of any party to the NAALC. However, the dispute-settlement procedure can be quite lengthy: over two years may elapse before measures such as the imposition of action plans, fines or trade sanctions can be enforced. In addition, trade sanctions are possible only in the areas of child labour, minimum wages and occupational safety and health, but not in cases relating to freedom of association, the right to bargain collectively, and forced labour (see the table below on the NAALC dispute-settlement process and time-frame). Furthermore, it must be noted that the NAALC refers not to internationally agreed minimum labour standards as does the European GSP system (see below), but to standards defined under the national legislation of the parties. In particular, complaints must be both trade-related and covered by mutually recognised labour laws, and there must have been a persistent pattern of non-enforcement of the relevant labour legislation (NAALC, Article 41).

Five cases have been submitted so far under the NAALC dispute-settlement procedure. Four submissions, alleging labour law violations in Mexico, have been filed with the US NAO[26] since its establishment in January 1994, the fourth of which was withdrawn in early 1995. The last submission was filed in 1995 with the Mexican NAO, alleging labour law violations in the United States. The first two submissions concerned subsidiaries of US firms in the Mexican *maquiladora* sector, and related to alleged violations of the right to freedom of association. A joint public hearing was held in September 1994 in Washington, D.C., and a public report was issued one month later. In the report, the US NAO recognised that the submissions raised strong concerns regarding the freedom to join independent unions, at the level of both the firm management and the Mexican labour authorities[27]. Nevertheless, the report concluded that it had not been established that the Government of Mexico failed to promote compliance with or to enforce the specific laws involved, and thus did not recommend Ministerial consultations on matters presented in the two submissions (US NAO, 1994 and 1995a).

NAALC dispute-settlement process

	Action	Timing
Step 1	Submission filed with NAO (full coverage of NAALC dispositions)	NAO must accept or reject submission for review within 60 days
Step 2	Review process: information gathering through consultation with other NAOs, and/or public hearing (in the US), final report published (in Mexico and the US)	Final report must be published within 120 days from acceptance of submission, with possible 60-day extension
	If unresolved:	
Step 3	Ministerial consultations (full coverage)	No set time limit
	If unresolved, and object of dispute is (i) trade-related; (ii) concerns mutually recognised labour laws in the areas of health and safety, child labour and technical labour standards; any consulting party may request:	
Step 4	Establish an Evaluation Committee of Experts, prepare draft evaluation report that may be reviewed by the Parties, and then present final evaluation report	Draft report shall be presented to the Parties within 120 days after establishment, and final report presented to the Council no later than 60 days later. Written responses by the Parties must be provided within 90 days, and submitted to the Council along with the final report at the next regular Council session.
	If unresolved AND related to health and safety, child labour or minimum wages:	

	Action	Timing
Step 5	Ministerial Council consultations	60 days
	If unresolved, within 60 days Party may request a Special Session of the Council to convene within 20 days and have 60 days to reach a resolution, and if unresolved, then at the request of any consulting Party and by a two-thirds vote, the Council shall:	
Step 6	Convene an Arbitrary Panel	Initial report presented to the Parties within 180 days after selection of the panelists. Final report due within 60 days after submission of initial report.
	If unresolved [(a) no action plan adopted by Parties or (b) Parties cannot agee on whether implemented]:	Under (a), request to reconvene between 60-120 days, under (b) no earlier than 180 days.
Step 7	Panel may be reconvened and may impose a monetary enforcement assessment	Under (a) Panel has 90 days to take action, under (b) 60 days.
	If a Party fails to pay a monetary enforcement assessment within 180 days after it is imposed by panel:	
Step 8	Complaining Party or Parties may suspend application of NAFTA benefits in an amount no greater than that sufficient to collect the monetary enforcement assessment (only for Mexico and the US).	

Sources: NAALC, Final Draft, 1993; *NAALC: A Guide*, US NAO, US Dept. of Labor, Washington, D.C., 1995, Appendix 1, Appendix 2.

The third submission concerned the *maquiladora* operations of a subsidiary of Sony Corporation in Mexico. Allegations involved freedom of association, the right to organise, and minimum employment standards relating to hours of work and holiday work[28]. The review revealed serious problems related to the workers' ability to obtain recognition of an independent union by local labour authorities. Therefore, the NAO recommended that Ministerial consultations would be appropriate in order to "further address the operation of the union registration process" (US NAO,1995b). The final agreement called for the Mexican authorities to meet (i) with workers at the subsidiary of Sony to inform them of remedies available to them under Mexican labour law regarding union registration and (ii) with local labour authorities to discuss union registration issues raised by the US NAO report. The agreement also included a series of public fora to discuss union registration and certification procedures in the three countries. Upon completion of the work programme set forth in this Ministerial consultations agreement, the United States and Mexico will release public reports.

The fifth submission, and the only one to date to be brought with the Mexican NAO, relates to the dismissal of about 200 workers and the shutting down of the "La Conexion Familiar" Sprint subsidiary in California, a week before a scheduled election of union representatives. In its public review report of 31 May 1995, the Mexican NAO recommended that Ministerial consultations be held in order to "further study the effects on the principles of freedom of association and the right to organize of workers of the sudden closure of a place of work". These consultations led to the adoption by the Mexican and US governments of a three-step action plan. First, the US Labor Secretary will keep his Mexican counterpart informed of any further legal developments in the case. Second, the Secretariat of the Commission for Labor Cooperation will conduct a study on the effects of the sudden closing of a plant on the principle of freedom of association and the rights of workers to organise in the three countries. Third, a public forum was held on 27 February 1996 in San Francisco to allow interested parties to express their views on the case.

Concluding remarks: Since the NAALC entered into force on 1 January 1994, and only five cases have been submitted so far, it is too early to draw conclusions on its effectiveness. All complaints involved alleged violations of the freedom-of-association right. As mentioned earlier, however, advanced steps of the dispute-settlement process are available to the Parties only on matters involving health and safety, child labour or minimum wages. Furthermore, only in two instances (Sony subsidiary and Sprint cases) did the dispute-settlement process reach the level of Ministerial consultations (see the table above), the results of which are being implemented at the time of this writing[29]. It remains to be seen whether this process will lead to effective improvements in the enforcement of the relevant national labour standards in the member countries.

Labour standards and trade preferences

i)   The US GSP Program

Legislation designed to promote better labour standards in developing countries has been added to several US trade and aid programmes over the past 12 years. These programmes include: the Caribbean Basin Economic Recovery Act (1983); the GSP Program (1984); the Overseas Private Investment Corporation (1985); the Multilateral Investment Guarantee Agency (1987); section 301 in the Omnibus Trade and Competitiveness Act (1988); the Andean Trade Preference Act (1991); section 599 of the Foreign Operations Appropriations Act (1992); and section 1621 of the Foreign Operations, Export Financing and Related Programs Act (1995). Among these programmes, the GSP is the most important in terms of promoting better labour standards. It contains a systematic review and decision process and suspension of GSP benefits potentially triggers action under the other workers' rights provisions in US trade law. This section concentrates on the US GSP Program because of its importance to advocacy groups and its 11 years in use. An overview of the Program's legislation, procedures and performance is followed by an assessment of its effectiveness.

The US GSP scheme was implemented on 1 January 1976, for a period of ten years, in conformity with the Trade Act of 1974[30]. It was reauthorised for another eight and one-half years until 4 July 1993, by the Trade and Tariff Act of 1984, which amended the GSP provisions in the 1974 Trade Act by adding stricter eligibility criteria for beneficiary countries. The criteria in the 1984 GSP legislation stipulated that in determining beneficiary status the President must take into account, among other things, (i) the extent to which the country in question provides adequate and effective protection of intellectual property rights and (ii) whether the country is taking steps to offer internationally recognised workers' rights to workers[31]. Since 1993, the GSP Program has been extended twice for around one year each time. The short-term renewals are due to budgetary concerns resulting from Congress' revenue offset requirements for US trade programmes[32].

The workers' rights provision in the GSP statute defines internationally recognised worker rights as including: the right of association; the right to organise and bargain collectively; a prohibition on the use of any form of forced or compulsory labour; a minimum age for the employment of children; and acceptable conditions of work with respect to minimum wages, hours of work, and occupational safety and health. The workers' rights criterion is one of "taking steps" to meet international standards, rather than being in full compliance with those standards.

The GSP statute does not define any of the rights in question, except for designating them as "internationally recognised", which is generally interpreted to refer to ILO norms. The GSP workers' rights standards are thus based on, but do not replicate, ILO Conventions. In interpreting the meaning of the five standards, the GSP Subcommittee takes into account the relevant ILO Conventions, e.g. Convention 87 in the case of freedom of association. The Subcommittee also examines the findings of ILO supervisory bodies for beneficiary countries under review in regard to the rights listed in the statute.

The 1984 renewal of the GSP Program required that the existing annual review process for products include "country practices" as well. According to this process, petitions to review workers' rights in particular beneficiary countries must be submitted by 1 June of each year to the GSP Subcommittee for subsequent evaluation. The Subcommittee, composed of representatives of the various government agencies responsible for trade policy making, bases its evaluation on information contained in several sources, including the State Department's annual Country Reports on Human Rights Practices, documents from the ILO, reports from the US embassy in the country, published studies by the US Labor Department and information provided by the petitioners and the beneficiary country.

Once a petition is filed, the Subcommittee can choose either to accept or to reject it. If it is accepted, a one-year review is conducted. After the review process, the Subcommittee can make one of three recommendations: (i) extend the review process for a period of time that is determined by the Subcommittee; (ii) terminate the review because the country is found to be "taking steps"; or (iii) suspend the country's eligibility for GSP benefits, because the country is not complying with GSP law. While the ultimate outcome of the review process is the recommendation of the Subcommittee, the bilateral negotiations or representations that are triggered by the filing of the petition are the real focus of the reviews[33].

The importance of the GSP Program for advocacy groups has grown in recent years[34] along with an interest in improving the system. Two problems with the present process are emphasized. The first is the fixed date (1 June) as the deadline for submissions of all GSP petitions for consideration during the annual review cycle. Workers' rights groups believe that they should be able to file petitions at any time during the year when a crisis occurs and receive expedited review. Frequently, country practice cases are held over to the next review cycle and take a long time to resolve.

The second problem concerns a lack of formal standards in GSP law or regulations for accepting country practice petitions for review. This has led to perceptions in advocacy groups that acceptance standards are subjective and highly political. They object particularly to two of the policies used to select petitions for review: (i) the classification of a petitioned offence into either a human rights or a workers' rights problem, which eliminates the human rights problems from reviews; and (ii) the use of the "new information" standards to deny re-petition of a case that has been dismissed previously, unless substantially new information is brought.

From 1984 through 1995, 40 countries have been named in petitions citing labour rights abuses according to GSP law. In almost half of the cases, the GSP Subcommittee recommended that a formal review of the country's situation be postponed until sufficient information could be gathered to evaluate the alleged abuses; many of these countries were later petitioned at least once more, and the monitoring period was prolonged even further. For the other cases, the countries were usually found to be in compliance with GSP law.

By far the most frequent petitioner has been the AFL-CIO, followed by the International Labour Rights Education and Research Fund although anyone is permitted to file a petition, including individuals and small interest groups. All petitions have cited freedom-of-association and collective bargaining violations; minimum age and work conditions violations have been mentioned in only about half, while forced labour abuses have received the least attention.

In reviewing workers' rights petitions, the GSP Subcommittee undertakes a thorough investigation in order to obtain a balanced view using information from a variety of sources. The Subcommittee looks in particular for evidence of progress in the country's legislation and in its practices, and relies on ILO Conventions and Recommendations as benchmarks for interpreting progress. The determination of "taking steps" is particular to each case. There are no guidelines, but the underlying criterion is that movement in the desired direction be taking place. While the link with ILO Conventions and Recommendations is indirect, complementarity between them and the Subcommittee's evaluation of progress is sought deliberately. In addition, the Subcommittee has regular contact with ILO staff and frequently recommends the ILO's technical assistance to countries where labour legislation is found to be in need of reform. The final recommendations of the Subcommittee note the positive actions taken but also record what additional steps the Subcommittee expects. This provides the "hook" for a new petition as well as a ruler for gauging progress in subsequent reviews.

The administration of the country practice reviews encourages improved workers' rights practices principally by raising consciousness and applying international peer pressure. A great deal of information about a country's labour regime is exposed during the GSP's review process. Beneficiary governments do not want to be judged negatively for fear of discouraging potential foreign investment.

The leverage provided by withdrawing tariff preferences, or threatening to, has been used only as a last resort. One of the main reasons for this is that once sanctions are applied, the leverage is lost.

The US GSP workers' rights provision is a unilateral trade programme according to GATT law. Its influence, however, depends not only on the sanctions mechanism that involves the withdrawal of one country's tariff preferences but also on the review process which is tied to ILO's international and tripartite agreements and procedures. In both cases, nevertheless, its effectiveness is clearly related to the fact that the US market is the largest for most of the GSP beneficiaries.

Concluding remarks: Progress in raising core standards has been made in most of the countries petitioned, particularly when the review period has been extended for several years. However, petitions focus frequently on specific workers' rights (freedom of association, collective bargaining) and sectors (export-processing zones). Other rights concerning minimum age of employment, work conditions, forced labour and informal sector activities receive less scrutiny.

ii)   The EU GSP

A direct link between trade and core labour standards is also established in the 1994 GSP of the European Communities[35]. The EC's approach consists of a mix of incentives, in the form of additional GSP benefits for countries implementing core labour standards, and of disincentives, i.e. the suspension of GSP benefits for countries denying some of the core labour standards.

On the one hand, starting on 1 January 1998, the Council Regulation establishing the GSP provides for "special incentive arrangements in the form of additional preferences", which may be granted at the written request of beneficiary countries, provided that they have adopted and apply the substance of ILO standards concerning freedom of association and collective bargaining (ILO Conventions 87 and 98), as well as the provisions on child labour laid down in ILO Convention 138. The actual implementation of these incentives, as well as the level of the supplementary preferential margin, will depend on a 1997 Commission report on the results of work on trade and labour standards carried out in the ILO, the WTO and the present OECD study.

On the other hand, trade sanctions in the form of a temporary suspension of the preference scheme can be taken in circumstances such as the practice of forced labour or export of goods made by prison labour[36]. Member states or any natural or legal persons or associations can signal such practices to the Commission, which then initiates consultations with the concerned parties before deciding whether to open an investigation. Sanctions, if any, cannot be implemented before a year of investigation and a decision by the (qualified) majority of the Council. Contrary to the special incentive clauses, this procedure became applicable as of 1 January 1995.

In January 1996, the European Commission initiated the first investigation of forced labour practices carried out in Myanmar. The complaint was filed jointly by the European Trade Union Confederation and the International Confederation of Free Trade Unions. The complainants allege that the various forms of forced labour practiced in Myanmar represent violations of international human rights, the ILO Conventions on Forced Labour and International Humanitarian Law, and are committed by or with the consent of the authorities of Myanmar in the context of forced labour exacted from the civilian population. The findings of the investigation could lead to the suspension of the country's GSP benefits[37].

Concluding remarks: This mechanism is being put into place, and it is not yet possible to discuss its effectiveness. The incentive approach is novel and interesting, in that an improved export performance should foster economic growth and this, in turn, tends to be correlated with higher levels of core labour standards. Nevertheless, its real value seems limited by the extent to which GSP preferences for developing countries are eroded under the implementation of the Uruguay Round of trade negotiations. The sanctions part has certain resemblances to the provisions set out in the US GSP, but there are also some differences. First, in the case of the European GSP, the labour standards referred to are defined in ILO Conventions, while the link is less explicit in the case of the US GSP. Second, the US GSP refers to a larger set of labour standards than the EU one, which coincides with the set of core labour standards referred to in this study.

iii) The relationship between trade and labour rights in the United States

The United States is probably the country that has enacted the most pieces of legislation linking trade and labour standards. This is a reflection of the US Constitutional system which gives strong regulatory powers to the Congress and of the high visibility given to labour standards issues in US legislation. A recent example of this can be found in the Omnibus Trade and Competitiveness Act of 1988[38]. Section 131 of the Uruguay Round Agreements Act (the US implementing legislation for the accords) further called for the establishment of a WTO working party "to examine the relationship of internationally recognized worker rights ... to the articles, objectives, and related instruments of the GATT 1947 and of the WTO, respectively." The provision proposed *inter alia* that the working party consider ways to address the effects that the systematic denial of these rights have on international trade, and "develop methods to coordinate the work program of the working party with the International Labor Organization". Congress directed the President to report within a year (i.e. by the end of 1995) on the progress made towards establishing this working party.

In addition, one proposed and one existing provision of US trade law could expand upon the historical experience with labour-related trade sanctions. As discussed below, the former refers to a proposed ban on the importation of goods produced with child labour, and the latter to the use of the principal US retaliatory trade law (i.e. section 301) against countries that deny internationally recognised workers' rights.

Child labour

There have been repeated but thus far unsuccessful efforts in the United States to impose a ban on the importation of products made by child labour. In the 102nd (1991-92) and 103rd (1993-94) Congresses, US legislators introduced a bill known as the Child Labor Deterrence Act, also known as the Harkin bill. Senator Harkin and other sponsors continue to press for approval of the bill, having reintroduced it in the 104th Congress (1995-96)[39].

Under the terms of this proposed legislation, the Secretary of Labor would be directed to compile a list of foreign industries that use children under the age of 15 in the manufacture or mining of exported products[40]. The bill would also prohibit the importation of any product made in whole or in part by children under the age of 15 in industry or mining. This ban would not apply if US importers take reasonable steps to ensure that the product is not made by child labour, and sign certificates of origin affirming that they have taken such steps. This provision is intended to promote programmes such as the Rugmark labelling initiative described below; importers in the United States could meet the "reasonable steps" test by complying with the Rugmark rules. The bill would also urge the President to seek an international agreement to impose an international ban on trade in products made by child labour.

Prison labour

Privately conducted investigations of prison labour in China, some of which were funded by the AFL-CIO (Southerland, 1994), revealed that goods produced by political prisoners and other incarcerated persons were being exported to the United States. Such imports are illegal under section 307 of the Tariff Act of 1930, and the threat of unilateral sanctions led to a series of bilateral disputes and negotiations.

The United States and the People's Republic of China reached a memorandum of understanding (MOU) on prison labour exports in August 1992. This agreement provides for investigation of suspected violations, exchanges of information and meetings between officials and experts, furnishing of evidence that can be used in judicial or administrative proceedings against violators, and facilitation of visits to relevant facilities[41]. Subsequent to the conclusion of this MOU, labour unions, human rights organisations and the State Department itself expressed dissatisfaction with Chinese compliance (Lord, 1993). These concerns have also led to new demands in Congress for more stringent legislation.

In addition, China's eligibility for receiving most-favoured-nation (MFN) status is being reviewed annually, partly on the basis of its record regarding prison labour and other workers' rights, as well as freedom of emigration under the 1974 Jackson-Vanick law.

Retaliation under section 301

Section 301 of the Trade Act of 1974 (as amended) gives the Office of the US Trade Representative (USTR) the authority to investigate foreign laws, policies and practices that are alleged to be unreasonable, unfair or discriminatory, and to negotiate with the country in question for redress. If an investigation determines that US trade rights have indeed been violated, and the foreign country does not take action to correct the problem, the USTR has the authority under section 301 to retaliate through the imposition of restrictions on imports from the country in question; penal tariffs of 100 per cent on a list of selected products have been the preferred means in recent cases.

Congress amended section 301 in 1988 to allow for the use of this mechanism in cases involving foreign countries' denial of internationally recognised labour rights. A provision in the Omnibus Trade and Competitiveness Act of 1988 did so by expanding the definition of "unreasonable" (and therefore actionable) acts, policies or practices to include "a persistent pattern of conduct that (I) denies workers the right of association, (II) denies workers the right to organize and bargain collectively, (III) permits any form of forced or compulsory labor, (IV) fails to provide a minimum age for the employment of children, or (V) fails to provide standards for minimum wages, hours of work, and occupational safety and health of workers". The provision further allowed the USTR to find that such a pattern was not unreasonable if either "the foreign country has taken, or is taking, actions to demonstrate a significant and tangible overall advancement in providing throughout the foreign country (including any designated zone within the foreign country) the rights and other standards" described in the law, or "such acts, policies, and practices are not inconsistent with the level of economic development of the foreign country".

This law has never been invoked. The USTR has not received any formal petitions asking that it do so, nor have allegations of labour rights violations been included in the USTR annual *National Trade Estimate Report on Foreign Trade Barriers* (1995).

Concluding remarks: It is difficult to evaluate these mechanisms since they have never been used directly. These Congressional initiatives may have contributed to the current debate on trade and labour standards.

International standards for the conduct of firms

The ILO Tripartite Declaration of Principles concerning MNEs and Social Policy

The ILO Tripartite Declaration of Principles concerning Multinational Enterprises and Social Policy (ILO, 1977) is a universal instrument adopted in 1977 by the ILO Governing Body in order to provide guidelines for MNEs, governments, employers and workers in areas of employment, training, conditions of work and life, and industrial relations. The Declaration urges the parties to respect the Universal Declaration of Human Rights and the corresponding United Nations Covenants, the constitution of the ILO and the principles laid down in the Declaration of Philadelphia on freedom of association and collective bargaining.

The Declaration, through references to UN and ILO Conventions, as well as explicit references, covers all the core labour standards listed in Part I of this study. It also contains an important direct reference to MNEs, i.e. that "where governments of host countries offer special incentives to attract foreign investment, these incentives should not include any limitation of the workers' freedom of association or the right to organise collectively" (ILO, 1977, par. 45).

A regular review procedure is established by the Declaration, which consists of a triennial survey conducted to monitor the extent of the application of the Declaration by governments, employers, workers and MNEs. The ILO Committee on MNEs analyses the parties' replies to the survey and formulates recommendations for decisions to be taken by the ILO Governing Body. Since 1986, there has also been a procedure for the examination of disputes concerning the application of the Declaration by means of interpretation of its provisions.

The sixth review is currently under way and a report is due by November 1996. The fifth review took place in 1992. The analysis of the parties' replies by the Committee on MNEs showed a "generally positive assessment of the valuable contribution that MNEs make to national economic and social development"[42]. Nevertheless, some workers' organisations signalled problems regarding the implementation of the Declaration, such as FDI legislation limiting the rights of unions, in particular in EPZs, and threats by firms to relocate in an attempt to influence the bargaining process.

Concluding remarks: The Tripartite Declaration represents a consensus statement of principles which "are commended to governments, the employers' and workers' organisations of home and host countries and to the multinational enterprises themselves" (par. 4 of the Declaration). Although it is a non-binding instrument, its implementation is nevertheless the object of regular reviews and there is a procedure for examining disputes concerning its application by means of an interpretation of its provisions. Since, however, it cannot be enforced in the same way as a Convention, the effectiveness of the Declaration has been questioned by some workers' organisations. Employers' organisations insist on the importance of its voluntary character.

The OECD Guidelines for Multinational Enterprises

The OECD Guidelines are recommendations to MNEs designed to ensure that they operate in harmony with the policies of the countries where they are located. These voluntary standards cover the full range of MNEs' operations.

An overview of the Guidelines

Features

The Guidelines are a part of the Declaration on International Investment and Multinational Enterprises. The Declaration constitutes a political commitment, adopted by the governments of OECD Member countries in 1976, with the objective of facilitating direct investment among OECD Members (see OECD, 1994a). The other parts of the Declaration deal with three related instruments, aimed at:

- providing national treatment to foreign-owned enterprises;

- promoting co-operation among governments in relation to international investment incentives and disincentives; and

- minimising the imposition of conflicting requirements on MNEs by governments of different countries.

The Guidelines are voluntary and, consequently, not legally enforceable. This, however, does not imply less commitment by OECD governments to encourage their observance. The system under which the Guidelines are implemented is described below.

The basic approach is that internationally agreed guidelines can help to prevent misunderstandings and build an atmosphere of confidence and predictability among business, labour and governments.

The Guidelines address the MNEs from OECD countries. However, reflecting the world-wide operations of MNEs, Member countries support international co-operation in this area to extend the Guidelines to all states, and in particular developing countries, with a view to improving the welfare and living standards of all peoples by encouraging the positive contributions of MNEs and minimising or resolving any problems which may arise in connection with their activities.

Coverage

The Guidelines are divided into separate chapters which cover the range of MNE activities. These chapters deal with: general policies, information disclosure, competition, financing, taxation, employment and industrial relations, environment, and science and technology. The introduction makes it clear that no different treatment between MNEs and domestic enterprises is sought. Wherever relevant, the Guidelines reflect good practice for all. The introduction also states that enterprises should take full account of countries' general objectives, co-operate with local community and business interests, and refrain from bribery and improper political activities.

The provision of information is an important theme of the Guidelines. For the public, this involves having information on the structure, activities and policies of the enterprise as a whole. For governments, this means access to information to ensure compliance with policies and regulations on taxes, competition and environmental standards. For employees, it means having information provided to their representatives for purposes such as meaningful negotiations on conditions of employment or the performance of the enterprise.

For the purpose of this study, it should be noted that a separate chapter addresses employment and industrial relations, where enterprises are encouraged to respect employees' rights to representation, refrain from unfair influence in labour negotiations or during organising campaigns, and to negotiate constructively on employment conditions. Enterprises are also encouraged to provide reasonable notice of changes in operations that would have major effects on employees and to co-operate to mitigate any adverse effects from such changes. In particular, enterprises should:

- respect the right of their employees to be represented by trade unions and other *bona fide* organisations and engage in constructive negotiations with them on employment conditions;

- provide assistance and information to employee representatives;

- provide information for a true and fair view of the performance of the enterprise;

- observe standards of employment and industrial relations not less favourable than those observed by comparable employers in the host country;

- utilise, train and prepare for upgrading their labour force;

- provide reasonable prior notice of changes in operations, in particular on intended closures and collective layoffs;

- refrain from discriminatory practices in their employment policies;

- not exercise unfair influence over *bona fide* negotiations with employee's representatives;

- enable authorised representatives of their employees to conduct negotiations on collective bargaining or labour-management relations with management representatives authorised to take decisions on the matters at hand.

Implementation

Institutional set-up

The institutional set-up of the Guidelines consists of three elements: (i) the National Contact Points; (ii) the OECD Committee on International Investment and Multinational Enterprises (CIME); and (iii) the advisory Committees of business and labour federations, BIAC and TUAC.

The National Contact Points (typically a government office in a Member country) serve to gather information on experience with the Guidelines, to promote them, to handle enquiries, to discuss matters related to the Guidelines and to assist in solving problems which may arise between business and labour in matters covered by the Guidelines. The CIME's responsibilities in the field of the Guidelines include: (i) providing clarifications on the interpretation of the Guidelines; (ii) reviewing and exchanging views on them; and (iii) responding to requests from Members, BIAC or TUAC on aspects of the Guidelines. BIAC and TUAC can request consultations with the National Contact Points on issues related to the Guidelines and can raise such issues at the CIME. They also inform their member federations about the Guidelines' development and seek their members' input in follow-up procedures.

Follow-up procedures

The Guidelines are drafted in general terms, so as to apply to the whole OECD area, with its diversity of legal systems and practices towards MNEs. Consequently, clarifications may be necessary in individual cases.

If a party is under the impression that, in an individual case, the Guidelines have not been observed, but is unclear about the Guidelines' applicability, that party should approach the National Contact Point. Member governments, labour and business organisations (through BIAC and TUAC) may raise such issues. The National Contact Point should contact the enterprise, either directly or through the appropriate business federation, to inform it that a Guidelines issue has been raised. The Contact Point and business and labour representatives should try to resolve the issue at the national level. If entities of the enterprise in another country are involved, the Contact Point should contact its counterparts in that country to exchange information and try to resolve the matter. The National Contact Point in the country where the enterprise has its headquarters should also be informed.

If no solution can be found through the National Contact Points, and a clarification seems necessary, the issue can be submitted to the CIME for consideration. Final responsibility for clarifications lies with the Committee, although matters discussed by the National Contact Points may involve questions of the scope and meaning of the Guidelines in specific circumstances. Whenever a Contact Point gives its opinion as to the relevance of the Guidelines to matters at hand, it should keep in mind the international character of the Guidelines and the overriding necessity of avoiding conflicting national interpretations. Where there is any doubt or where there are divergent views as to the consistency of an interpretation under consideration by a Contact Point with clarifications adopted by the OECD, the matter should be brought to the attention of the Committee before the Contact Point gives the final answer.

In order to speed up such proceedings, these matters can be referred directly to the CIME's Working Group on Investment Policies and the Guidelines for preliminary consideration. After considering the question, and consulting with BIAC and TUAC, the CIME may then provide a clarification. It is important to note that the clarification refers to how the Guidelines would apply to the issue raised. It is not a judgement on the behaviour of an individual enterprise and thus does not refer to it by name. This being said, the enterprise concerned may express its views orally or in writing on Guidelines issues involving its interests. Such an enterprise may, alternatively, use the offices of BIAC for this purpose.

Labour and business organisations may, through BIAC and TUAC, submit cases that raise issues for clarification, but an attempt should be made first to resolve the issues at the national level.

Experience

In the two decades of their existence, the OECD Guidelines have become a respected point of reference for a great majority of MNEs. Although the Guidelines are a voluntary instrument, they carry the weight of a joint Recommendation of OECD governments. Along with national laws, the Guidelines form part of a legal infrastructure which promotes responsible behaviour of MNEs. In addition, their language has influenced considerably the other codes of conduct for multinational enterprises, such as the ILO Tripartite Declaration (see above) and the Code of Conduct for Transnational Corporations of the United Nations.

Since the adoption of the Guidelines, around 30 cases of alleged violations have been introduced to the CIME, mostly by TUAC, but also by the Belgian, Danish, Netherlands and French governments, most of them referring to the provisions of the industrial relations chapter.

Issues have related, in particular, to infringements of the right of employees to be represented by trade unions (section 1); to the provision of reasonable notice in case of major changes in company operations (section 6); and to the provision of information to employee representatives to enable them to obtain a true and fair view of enterprise performance (section 3). Since the Committee does not reach conclusions on the conduct of individual enterprises, these cases have been raised as requests for "clarification" of the Guidelines. As in the past, the CIME has issued clarifications in response to questions raised, explaining in more detail the meaning of existing provisions in concrete situations in order to assist the parties concerned when using the Guidelines.

The CIME periodically reviews the efficiency of the Guidelines. The geographical expansion of the Guidelines to countries in Central and Eastern Europe, Asia and Latin America will reinforce the role of this OECD instrument. By endorsing the OECD Guidelines, non-member countries would indicate to all investors their clear interest in the respect of internationally recognised standards.

As with any internationally negotiated instrument, the Guidelines have sometimes been criticised, for being either too general or too detailed. Some have argued, for example, that they do not go far enough in ensuring that MNEs comply with national law and practice, while others have suggested that the Guidelines go beyond those standards in some areas. Another area of debate involves the follow-up, which some say needs to be made stronger, while others argue that it is too juridical. To date, no formal evaluation of these criticisms has been made. In particular, further study is needed in order to assess whether the Guidelines have had any impact on the observance of core labour standards by MNEs in developing countries.

When Guidelines issues arise, the onus of attempting a settlement is particularly on the National Contact Point; hence, the effectiveness of the Guidelines depends to a large degree on that of the Contact Points. This effectiveness differs from country to country.

The OECD Guidelines for Multinational Enterprises have a role to play as a voluntary instrument to promote responsible behaviour of MNEs. This role would be enhanced if home and host countries made it known that they expect foreign investors to follow the Guidelines world-wide and if non-member countries were encouraged to endorse the Guidelines. Consideration could also be given to revising the Guidelines to include those core standards which are not explicitly covered, namely prohibition of forced labour, exploitation of child labour and discrimination. This would send a clear message of the importance OECD governments attach to the respect of these standards.

Private-sector codes of conduct

Ethical standards for firms emerged mainly during the lengthy campaign to eliminate apartheid in South Africa. In the European Union, these pressures produced the Code of Conduct (Redleaf, 1992); in the United States, companies were urged to adhere to the voluntary Sullivan Principles. These standards stemmed from broader human rights concerns but core labour standards are clearly included in these measures.

The Sullivan Principles are named after the Reverend Leon Sullivan, who is a member of the board of directors of General Motors. When in 1977 Sullivan was unsuccessful in his efforts to convince his fellow board members to pull the company's operations out of South Africa, he proposed instead that the firm agree to a series of six pledges regarding its treatment of South African workers[43]. These principles of fair employment and non-segregation soon spread to other companies, with a dozen adhering to them in the first year, and 120 by 1983 (Clark, 1983, p. 362). The accounting firm of A.D. Little was given the responsibility for policing companies' adherence to the principles, issuing annual reports on each signatory's compliance. The European Code of Conduct was based on similar principles.

These principles inspired several comparable initiatives. Prior to the breakup of the Soviet Union, for example, the Slepak Principles provided a voluntary code of conduct for Western businesses (Hansen, 1989). These principles offered guidance on issues ranging from labour rights (e.g. pledge not to use the products of forced labour) to strategic industries (e.g. pledge not to aid the Soviet military).

The MacBride Principles provide guidance for US companies that invest in Northern Ireland, in order to prevent employment discrimination on the basis of religion[44]. In the United States, 16 states and over 40 cities have laws or resolutions in support of these principles (Gilman, 1995), some of which are linked to investment of pension funds or rules governing government procurement of goods and services. The MacBride Principles bill (H.R. 470) pending in Congress would prohibit US companies operating in Northern Ireland from exporting their products to the United States unless they are in compliance with the MacBride Principles; similar legislation has been repeatedly introduced, but not enacted, since the mid-1980s[45].

Another set of principles is variously known as the Minnesota Principles (for the Minnesota Center for Corporate Responsibility), the Caux Principles (for the Caux Round Table) or the Kyosei Principles (for the Japanese term meaning "living together"). They establish "stakeholder principles" for dealing with customers, employees, owner/investors, suppliers, competitors and communities. Included among the principles for dealing with employees are the responsibilities to "provide jobs and compensation that improve workers' living conditions" and to "engage in good faith negotiation when conflict arises". The principles have been backed by business leaders in the European Union, Japan and the United States (Skelly, 1995).

Finally, the US administration released its own "Model Business Principles" destined to US business companies operating overseas in mid-1995. Included in this five-point set of recommendations is a call for "fair employment practices, including avoidance of child and forced labour and avoidance of discrimination based on race, gender, national origin or religious beliefs; and respect for the right of association and the right to organize and bargain effectively". It is the intention of the administration that these principles be adopted by companies on a voluntary basis.

Concluding remarks: Are privately adopted standards effective? Because they are voluntary, firms remain free not to follow the standards. Another weakness lies in the lack of satisfactory review procedures. However, there are indirect ways in which voluntary codes of conduct can make a real contribution to the promotion of core labor standards. First, if adhering to such standards improves a firm's image, making consumers more willing to buy its products, other firms may want to join in for fear of losing market shares[46].

Second, voluntary adherence to ethical codes of conduct by large firms may lead them to insist that their suppliers, which often consist of small subcontracting firms located in least developed countries, also respect core labour standards. For example, in 1983 the Swiss retail stores chain Migros signed an agreement with Del Monte, its Philippine pineapple supplier, guaranteeing that "production conditions for workers are above average on the social and economic level"[47].

Private-party mechanisms

Many of the policy instruments examined in this study are in the hands of governments and international organisations. They are not the only actors in this field, however. Consumers, investors and firms can also influence directly the promotion of core labour standards, both at home and abroad.

Moral suasion

The basic principle of what is sometimes called "ethical consumption" is to persuade consumers to base their consumption decisions not only on price considerations but also on moral principles, relating to the conditions of production. Some activists encourage consumers to reward socially responsible firms by directing their purchases towards companies that meet certain social criteria (Council on Economic Priorities, 1994). Others urge boycotts of goods that are produced under conditions of poor labour standards.

In the United States, the AFL-CIO officially sanctions national boycotts of non-union products. From a legal perspective, campaigns of this sort are a form of "secondary boycott". Some types of secondary boycott are illegal under US labour law, but the law explicitly permits advertising campaigns that urge consumers not to purchase non-union products[48]. A secondary boycott is illegal if it encourages consumers to avoid all purchases from a secondary employer (e.g. an otherwise unrelated retailer), and the law has been interpreted to bar US labour unions from asking foreign labour unions to participate in a boycott.

There are also children's advocates based in developing countries who have adopted this tactic, such as the South Asian Coalition on Child Servitude (Harvey and Riggin, 1994).

Concluding remarks: Is this approach effective? Boycott campaigns mobilise consumers, by disseminating information about work conditions in certain export industries and encouraging them to reward good corporate practice. Nevertheless, the utility of this tactic may be limited by the substantial informational and organisational problems faced by those who seek to organise collective action by consumers. The difficulty here is even greater than that faced in the classic case of organising consumers to oppose protectionist policies. In the case of a boycott organised for the promotion of labour rights abroad, it means convincing consumers to act *against* their narrow economic interests (i.e. asking that they voluntarily restrict their choice or be willing to pay higher prices).

In addition, boycotts can have an impact on trade, and indeed a danger is that they could be manipulated for protectionist purposes. This issue hinges upon the type of good being boycotted, and the groups that are behind the campaign. If the good in question is produced in the consuming country, there may be an incentive for a local industry to take advantage of the calls for a boycott.

Labelling of consumer goods

The main tool of the organisations attempting to induce consumers to stop buying some products and start to buy others according to ethical criteria is of course the gathering and diffusion of information regarding the conditions of production. This is why "social labelling" programmes have grown in number and importance. The principle is to provide consumers with information that enables them to choose to reward goods that meet certain standards deemed to be socially desirable. Examples of social labelling programmes include (i) the Rugmark campaign, under which certain hand-made carpets are labelled to indicate that they were not produced with child labour; and (ii) the union label, indicating that the product in question was produced by members of a labour union.

The Rugmark campaign is directed specifically at the hand-knotted rug industry (Harvey and Riggin, 1994). Founded in 1994, the Rugmark Foundation is the joint effort of the Indo-German Export Promotion Council, carpet manufacturers, and child welfare and human rights organisations. Rugmark has a small staff of inspectors, and has thus far certified several dozen

Indian companies; many more have applied for membership. The programme also entails a levy of 1 to 2 per cent of the export value of these rugs, with the funds being used for the rehabilitation of former child labourers in the industry. Although the initiative is relatively new, it has received considerable publicity and achieved early progress. The Rugmark programme has thus far been most successful in Europe. Germany is the leading importer of oriental carpets, and several major German retailers have pledged to honour the campaign. The programme has made limited inroads in the United States.

The union label approach has a lengthy history in the United States, where it extends as far back as 1869. The observation that some manufacturers have tried to apply counterfeit union labels may be taken as an indication of their economic value. The union label is in fact a protected trade mark, and one of the principal responsibilities of the union label department of the AFL-CIO is the discovery of such false representations.

Concluding remarks: Is social labelling an effective means of promoting core labour standards? This approach is useful only for products that meet the twin criteria of being (i) exported and (ii) purchased directly by consumers. It would not work for goods or services that are sold solely in the country of origin, such as household services or locally consumed construction materials. Similarly, it would be too unwieldy to use for raw materials or semi-finished goods that are incorporated in the manufacture of other products overseas. However, labelling requirements on the finished product may induce some producers to require from their suppliers that they respect core labour standards in their production of inputs, thus starting a dynamic of self-discipline. In this way, it could make a positive contribution to fostering core labour standards world-wide.

Could social labelling programmes constitute a barrier to trade? Some argue that social labelling constitutes a non-tariff barrier to the extent that it appeals to the latent economic nationalism of consumers. It is true that the implementation of social labelling programmes raises delicate issues, including the unequal accessibility of labelling schemes to foreign versus domestic firms, the incentives to develop competitive and/or counterfeit labels and, finally, whether voluntary labelling schemes would be subject to the disciplines of the WTO Agreement on Technical Barriers to Trade. This last question, however, goes beyond social labelling *per se* and is currently debated in the WTO. Without prejudging the outcome of this discussion, it should be noted that the impact on trade, if any, is likely to be small, since labels would be awarded to a limited number of products representing a relatively small share of the market. The potential trade distortions generated by a proliferation of social labels will be further diminished if they refer to international standards, agreed to by both developed and developing countries. In any case, labels represent an improvement upon, as well as a potential substitute for, unilateral trade action. An advantage of social labelling programmes is that they cause a minimum of economic distortions, since the incentives are likely to be most directly and appropriately related to the producers concerned.

Socially responsible investing

Known as "socially responsible investing" (SRI) in the United States and "ethical investing" in the United Kingdom, this is a practice under which those who purchase stocks and other securities make their investment decisions on the basis of social as well as economic criteria. Practitioners of SRI hope that by steering capital towards what are deemed to be socially responsible firms and away from those deemed to be socially irresponsible, they can wield a positive influence on issues of importance to them. There are active and growing associations of SRI practitioners who share information and ideas through newsletters, investment clubs, computer networks and organisations such as the Social Investment Forum in the United States and the Ethical Investment Research Service in the United Kingdom. SRI is also expanding to several other countries. The International Association of Investors in the Social Economy (founded in 1989) is a Brussels-based organisation that has 35 member organisations in 15 countries. Other NGOs and firms involved in this field are located in Austria, Australia, Canada and Germany, and in other countries as well.

The most important forms of SRI, for the purposes of this study, are investment in stocks of socially responsible companies through (i) screened mutual funds, (ii) divestment of stocks in socially irresponsible companies and (iii) the promotion of shareholder resolutions that deal with social issues. These operate in the following ways:

- In screened mutual funds, in addition to employing traditional economic criteria in picking stocks, the managers employ various types of "social screens" to choose specific companies. A "positive screen" actively seeks companies that are believed to produce a socially desirable good, or are otherwise deemed to be exceptionally good corporate citizens. More common is the "negative screen" approach under which companies are rejected if they violate one or more of the criteria set by the fund managers.

Are screened mutual funds an effective means of promoting core labour standards? Among the SRI funds that are currently offered in the United States, relatively few focus specifically — and none of them exclusively — on the *foreign* labour practices of companies. For most SRI practitioners, both charity and investment begin at home. It is much more common for these funds to examine the domestic labour relations of a company, as measured by such criteria as its degree of unionisation or the generosity of its benefits packages, than it is to scrutinise their overseas labour practices, let alone focus on core labour standards. Finally, screened mutual funds seem too small and diverse to have wielded much influence on core labour standards.

– Divestment by institutional investors might be seen as the reverse image of screened mutual funds. This approach is based not on investing in stocks, but instead on urging or obliging large institutions to sell off any stock that they might hold in companies that are deemed to violate some social standards. The classic example of divestment was the campaign in the 1970s and 1980s to require that universities, labour unions, government pension services and other institutional investors divest any stocks in companies that had operations in South Africa. More than 150 municipal and state governments in the United States adopted divestment polices, some of which forced the sale of billions of dollars worth of securities. These restrictions were lifted after Nelson Mandela requested an end to sanctions in 1993. Another divestment campaign sprouted in 1989, following the Tiananmen incident in China.

– The introduction of shareholder resolutions at annual meetings was popularised in the early 1970s by consumer organisations in the United States. For example, activists used the annual shareholder meetings of automotive producers to promote labour rights and product-safety issues. Shareholder resolutions moved into entirely new territory with the controversy over apartheid; while previous resolutions had dealt specifically with the nature of the products or services offered by a firm, or direct consequences of their production and use (e.g. pollution), resolutions concerning apartheid dealt with the broader political and social environment in which companies operate. There are now literally dozens of social and environmental issues that are frequently raised at annual meetings. As in the case of screened mutual funds, however, it appears that domestic issues, both social and environmental, are much more attractive targets of interest than is the protection of labour rights abroad, let alone core labour standards. There are relatively few shareholder resolutions that deal with this topic, and fewer still that are adopted.

Concluding remarks: Consumer-driven mechanisms, such as boycotts of specific products or social labelling schemes, can constitute a potentially useful, albeit limited means of promoting core labour standards. One advantage is that they allow consumers to express their views on appropriate levels of core standards by paying for the social content of goods. Another advantage is the potential utility of incentives or penalties being channelled through more market-oriented forces. In this way any economic benefits stemming from the violation of core labour standards could be diminished by the effect of market-based mechanisms that would create correct incentives. Under certain conditions[49], programmes such as social labelling schemes could constitute a useful complement to other types of governmental action.

That said, specific measures generally focus on only one or two labour standards, such as child labour or freedom of association, and/or they are targeted at only a few firms or countries. The standards may or may not be internationally defined, and broader motives than the promotion of core labour standards may explain specific measures. Furthermore, boycotts or selective investment/divestment may, if they operate on a large enough scale, have a disruptive and spillover effect on trade and/or investment flows, which in turn may lead the affected countries to retaliate in some way. Finally, there is a danger that these mechanisms will not distinguish adequately between low standards which are poverty-related and those that are not, i.e. child labour versus exploitation. Where child labour is poverty-related, boycotts risk exacerbating the problem.

NOTES

1. See 1995 Report of the Committee of Experts of the ILO, page 27.

2. These proposals are presented in ILO (1995), GB.264/6.

3. State parties are the countries that have committed themselves to the Convention through ratification (after signature) or accession (without signing). Signatories (presently nine countries) are those that have signed the convention, and are presumably considering ratification.

4. The World Declaration on Education for All, Jomtien 1990, adopted by 155 UN Member states, including OECD countries, calls for a renewed commitment and mobilisation of financial and technical assistance to basic education.

5. UNESCO (1993).

6. See DAC Orientations for Development Co-operation in Support of Private Sector Development (OECD, 1995d).

7. The DAC Guiding Principles for Women in Development (1989) provide a framework for assistance in this area. They are reproduced in OECD (1992c).

8. NGOs doing notable work on child labour include, among others: Bureau International Catholique de l'Enfance; Save the Children; Childwatch; Childhope; Concerned for Working Children; Norwegian Centre for Child Research; Education International, a world teachers' union; Terre des Hommes; Enda-Tiers-Monde, Dakar; Child Asia, Thailand; Bonded Labour Liberation Front of Pakistan; Child Workers in Nepal Concerned Centre; Childworkers in Asia, Bangkok; Committee for Eradication of Child Labour, India.

9. Key countries funding the IPEC programme are Germany (by far the largest contributor), Australia, Belgium, France, Norway, Spain and the United States. Countries where IPEC has conducted action programmes include: Bangladesh, Brazil, Cameroon, Colombia, Egypt, India, Indonesia, Kenya, Nepal, Pakistan, the Philippines, Tanzania, Thailand and Turkey.

10. See IPEC (1995).

11. See OECD (1995e).

12. OECD (1993b).

13. The ITO was not set up. GATT 1947 took its place and was seen originally as an interim Agreement setting the stage for possible later consideration of the more comprehensive provisions in the Havana Charter. When that in fact did not occur, the GATT CONTRACTING PARTIES undertook to refine and considerably expand this interim Agreement which in 1948 was principally focused on cross-border trade in goods. For many years, revisions to the Agreement were accomplished through a series of "rounds" of negotiations focused principally on reductions of tariffs, although anti-dumping and some non-tariff barriers were also the subject of negotiations.

    The Tokyo Round shifted the focus of negotiations and explicitly recognised that other measures, principally non-tariff measures, affected trade flows. The September 1973 Ministerial Declaration launching the Tokyo Round stated that the negotiations should aim to, *inter alia,* "reduce or eliminate non-tariff measures or, where this is not appropriate, reduce or eliminate their trade restricting or distorting effects, and to bring such measures under more effective international discipline". Agreements negotiated under this section of the Declaration dealt with customs valuation and import licensing practices; reduction of technical barriers to trade; countries anti-dumping, subsidies and countervailing duty measures; government procurement practices; trade in civil aircraft and trade in dairy and bovine meat products.

    GATT 1947 CONTRACTING PARTIES also explored and considered expanding the scope of the agreement in narrower and less formal settings than the general rounds of negotiations, such as the Tokyo and Uruguay Rounds. Various working parties were established in the GATT to consider subjects such as trade and the environment, restrictive business practices and other matters. For example, a Working Party on Environmental Measures in International Trade was first formed in 1972 and reconstituted in 1991.

In September 1986, GATT CONTRACTING PARTIES initiated the Uruguay Round of negotiations which dramatically expanded the subject matter subject to "international trade" discipline. GATT 1947, which dealt primarily with matters affecting trade in goods, was subsumed into an agreement that encompasses trade in services, including financial services and trade-related aspects of intellectual property rights. The results of these negotiations were then put under the auspices of a "formal" international trade organisation -- the World Trade Organisation.

In the WTO, Members have agreed that this new organisation shall provide the forum for negotiations among its Members concerning their multilateral trade relations in matters dealt with under the agreements in the Annexes to the Agreement. The WTO may also provide a forum for further negotiations among its Members concerning their multilateral trade relations, and a framework for the implementation of the results of such negotiations, as may be decided by the Ministerial Conference (WTO Agreement, Art. III:2).

The WTO Agreement also provides a mechanism for adding new plurilateral trade agreements or amending the scope of the Multilateral Trade Agreements (Art. X:9 and X generally). It also authorises the formation of committees and other bodies which can serve as a forum for consideration of issues of interest to Members. The first concrete example of this was the creation of the Committee on Trade and Environment which Ministers agreed to do at the 1994 Marrakesh Implementation Conference.

14. Resolution of the European Parliament of 28 October 1983, par. 12, reiterated in the Resolution of 9 September 1986, pars. 64-65.

15 . US House of Representatives Doc.102-51 (1991), pp. 111-112.

16. Resolution of the European Parliament on the Introduction of a Social Clause in the Unilateral and Multilateral Trading System, *Official Journal of the European Communities,* No. C61, 28 February 1994, p.89. The Resolution further suggested that the ILO be associated with any

surveillance of the respect of core labour rights undertaken by the WTO; and that an advisory committee composed by the ILO and concerned countries be able to lodge complaints against MNEs or countries violating the provisions incorporated in the social clause.

17. ILO (1994d), p. 57.

18. Agreement on Subsidies and Countervailing Measures, Art. 1.1, (a)(1).

19. The 1992 Sugar Agreement provides in Article 29 that "Members shall ensure that fair labour standards are maintained in the respective sugar industries and, as far as possible, shall endeavour to improve the standard of living of agricultural and agricultural workers in the various branches of sugar production and of growers of sugar cane and sugar beet". The 1993 Cocoa Agreement provides in Article 49 that "Members declare that, in order to raise the levels of living of populations and provide full employment, they will endeavour to maintain fair labour standards and working conditions in the various branches of cocoa production in the countries concerned, consistent with their stage of development, as regards both agricultural and industrial workers employed therein". The 1987 Natural Rubber Agreement provides in Article 53 that "Members declare that they will endeavour to maintain labour standards designed to improve the levels of living of workers in their respective natural rubber sectors" (this text remains unchanged in the draft under renegotiation). Once a "fair labour standards" clause has obtained entry to an agreement, in each case it has been included in the renegotiations as a non-controversial element without any amendments. However, these provisions have not been of major operational importance compared with the mostly very detailed economic provisions of the agreements.

20. US Commission on Foreign Economic Policy Staff Papers, February 1954, pp. 437-438.

21. WTO Article XIII generally operates on the same principles as did GATT Article XXXV. One difference concerns the restraints placed on a WTO Member's right to invoke the provision: a CONTRACTING PARTY could not invoke GATT Article XXXV if it had engaged in tariff negotiations with the acceding country, but there is no such restriction in the operation of WTO Article XIII.

22. Section 526(e) of Public Law 103-306: Foreign Operations, Export Financing and Related Programs Appropriations Act.

23. Annual Report to Congress on Labor Issues and the International Financial Institutions, 1995.

24. In particular, labour law includes laws and regulations pertaining to:
    - freedom of association and protection of the right to organise;
    - the right to bargain collectively;
    - the right to strike;
    - prohibition of forced labour;
    - labour protections for children and young persons;
    - minimum employment standards, such as minimum wages and overtime pay;
    - elimination of employment discrimination;
    - equal pay for men and women;
    - prevention of occupational injuries and illnesses;
    - compensation in cases of occupational injuries and illnesses;
    - protection of migrant workers.

25. In the case of Canada, however, a special procedure defined in an annex to the Agreement shall apply instead of the provisions relating to the suspension of NAFTA's trade benefits (NAALC, Annex 41A).

26. The National Administrative Offices (NAOs) administer the agreement and serve as a liaison between the Commission and the national governments.

27. Workers supposedly linked with independent unions were fired and had to waive their right to file claims against their former employer in order to collect severance payments. In addition, the employer is accused of having used coercive measures in order to gain information about other pro-union employees. The second submission also asserts that the Government of Mexico failed to enforce its labour law, especially in the *maquiladora* sector.

28. In particular, the submission documents violations of workers' rights in the area of freedom of organisation, involving intimidation, firing and other repressive actions against independent union activists as well as failure by the Mexican government to allow the registration of an independent union (Submission #940003, before the US NAO).

29. Regarding the Sony submission, the consultations have led to a review by a panel of independent experts of the overall union registration process in Mexico and in the Sony case in particular. Meetings between federal Mexican labour authorities and the parties concerned (Sony workers, Sony managers, and local labor authorities) will also be held during the summer of 1996 (Daily Labor Report, Bureau of National Affairs, Washington, D.C., 27 July 1995).

30. In June 1971, the GATT CONTRACTING PARTIES established the legal basis for GSP schemes by approving a waiver to GATT Article I, which requires that trade policy measures be applied without discrimination to all contracting parties (OECD, 1983). Under the waiver, developed CONTRACTING PARTIES were permitted to accord more favourable tariff treatment to products imported from developing countries, for a period of ten years. Over time, OECD and most East European countries have modified their respective schemes according to different criteria and time schedules.

31. Section 502 (b) of the US Trade and Tariff Act of 1984. The President may waive this condition for a particular country if he/she determines and reports with reasons to Congress that such a waiver is in the US national economic interest.

32. Under the "offset" programme, a long-term renewal of the GSP requires a cut of US$500 million in other programmes. This is because the GSP, according to government accounts, leads to a loss of tariff revenues of US$500 million.

33. Law cases associated with such negotiations or representations are reported to be relatively inexpensive, or about one-tenth the cost of anti-dumping cases, on average.

34. According to labour advocacy groups, successive cuts in the financial benefits available under the Trade Adjustment Assistance programme

have led them to rely more heavily on the GSP workers' rights review process as a vehicle to defend their interests, in spite of the overall decline in the value of GSP preferences resulting from the Uruguay Round agreement on MFN tariff cuts.

35. *Official Journal of the European Communities* N.L 348, Council Regulation N.3281/94.

36. Other circumstances where preferences may be withdrawn relate to drug trafficking and money laundering, fraud or failure to co-operate regarding verification of certificates of origin, and manifest cases of unfair trading practices (See *Official Journal of the European Communities* N.L.348, Council Regulation N.3281/94, Art. 9).

37 *Official Journal of the European Communities* No. C 15/3, 20 January 1996.

38. Section 2901(b)(14) of the Act provides that, "The principal negotiating objectives of the United States regarding worker rights are:

   - to promote respect for worker rights;

   - to secure a review of the relationship of worker rights to GATT articles, objectives, and related instruments with a view to ensuring that the benefits of the trading system are available to all workers; and

   - to adopt, as a principle of the GATT, that the denial of worker rights should not be a means for a country or its industries to gain competitive advantage in international trade."

39. In the Senate it is designated S.706 (introduced 6 April 1995); the version in the House of Representatives is H.R. 2058 (introduced 19 July 1995). Similar legislation has been sponsored in the German Bundestag and in the European Parliament (Brown, 1994).

40. The decision to place an industry on the list would be based on consideration of (i) whether it complies with the applicable national laws prohibiting child labour; (ii) whether it utilises child labour in the export of products; and (iii) whether it has on a continuing basis exported the products of child labour to the United States.

41. The text of the MOU is published in Volume 3, Number 3, of the State Department's journal *Dispatch* (17 August 1992).

42. ILO, GB.254/MNE/1/4, p. 18.

43. The Sullivan Principles called for:

    - non-segregation of the races in all eating, comfort and work facilities;

    - equal and fair employment policies for all workers;

    - initiation of training programmes to bring blacks into supervisory, administrative, clerical and technical employment;

    - recruitment and training of minorities for management and supervisory positions;

    - improving the quality of life for minorities outside the work environment in areas such as housing, health, transportation, schooling and recreation.

44. The MacBride Principles provide for:

    - Increasing the representation of individuals from under-represented religious groups in the work force including managerial, supervisory, administrative, clerical and technical jobs.

    - Adequate security for the protection of minority employees both at the work place and while traveling to and from work.

    - The banning of provocative religious or political emblems from the work place.

    - All job openings should be advertised publicly and special recruitment efforts made to attract applicants from under-represented religious groups.

    - Layoff, recall and termination procedures should not in practice favour a particular religious group.

    - The abolition of job reservations, apprenticeship restrictions and differential employment criteria which discriminate on the basis of religion.

    - The development of training programmes that will prepare substantial numbers of current minority employees for skilled jobs, including the expansion of existing programmes and the creation of new programmes to train, upgrade and improve the skills of minority employees.

- The establishment of procedures to assess, identify and actively recruit minority employees with potential for further advancement.

- The appointment of a senior management staff member to oversee the company's affirmative action efforts and the setting up of timetables to carry out affirmative action principles.

45. A less radical approach, but one more likely to be enacted into law, is offered by a provision of the American Overseas Interests Act of 1995 (H.R.1561). As approved in the House of Representatives, and now pending in the Senate, the bill provides that any US company accepting funds from the International Ireland Fund must comply with the MacBride Principles. This fund was established in 1986, and provides grants and loans for business enterprises in Northern Ireland.

46. In particular, the companies that signed on to the Sullivan Principles often did so out of concern that they would otherwise be subject to divestment campaigns or even boycotts, while the Irish National Caucus in the United States has organised boycotts against three firms that are alleged to operate in violation of the MacBride Principles (i.e. Coca Cola, Ford Motor and Timex).

47. Cited in the report of the European Parliament Commission on Social Affairs, Employment and Work Environment on the introduction of a social clause in the multilateral trading system, A3-0007/94, 6 January 1994. A follow-up on the agreement took place in 1987, when a Swiss Parliament Representative and a US law professor went to the Philippines to check on local conditions. They verified that the clause was indeed respected.

48. There is an important distinction to be drawn here. Campaigns that urge consumers not to purchase certain products are considered a form of "secondary boycott" under US labour law, when the product in question is sold to the consumer by a firm other than the one that produces it (e.g. a pair of shoes is produced by one manufacturer, but then sold by a shoe store that carries the products of many different shoe manufacturers). It is lawful under the National Labor Relations Board Act (as amended) for a union to engage in such a secondary boycott through advertisements in the public media or through handbilling (i.e. the distribution of literature).

The law also permits the use of pickets (i.e. persons carrying signs outside the secondary establishment) urging consumers not to purchase the product in question, but it is illegal to picket when the aim is to urge consumers to cease *all* purchases from the secondary establishment. Moreover, it is lawful for a union to request that a retailer stop handling goods produced by the primary employer, provided that the request does not threaten or coerce.

49. In particular, to ensure a universal definition of the standards and uniform application of social labelling schemes, an international institution such as the ILO or the International Organisation for Standardisation could be asked to oversee their implementation.

ANALYTICAL APPENDIX

CORE LABOUR STANDARDS,
ECONOMIC EFFICIENCY AND TRADE

This note provides a formal framework for analysing how core labour standards might possibly affect economic efficiency, judged mainly from the standpoint of production. The issue of how core standards might enter the consumers' utility function is not addressed, largely because it would pose serious analytical and methodological problems. First, in order to take into account core standards in the utility function, one would need to expand the conventional two-goods model to include a third good, thus making the diagrammatic presentation a very complex one. Second, if core standards were to be introduced in the utility function as normal (private) goods, then the issue of whether and how core standards might be traded off against other goods would have to be addressed. This, in turn, raises the question of whether core standards are divisible; if they are not, the analysis must focus on a comparison between a situation where there are (fully enforced) core standards and a situation where there are no core standards. It is unclear, however, which criteria could be used to judge the two situations. Third, alternatively, core standards could be included in the utility function as a public good, i.e. as a good that can be consumed by all individuals at the same time; consumption of the good by one individual does not reduce consumption by the others. As is well known, optimality conditions in a public goods case are especially complicated.

Conditions under which economic outcomes are efficient are first described. Thereafter, the extent to which core labour standards affect these conditions, in particular the allocation of resources and their availability, is addressed. Finally, the note discusses the possibility of a relationship between core standards and trade.

Equilibrium in the absence of distortions

In a neo-classical framework, it can be shown that the economy maximises the level of output when relative factor prices are allowed to reflect supply and demand forces and all factors are fully utilised. For instance, suppose the economy comprises two representative firms, each producing one good, with two factors of production, labour and capital. For a given level of output, each firm will select a combination of labour and capital that will minimise its costs[1]:

- The objective function is
  min wL+rK
    s.t. f(L,K)=y,
  where L and K represent the available quantities of labour and capital, respectively (assumed for convenience to be in fixed supply), w and r labour and capital factor prices, f the production function and y the level of output.

- First-order conditions for cost minimisation lead to:
  MPL/MPK = w/r

That is, the technical rate of substitution between labour and capital (the rate at which capital can be substituted for labour while maintaining output constant) is equal to the factor-price ratio, (the rate at which capital can be substituted for labour while maintaining a constant cost). If the technical rate of substitution is less than the factor-price ratio, it is possible to use one less unit of labour and one more unit of capital, while maintaining output essentially unchanged and reducing costs. The equilibrium condition is represented in the diagram below. The curved isoquant I(y) gives the combinations of capital and labour that yield a constant volume of output y. The straight line gives the combinations of capital and labour associated with a constant cost. Cost minimisation is achieved at a point (P) where the slope of the iso-cost line (the ratio of factor prices) is equal to the slope of the isoquant (the technical rate of substitution). At point P, the iso-cost line is as close to the origin as is feasible.

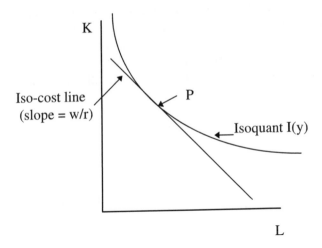

In the absence of market distortions, the factor-price ratio will be the same for both firms. Under such circumstances, the equilibrium for the economy will be such that the technical rate of substitution is the same for both firms and is equal to the factor-price ratio. Such an equilibrium is termed efficient. This can be illustrated in an Edgeworth-Bowley box diagram:

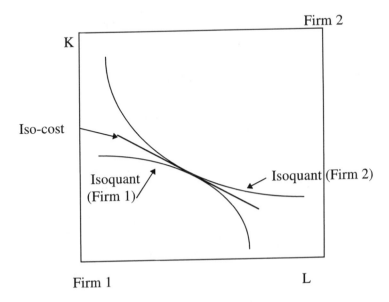

Therefore, in the absence of distortions, the level of output in the economy reaches the production possibility frontier. As shown in the following diagram, the production possibility frontier gives the maximum levels of output of both firms that can be attained given available factor resources. The economy will reach the frontier of production when factors are well allocated and fully utilised.

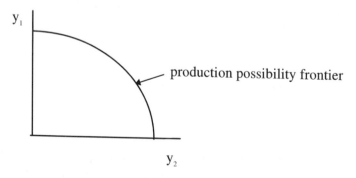

Core labour standards and allocation of production factors

One channel through which core labour standards might operate is through their impact on the factor-price ratio and the allocation of production factors. It turns out that employment discrimination, forced labour and child labour exploitation can distort the allocation of factors, so that core labour standards may need to be enforced to correct these distortions. The impact of freedom-of-association and collective bargaining rights on the allocation of factors and economic efficiency is more ambiguous.

Economic efficiency and employment discrimination

Employment discrimination is a practice whereby certain workers are not allowed to work in the occupation or sector of their own choosing. Restrictions on (or prohibition of) female work in Islamic societies is an example of employment discrimination. It can be shown that discrimination in terms of employment can be assimilated to an economic distortion, thus leading to a loss of economic efficiency. This is most clear when workers are simply not allowed to work, in which case the quantity of labour available for production is reduced, thus leading to a situation that is not efficient (see below). When employment discrimination takes the form of restrictions that impede certain workers from fulfilling particular jobs, a loss in efficiency will also arise because, in the presence of employment discrimination, labour cannot be allocated to the sectors or occupations where it is most productive. To see this, suppose that there are two types of labour, female and male. Female labour is subject to employment discrimination in Firm 1, but not in Firm 2[2], while male labour is not subject to any such discrimination. In other words, there is a limit to the number of female workers Firm 1 can hire.

- The objective function for Firm 1 can be written as follows[3]:

  $\min w_f L_f + w_m L_m$

  s.t. $f(L_f, L_m) = y$

  $L_f \leq c$,

  where c is the maximum number of female workers.

- This leads to the following first-order condition:

  $TRS = (w_f + \lambda)/w_m$,

  that is, the technical rate of substitution is no longer equal to the relative price of inputs, as there is a constraint on the use of female labour (λ is the multiplier attached to the constraint that the number of female workers is less than or equal to c).

- The objective function of Firm 2 is unchanged compared with the standard case:

  $\min w_f L_f + w_m L_m$

  s.t. $f(L_f, L_m) = y$

- And the first-order condition for Firm 2 is:

  $TRS = w_f/w_m$

It follows that the two firms have different technical rates of substitution. Therefore, both firms would be better off if Firm 1 could hire some more female workers in exchange for fewer male workers. This can be seen by calculating the number of male workers that Firm 1 is prepared to give to Firm 2 in exchange for one more female worker, while keeping output constant $[dL_m(1) = (w_f + \lambda)/w_m]$. This is higher than the number of male workers that Firm 2 needs in order to compensate for the transfer of one female worker to Firm 1 while keeping its output constant $[dL_m(2) = w_f/w_m]$

Since $dL_m(1) > dL_m(2)$, employment discrimination reduces the level of output compared with an efficient situation. The equilibrium point (P) with employment discrimination is represented in the following Edgeworth-Bowley box. The two firms can engage in an exchange of inputs so that both are better off: any point that lies in the region delimited by the two isoquants improves output for both firms.

219

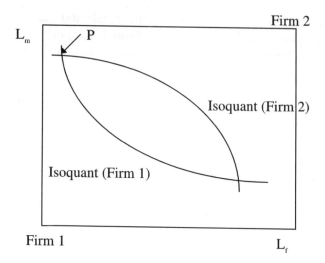

The loss of output resulting from discrimination can be shown in the output diagram below. Because of the distortion, output of the two goods is at point A, which lies below the production possibility frontier.

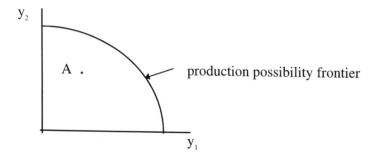

If employment discrimination makes both firms worse off, the issue arises as to why there is discrimination in the first place. This issue is discussed in the main text. Socio-cultural habits can explain such economically irrational behaviour. Hence, although output may be higher in the absence of employment discrimination, social welfare may in fact be lower. Another explanation may be the fact that societies where there is employment discrimination are dominated by a particular social group, whose interests do not coincide with those of the society at large. In the example developed here, it may be the case that male workers have an interest in discriminating against female workers, even though non-discrimination is better for the society as a whole.

Economic efficiency and forced labour

Forced labour produces similar effects to employment discrimination. Suppose some female workers are forced to work in Firm 2, i.e. they are not allowed to work in Firm 1. This situation can arise because Firm 2 has property rights on some female workers, as in the case of slavery, or because of debt bondage, forced prison labour, etc. In these circumstances, forced workers will be paid less than under free market conditions; for instance, the wage of female workers in Firm 2 will come close to the minimum subsistence wage, that is below the marginal product of female workers[4].

- As in the case of non-discrimination, Firm 1 will have a constrained objective function:
  $$\min w_f L_f + w_m L_m$$
  $$\text{s.t. } f(L_f, L_m) = y$$
  $$L_f \leq L\text{-}S$$
  where L-S is the maximum number of female workers Firm 1 can hire.

- The first-order condition for Firm 1 will be:
  $$TRS = (w_f + \lambda)/w_m$$

- The objective function of Firm 2 is slightly more complicated:
  $$\min s\, S + w_f L_f + w_m L_m$$
  $$\text{s.t. } f(S + L_f, L_m) ,$$
  where s is the minimum subsistence wage and S the number of female forced workers.

- The first-order condition for Firm 2 will be:
  $$TRS = w_f/w_m$$

It emerges that, as in the case of employment discrimination, forced labour reduces the volume of output compared with an efficient situation. Again the issue of why forced labour exists arises. For Firm 1, forced labour means lower output but higher profits, because this firm realises a rent which is equal to the difference between the subsistence wages paid to forced workers and the wages that would have to be paid in the absence of forced labour. The existence of this rent can explain why Firm 1 would be reluctant to accept free labour.

Economic efficiency and child labour exploitation

Child labour exploitation is a special case of forced labour. Besides the economic effects associated with forced labour, child labour exploitation can be expected to undermine long-term economic prospects to the extent that such practices strongly hamper children's educational possibilities.

Economic efficiency and freedom of association

The economic effects of freedom of association are considerably more complex than is the case for the other core labour standards. Whereas the presence of other core standards is likely to be associated with efficiency, the effects of freedom of association are ambiguous:

- On the one hand, in the absence of freedom-of-association rights, it may be difficult to protect other core labour standards. When workers cannot organise themselves, they may be easier to exploit. Certain groups of workers are more vulnerable than others, for example when they are not educated or when they are simply too poor to refuse a job or look for a better-paid job. In this case, denial of freedom of association will produce similar results to either employment discrimination or forced labour.

- On the other hand, in the presence of freedom of association, a new distortion may be introduced into the labour market: when certain workers are better organised than others, this gives them the power to raise wages above market levels, thus preventing other workers from joining the enterprise. There are also cases where unions impose direct restrictions to join an enterprise, for example through the requirement that new workers must be union members. However, these negative effects on efficiency can be outweighed by the favourable impact of freedom of association on workers' motivation and productivity. The latter effects can be reinforced if freedom of association facilitates the establishment of a stable social climate and the creation of collective bargaining institutions which are conducive to better relations between management and workers[5].

It is possible to use the framework developed here to analyse the various effects of freedom of association. Assume that there is freedom of association and that workers of Firm 1 are unionised, while workers of Firm 2 are not. Moreover, unionised workers enjoy a pay premium compared with non-unionised ones. On the other hand, the presence of a union increases workers' productivity in Firm 1.

- The objective function of Firm 1 can be written as follows:
  min $(w + u)L + rK$
  s.t. $f(e.L, K)$
  where u is the pay premium of unionised workers and e denotes technical progress and captures labour-productivity gains associated with the presence of unions[6].

- The first-order cost-minimisation condition for Firm 1 is:
  $TRS = ((w+u)/e)/r$

- The objective function of Firm 2 is unchanged compared with the standard case. Hence the first-order condition for Firm 2 is:
  $TRS = w/r$

The technical rate of substitution is equal for both firms only if the productivity effect of the union offsets the pay premium effect. In general, the pay premium will be at least equal to the gain in productivity, because unionised workers will be in a strong position to bid for higher wages, so capturing part or all of the productivity gains. Therefore, the technical rate of substitution for Firm 1 is likely to be higher than or equal to the technical rate of substitution for Firm 2, and the output effects are ambiguous, as illustrated in the output diagram:

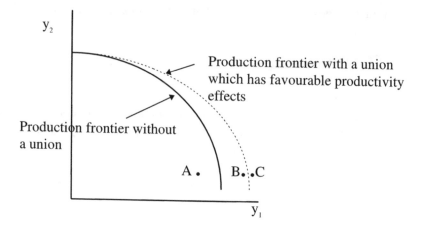

If the presence of a union yields technical progress in Firm 1, the production possibility frontier moves right-ward, i.e. at any given level of output in Firm 2, Firm 1 can produce more than in the absence of the union. It is unclear, however, whether the new production possibility frontier will be reached. If the productivity effect recorded in Firm 1 is less than the union pay premium, then the economy will not reach the production frontier: equilibrium will be at A if the pay premium is very high (in which case the total level of output in the economy will decline compared with the no-union situation); equilibrium will be at B if the pay premium is higher than the productivity effect, but not too high (in which case the total level of output will be higher than in the non-union situation, but not efficient, i.e. lower than what is technically feasible). Finally, only when the pay premium is equal to the gain in productivity associated with the presence of a union does the economy reach the production frontier (point C), leading to efficiency.

Equilibrium when core labour standards affect the availability of factor inputs

Besides their effects on the allocation of resources, core standards might also influence the available quantity of inputs. Labour standards can be labour-using, i.e. they might reduce the availability of labour for the purposes of producing goods and services. Prohibition of forced labour and child labour exploitation are examples of labour-using standards. Their enforcement will make part of the potential labour force unavailable for production. In this case, the production possibility frontier will shift inwards. If forced labour and child labour exploitation are concentrated in the production of good 1, their elimination will produce a shift inwards in the production frontier, as shown in the following diagram.

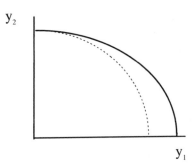

On the other hand, another core standard, namely prohibition of employment discrimination, can be labour-augmenting and not labour-using. The implications for the production frontier are the opposite of those for prohibition of forced labour and child labour exploitation: it will move outwards. Finally, freedom of association will not modify the availability of resources unless it helps improve enforcement of other core labour standards.

This analysis ignores any dynamic efficiency benefits from elimination of exploitative child labour, forced labour and employment discrimination. To the extent that such dynamic gains materialise, the production frontier would shift out in future periods.

Why do some firms not enforce core standards?

If most core standards are likely to improve economic efficiency and are therefore in the interest of enterprises taken as a whole, why are they not enforced in all cases? The main explanation to this puzzle is that the enforcement of core standards might imply some transitory costs, whereas the benefits are likely to manifest themselves over the longer run.

Core labour standards and trade

So far, the analysis was carried out in a closed-economy context. In this section, the framework will be extended to include trade and the impact of core labour standards will then be analysed. In the two-good, two-factor economy described above, equilibrium in production is determined by the production possibility frontier and the relative price of the two goods. In the absence of trade, production is equal to consumption at point C, where the community indifference curve is tangent to the production possibility frontier in the diagram below. When the economy opens to trade, the relative price of the two goods will change as it converges to the world market level. This will lead to a change in the relative production of the two goods (the production equilibrium point moves along the production frontier to point P′). As the diagram shows, consumption no longer corresponds to production: in the country examined here, consumption of product 1 is less than production, while the opposite occurs for product 2. Therefore, the country is an exporter of product 1 and an importer of product 2; the volume of trade is represented by the trade triangle C′GP′. It is important to note that the change in consumption patterns arising from trade leads to a rise in consumers' utility, which is represented in the diagram by a higher indifference curve than in the no-trade situation. This result illustrates the gains from trade.

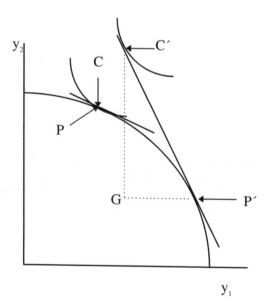

The gains from trade will arise irrespective of whether core labour standards are observed in the country. These gains arise because of the change in the relative price of the two goods. If two countries have different relative goods prices, they will always have an incentive to trade with each other and will specialise in those goods in which they have a comparative advantage. Suppose that in the presence of employment discrimination or forced labour the economy produces at a point inside the production possibility frontier. Under free trade, the economy will specialise, thus reaching a higher consumers' utility compared with the no-trade situation. In the case of freedom of association, the same result will obtain, independently of whether freedom of association leads to sub-optimal production patterns.

Even though trade will improve consumers' utility in all cases, the non-observance of particular core standards may still lead to sub-optimal production patterns. In other words, the equilibrium production point can remain within the production frontier.

It is sometimes argued that the non-observance of core standards shapes the patterns of international specialisation and consequently that an improvement in core standards would change specialisation. This is why it is claimed that the pattern of international specialisation can be partly artificial in the absence of core standards. However, such assertions have little foundation. First, specialisation in production is determined by many factors, including relative resource endowments, technology, consumers' preferences, economies of scale, etc. The role of core standards depends on their incidence on these factors. The only factor of specialisation that might possibly be affected by the degree of observance of core standards is relative resource endowments. For instance, if employment discrimination reduces the amount of labour available for production, the capital/labour ratio will be higher than in the absence of discrimination. Second, even if core labour standards do change relative resource endowments, specialisation is unlikely to be affected significantly.

The effects of changes in relative factor endowments can be traced out using the standard Heckscher-Ohlin-Samuelson general equilibrium model[7]. The model comprises two countries, two tradable goods and two factors of production, capital and labour. Each country produces both goods, using both factors. Production technologies are assumed to be identical in both countries, with production functions exhibiting constant returns to scale. The only difference is in relative factor endowments, i.e. one country is assumed to have proportionately more labour than the other. Also, one of the goods uses proportionately more of one factor than the other. As is well known, trade patterns in this model are determined by relative factor endowments and the relative factor intensity of production of each good.

The model is extended to include core labour standards. It is assumed that the imposition of such standards leads to a withdrawal of part of the factors that would otherwise be used for production of the two tradable goods: labour standards are assumed to be relatively labour-using[8]. Initially, it is assumed that the labour-abundant country does not observe core labour standards, whereas the capital-abundant country does.

Suppose country A is labour-abundant. Equilibrium under free trade, in the absence of labour standards, is characterised by country A's exporting the labour-intensive good x, while importing good y (panel A in the diagram below). Consumption and production patterns are given by point C which lies on the highest possible community indifference curve and point P which lies on the production possibility frontier AB. Given the country's production possibility frontier between the two tradable goods, the introduction of a labour-using standard causes a shift in the curve in a direction that depends on the factor intensity of the standard. If the labour standard is labour-using, the curve will shift inward to AB"[9]. The labour standard will lead to a reduction of country A's output and trade. The new consumption and production patterns are C' and P', respectively. But the diagram also shows that the terms of trade have improved (line TT shifts to TT'), thus making the country better off compared with a situation characterised by constant terms of trade (without the terms-of-trade improvement, consumption would be at C", that is, less than C').

By contrast, country B already respects core standards in the initial situation. The only change will be the deterioration in its terms of trade (reflecting the improvement in country A's). This will make the production of the labour-intensive good more profitable compared with that of the capital-intensive good (production patterns move from P to P' in panel B of the diagram below). At the same time, the worsening of its terms of trade will affect consumption, because country B cannot import as many goods as in the initial situation. Consumption falls from C to C'.

One interesting result is that the introduction of core labour standards in the low-standards country appears to lead to a reduction in consumption and welfare for both countries: C' is less than C in both cases. This result is an artefact of the analysis, however, because the level of welfare would likely be different if core standards were taken into account in the utility function. As explained above, in such a setting the analysis would be greatly complicated and this extension is not attempted here[10].

In sum, if core labour standards are relatively labour-using and countries have some monopoly power in trade, a levelling-up will be more beneficial (or less detrimental) for labour-abundant countries than for capital-abundant countries.

**Trade effects of core labour standards:
the large-country case**

A. Labour-abundant country

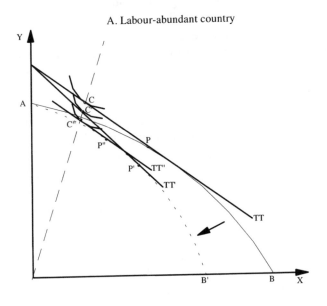

B. Capital-abundant country

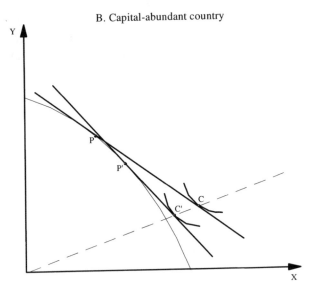

Conclusions

This note has developed a framework to analyse some economic properties of core labour standards. It emerges that employment discrimination unambiguously reduces economic efficiency. The reason is that such a practice causes a misallocation of resources while also reducing the availability of production factors. Forced labour and child labour exploitation also cause a misallocation of resources, thus reducing economic efficiency, but they might also raise the quantity of labour available for production. Child labour exploitation undermines long-term economic prospects to the extent that it hampers children's educational possibilities. In countries where such practices exist, the enforcement of core labour standards would improve economic efficiency.

The economic effects of freedom of association are more difficult to gauge. On the one hand, freedom of association can help upgrade production processes, while also raising workers' motivation and productivity. On the other hand, freedom of association can introduce a new distortion in the market to the extent that unionised workers succeed in raising their wages above market levels. The net effect on economic efficiency depends on the relative importance of these two effects.

The framework also confirms that, under certain assumptions, trade improves economic welfare, irrespective of whether core standards are observed in all trading partners: both high-standards countries and low-standards countries have an interest in trading with each other. Moreover, in general, the patterns of international specialisation are likely to be determined by fundamental factors such as relative factor proportions, technology and economies of scale, rather than the degree of observance of core standards.

NOTES

1. Throughout the discussion, relative product prices are assumed to be fixed (the "small-country" assumption in the Heckscher-Ohlin-Samuelson model).

2. If female employment is constrained in both firms, there is a case of prohibition, whose effects have just been described.

3. For simplicity, the capital input is ignored here, as its inclusion would unnecessarily complicate the analysis.

4. If the wage of forced workers is equal to their marginal product, there is no economic inefficiency (however, the workers might still regard themselves as being "forced" to work).

5. There is a vast literature on the economic effects of unions (see for example Freeman and Medoff, 1984). In general, available empirical research points to the existence of both pay premium effects and productivity effects.

6. Technical progress is assumed to be neutral in the sense of Harrod. In other words, technical progress increases labour productivity only, thus leaving capital productivity unchanged. This assumption is consistent with the observed long-term stability of factor shares.

7. See Brown et al. (1993) for a discussion of how this model can be used to address the trade and labour standards issue.

8. As discussed above, this is a reasonable assumption in the case of prohibition of forced labour and child labour exploitation. By contrast, the elimination of employment discrimination is likely to be labour-augmenting.

9.   In the diagram, it is assumed for simplicity that the production of the capital-intensive good is not affected by the introduction of core standards. Making allowance for this would complicate the story slightly but not change the essential results.

10.   The analysis of Brown *et al.* (1993) also focuses on the effects of labour standards on the production and consumption of physical goods.

ANNEX

METHODS APPLIED IN PART II,
"CORE LABOUR STANDARDS AND TRADE LIBERALISATION"

Index of compliance with ILO Conventions 87 and 98

The method used to gauge countries' compliance with the requirements of ILO Conventions 87 and 98 is based on information contained in the ILO's new computerised data base (ILOLEX, 1995). Along with extensive information on ILO Conventions and procedures, the annual reviews carried out by the ILO Committee of Experts on the Application of Conventions and Recommendations (CEACR) and the Conference Committee on the Application of Conventions and Recommendations (ILC) are recorded by country and Convention for each year from 1980 through 1994.

An important feature of the data base is that the information is presented in the same format each year. For example, country reviews begin with a list of the observations made by the Committees in the previous reviews, in several cases going back as far as the 1970s. This is followed by an evaluation of the changes made since the previous review of the country's legislation and enforcement practices. The Committees' evaluation ranges from finding that "no efforts" have been made to improve the situation to finding "with satisfaction" that the changes bring the country's standards of freedom-of-association and collective bargaining rights into conformity with ILO requirements. Finally, a new list of remaining problems is presented and for each problem the Committees make specific recommendations for improvement. This process provides a grid for evaluating progress in the next annual review.

The systematic presentation of information in the reviews permits the calculation of an index for each country, each year, of compliance with Conventions 87 and 98. Three steps are followed. First, observations are classified according to the type of restriction observed. Five broad categories are defined and assigned a number that ranges from 5 for the most severe (murder and physical violence) to 1 for the least severe (restrictions on political or religious activity). Within the five broad categories, certain restrictions are deemed worthy of a lower or higher value than the category as a whole. Values for these restrictions are shown in parentheses. Second, the Committees' evaluations of the restrictions observed are also assigned a number that ranges from 4 for greatest dissatisfaction to 0 for stated satisfaction. A complete list of the types of observations made by the Committees and of the variations in their evaluations is presented below. Finally, an index is calculated according to the formula:

$$\text{Index}^{ct} = \Sigma i [A \times B] i^{ct}, \text{ where}$$

A = category of observation, ranging from 5 to 1:
   5 = most severe violation (e.g. murder, attacks on union members)
   4 = severe violation (e.g. prohibition of union activity or collective bargaining)
   3 = major restriction (e.g. unjustified exclusion of certain sectors or categories of workers)
   2 = moderately severe restriction (e.g. eligibility requirements for union leaders)
   1 = least severe restriction (e.g. prohibition of political or religious activity)

B = category of evaluation, ranging from 4 to 0:
   4 = most critical evaluation (e.g. situation is inconsistent with ILO requirements; no government response)
   3 = critical evaluation (e.g. situation is inconsistent with ILO requirements; government plans to amend labour laws)
   2 = moderately critical evaluation (e.g. labour law amended; information requested on enforcement)
   1 = least critical evaluation (e.g. labour law amended and enforcement is improving; further information requested)
   0 = favourable evaluation (e.g. situation is consistent with ILO requirements)

i = number of observations made per annual country review;
c = country;
t = year, ranging from 1980 through 1994.

A decline (rise) in the index over time is then taken to designate an improvement (deterioration) in the country's compliance with the Conventions. Until recently, greatest emphasis was placed by the Committees on bringing countries' legislation into conformity with the Conventions. In recent years, however, account is increasingly taken in country reviews of improvements in implementation. A special project is under way in the ILO to quantify countries' expenditure on inspection and on penalties for non-enforcement.

While the index is based on published information, it inevitably embodies an element of Secretariat judgement. The element of judgement is limited, however, to the initial categorisation of types of restrictions and evaluations, as listed above. From this point on, the identification of types of restrictions and evaluations in the Committee's annual reviews is practically automatic since the wording used generally corresponds to set patterns. This means that for a given type of restriction or evaluation, the numerical value assigned to it will always be the same across countries and over time.

Classification of restrictions on freedom-of-association rights
(with examples of frequently observed restrictions)

I.	Physical violence against union members, their belongings, publications	4
	* murder, violence	(5)
	* seizure of union locales	(4)
	* seizure of publications	(3)

II.	Violation of right to organise	4
	(Articles 2 & 11, C. 87)	
	* preventing union establishment	
	* mandatory single union structure	
	* exclusions of categories of workers/sectors	(3)
	* prior authorisation requirements	(1)
	* membership/establishment requirements	(2)
	* single international union affiliation	(1)

III.	Violation of union activity rights	4
	(Article 3, C. 87)	
	* restriction of setting by-laws	
	* eligibility requirements for leaders	(2)
	* restriction of strikes	
	* unjustified government interference in internal affairs, elections	
	* prohibition of political/religious activity	(1)

IV.	Dissolution, suspension of a union (Article 4, C. 87)	4

V.	Restriction on joining federations, confederations (Article 5, C. 87)	2

VI. Anti-union discrimination (Article 1, C. 98) 2

VI. Employer interference (Article 2, C. 98) 3

VII. Restriction of collective bargaining (Article 4, C. 98) 3
   * wage setting
   * scope

Classification of evaluations by ILO CEACR and ILC Committees

Situation is inconsistent with Conventions 87 and 98; government 4
  has made no effort to change
Law amendment is requested; government has demonstrated efforts to do so 3
Information pending; law amended but has not yet been enforced 2
Information pending; law amended and enforcement is improving 1
Satisfaction 0

Indicators of trade liberalisation

The method used to gauge the restrictiveness of countries' tariff and quantitative restriction (QR) regimes is presented in IMF (1995), pp. 34-35. According to the IMF, the standards used in its 1995 report are stricter than in its previous trade surveys and take account of the coverage and intensity of QRs as well as the average level of (all-inclusive) statutory tariffs. Increased availability of information and progress in liberalising trade regimes in developing and transition economies are cited as the factors responsible for the toughening of criteria for evaluation. An overview of the IMF method is presented below.

The tariff regime is classified into three categories: "restrictive", "moderate", and "open", based on the experience of the successful trade reformers (e.g. in Latin America) and taking into account the average tariff of less than 5 per cent prevailing in the major industrial countries:

Classification of tariff regime

	Restrictive	Moderate	Open
Average tariffs	>25 per cent	11 to 25 per cent	≤10 per cent

The assessment of QR regimes is based on the import and export coverage and the intensity of the respective QRs. Coverage is measured as the proportion of tariff lines covered by QRs; where this information is not available, the share of imports affected by the QR is used as a proxy. The intensity of the QR is also taken into account because various QRs differ in their protective effects. Thus, QRs are classified as high-, medium-, or low-intensity items. The resulting QR classification is as follows:

Classification of QR regime

	Restrictive	Moderate	Open
Import and export coverage	>25 per cent and any intensity (high, medium, or low)	0 to 10 per cent and high intensity	0 to 25 per cent and low intensity
	>10 per cent and high intensity	10 to 25 per cent and medium intensity	10 per cent and medium intensity

The overall stance of the trade regime reflects the combined effect of QRs and tariffs. If one area is liberalised more than the other, whether QRs or tariffs, the more restrictive measure determines the overall stance. Thus, a "restrictive" tariff regime (with average tariffs above 25 per cent) combined with an "open" QR regime would yield a characterisation of the overall trade regime as being "restrictive". Accordingly, the following matrix guides the determination of the overall trade policy stance:

Combined trade policy stance

	Quantitative restrictions		
	Open	Moderate	Restrictive
Tariffs	Open	Moderate	Restrictive
	Moderate	Moderate	Restrictive
	Restrictive	Restrictive	Restrictive

REFERENCES

AGGARWAL, M. (1995), "International Trade and the Role of Labor Standards", *International Economic Review*, US International Trade Commission, August.

ASHAGRIE, K. (1993), "Statistics on Child Labour: A Brief Report", *Bulletin of Labour Statistics*, ILO.

BALASSA, B. (1966), "Tariff Reductions and Trade in Manufactures among the Industrial Countries", *American Economic Review*, Vol. 56.

BALDWIN, R. (1995), "The Effects of Trade and Foreign Direct Investment on Employment and Relative Wages", *OECD Jobs Study Working Paper Series*, No. 4.

BHAGWATI, J. (1994), "A View from Academia", in Schoepfle, G. and Swinnerton, K. (eds.), *International Labor Standards and Global Integration: Proceedings of a Symposium*, US Department of Labor, Washington, D.C.

BHAGWATI, J. (1995), "Trade and Wages: A Malign Relationship?", mimeo.

BHALLA, S. (1994), "Freedom and Economic Growth: A Virtuous Cycle?" paper presented at the Nobel Symposium on Democracy's Victory an Crisis, Uppsala University, August.

BLANPAIN, R. (1991), *Labour Law and Industrial Relations of the Europe Community*, Kluwer Law and Taxation Publishers, Deven (Netherlands).

BOUHDIBA, A. (1982), *Exploitation of Child Labour*, United Nations, I York.

BROWN, D.K., DEARDORF, A.V. and STERN, R.M. (1993), "Interna Labour Standards and Trade: A Theoretical Analysis", paper presen Fairness Claims and Gains from Trade Project Meeting, Univers Minnesota Law School, 29-31 July.

BROWN, G.E. Jr. (1994), Statement on the introduction of the "Chil Deterrence Act of 1994", *Congressional Record,* Vol. 140, (1 July 1994), p. E1420.

BURNIAUX, J.-M. and WOELBROECK, J. (1996), "The Intera Enhanced Competition with a 'Kind' Social System", paper pr the A.E.A. conference, Paris, 11-12 January.

BURTLESS, G. (1995), "Widening US Income Inequality and the Growth in World Trade", unpublished paper, The Brookings Institution, Washington, D.C., October.

BURTT, E.J. (1972), *Social Perspectives in the History of Economic Theory*, St. Martin's Press, New York.

CALMFORS, L. (1993), "Centralisation of Wage Bargaining and Macroeconomic Performance -- a Survey", *OECD Economic Studies*, No. 21, Winter.

Calvert Group (1995a), Calvert Social Investment Fund prospectus, Bethesda, Maryland.

Calvert Group (1995b), Calvert World Values Global Equity Fund prospectus, Bethesda, Maryland.

CASELLA, A. (1994), "On Standards and Trade: A Review of Simple Results", paper prepared for a conference, "Domestic Policy Divergence in an Integrated World Economy: Fairness Claims and the Gains from Trade," sponsored by the American Society of International Law and funded by the Ford Foundation, Washington, D.C., 30 September and 1 October.

CLARK, B.J.F. (1983), "United States Labor Practices in South Africa: Will a Mandatory Fair Employment Code Succeed Where the Sullivan Principles Have Failed?", *Fordham International Law Journal*, Vol. 7, No. 2, pp. 358-387.

CORTES, O., JEAN, S. and PISANI-FERRY, J. (1995), "Trade with Emerging Countries and the Labour Markets: The French Case", CEPII-ECARE Workshop, "International Trade and Employment: The European Experience", Paris, 25 September.

Council on Economic Priorities (1994), *Shopping for a Better World*, New York, Sierra Club Books.

COURAKIS, A., MASKUS, K.E. and WEBSTER, A. (1995), "Occupational Employment and Wage Changes in the UK: Trade and Technology Effects", International Economics Study Group Annual Conference, 22-24 September.

CROPPER, M. and GRIFFITHS, C. (1994), "The Interaction of Population Growth and Environmental Quality", *American Economic Review*, May.

Daily Labour Report (1995), Bureau of National Affairs, Inc., Washington, D.C., 10 February.

DEWATRIPONT, M., SAPIR, A. and SEKKAT, K. (1995) "Labour Market Effects on Trade with LDC's in Europe", CEPII-ECARE Workshop, "International Trade and Employment: The European Experience", Paris, 25 September.

DUNNING, J.H. (1993), *Multinational Enterprises and the Global Economy*, Addison-Wesley.

EHRENBERG, R.G. (1994), *Labor Markets and Integrating National Economies*, The Brookings Institution, Washington, D.C.

EHRENBERG, R.G. and SMITH, R.S. (1994), *Modern Labor Economics: Theory and Public Policy*, Fifth Edition, Harper Collins College Publishers.

FIELDS, G. (1994), *Trade and Labour Standards: A Review of the Issues*, OECD.

FOLLOWS, J.W. (1951), *Antecedents of the International Labour Organization*, Clarendon Press, Oxford.

FREEMAN, R.B (1994), "A Hard-headed Look at Labour Standards", in Sengenberger, W. and Campbell, D. (eds.), *International Labour Standards and Economic Interdependence*, ILO, Geneva.

FREEMAN, R.B (1995), "Are Your Wages Set in Beijing?", *Journal of Economic Perspectives*, Vol. 9, No. 3, Summer.

FREEMAN, R.B. and MEDOFF, J. (1984), *What Do Unions Do?*, Basic Books.

GASTON, N. and TREFLER, D. (1995), "Union Wage Sensitivity to Trade and Protection: Theory and Evidence", *Journal of International Economics*, August.

GATT Secretariat (1987), "Article XXXV; Note by the Secretariat", MTN.GNG/NG7/W/30.

GATT Secretariat (1990), "Article XXXV; Note by the Secretariat; Corrigendum", MTN.GNG/NG7/W/30/ Corr.6.

GILMAN, B.A. (1995), Remarks on the floor of the US House of Representatives upon the introduction of the MacBride Principles Bill (H.R. 470), 11 January 1995.

GOLDSMITH, S. (1994), "Abdul Moment's Mission: One Man's Crusade to End the Slave Trade in Asia and the Middle East", *Student Lawyer*, Vol. 22, No. 8, pp. 31-33.

GRAHAM, E.M. (1995), *Foreign Direct Investment in the World Economy*, International Monetary Fund, Washington, D.C.

GRIMSRUD, B. and A. MELCHIOR, eds (1996), *Child Labour in International Trade and Norwegian Imports*, Norwegian Trade Union, Center for Social Science and Research and Norwegian Institute for International Affairs, Oslo.

HANSEN, C.R. (1989), "The Slepak Principles: No Threat to American Traders", *Whittier Law Review*, Vol. 2, No. 2, pp. 459-472.

HARVEY, P. and RIGGIN, L. (1994), *Trading Away the Future: Child Labor in India's Export Industries*, International Labor Rights Education and Research Fund, Washington, D.C.

HINE, R.C. and WRIGHT, P. (1995), "The Impact of Changing Trade Patterns on the Demand for Labour in the United Kingdom", International Economics Study Group Annual Conference, 22-24 September.

HUFBAUER, G.C., SCHOTT, J.J. and ELLIOTT, K.A. (1990), *Economic Sanctions Reconsidered: History and Current Policy*, Institute for International Economics, Washington, D.C.

ILO (1977), Tripartite Declaration of Principles concerning Multinational Enterprises and Social Policy, Geneva.

ILO (1985), *Freedom of Association*, Geneva.

ILO (1991), *International Labour Standards Concerned with Labour Inspection*, Geneva.

ILO (1993), *Multinationals and Employment*, Geneva.

ILO (1994a), *The Social Dimensions of the Liberalisation of World Trade*, GB.261/WP/SLD/1 November, Geneva.

ILO (1994b), *Freedom of Association and Collective Bargaining*, Geneva.

ILO (1994c), ILOLEX.

ILO (1994d), *Defending Values, Promoting Change*, Report of the Director-General to the 81st International Labour Conference, Geneva.

ILO (1995), *Child Labour*, GB.264/ESP/1, November, Geneva.

IMF (1992), *International Issues and Developments in International Trade Policy*, Washington, D.C.

IMF (1995), *International Trade Policies: The Uruguay Round and Beyond*, Vols. 1 and 2, Washington, D.C.

International Confederation of Free Trade Unions (1994), *Annual Survey of Violations of Trade Union Rights*, Brussels.

International Economic Review (1995), "International Trade and the Role of Labor Standards", US International Trade Commission, August.

IPEC (1995), *Strategies, Priorities and Lessons for the future: A Summary*, Geneva.

KRUEGER, A.B. (1995), *Labour Market Shifts and the Price Puzzle Revisited,* unpublished paper, Princeton University, October.

KRUGMAN, P. and OBSTFELD, M. (1991), *International Economics*, Harper Collins.

LAL, D. (1981), "Resurrection of the Pauper-Labour Argument", *Thames Essay* No. 28, London.

LARRE, B. (1995), "The Impact of Trade on Labour Markets: An Analysis by Industry", *OECD Jobs Study Working Paper Series*, No. 6.

LARRE, B. and TORRES, R. (1991), "Is Convergence a Spontaneous Process? The Experience of Spain, Portugal and Greece", *OECD Economic Studies*, Spring.

LAWRENCE, R.Z. (1994), "Trade, Multinationals & Labor", *NBER Working Paper No. 4836*, August.

LAWRENCE, R.Z. (1996), *Global Economy, Divided Nations? International Trade and OECD Labour Markets,* OECD Development Centre, Paris, forthcoming .

LAWRENCE, R. Z. and SLAUGHTER, M. J. (1993), "Trade and US Wages in the 1980s: Giant Sucking Sound or Small Hiccup?", *Brookings Papers on Economic Activity: Microeconomics.*

LEAMER, E.E. (1996), *In Search of Stolper-Samuelson Effects on US Wages,* NBER Working Paper No. 5427.

LIZONDO, J.S. (1991), "Foreign Direct Investment", in *Determinants and Systematic Consequences of International Capital Flows*, International Monetary Fund, Washington, D.C.

LLOYD (1995), Regional Integration Arrangements in East Asia, unpublished paper, Monash University.

LORD, W. (1993), "Chinese Compliance with MOU Governing Prison Labor Exports", *Dispatch,* Vol. 4 No. 40 (4 October 1993), pp. 681-683.

NAALC: A Guide, (1995) US National Administrative Office, Bureau of International Labor Affairs, US Department of Labor, Washington, D.C.

North American Agreement on Labor Cooperation (1993), Final Draft, 13 September 1993.

OECD (1983), *The Generalised System of Preferences: Review of the First Decade*, Paris.

OECD (1991), *Employment Outlook*, Paris.

OECD (1992a), *Industrial Policy in OECD Countries: Annual Review 1992*, Paris.

OECD (1992b), *International Direct Investment: Policies and Trends in the 1980s*, Paris.

OECD (1992c), *Development Assistance Manual: DAC Principles for Effective Aid*, Paris.

OECD (1993a), *Employment Outlook*, Paris.

OECD (1993b), *Directory of the Development Activities of Trade Unions Based in OECD Countries*, Paris.

OECD (1994a), *The OECD Guidelines for Multinational Enterprises*, Paris.

OECD (1994b), *Employment Outlook*, Paris.

OECD (1994c), *The Benefits of Freer Trade: East Asia and Latin America*, Paris.

OECD (1994d), *Assessing Investment Opportunities in Economies in Transition*, Paris.

OECD (1995a), *Foreign Direct Investment, Trade and Employment*, Paris.

OECD (1995b), *International Direct Investment Statistics Yearbook*, Paris.

OECD (1995c), "Special Features: Recent Trends in Foreign Direct Investment", *Financial Market Trends*, Paris.

OECD (1995d), *BIAC Workshop on Corporate Strategy in a Global Economy*, Paris.

OECD (1995e), *DAC Orientations for Development Co-operation in Support of Private Sector Development*, Development Co-operation Guidelines Series, Paris.

OECD (1995f), *DAC Orientations on Participatory Development and Good Governance*, Development Co-operation Guidelines Series, Paris.

Office of the United States Trade Representative (1995), *National Trade Estimate Report on Foreign Trade Barriers,* US Government Printing Office, Washington, D.C.

OLIVEIRA-MARTINS, J. (1994), "Market Structure, Trade and Industry Wages", *OECD Economic Studies,* No. 22, Spring.

OLSON, M. (1982), *The Rise and Decline of Nations,* Yale University Press, New Haven, Connecticut.

OMAN, C. (1994), *Globalisation and Regionalisation: The challenge for Developing Countries,* OECD Development Centre, Paris.

PARISOTTO, A. (1995), "Recent Trends in Employment in Transnational Corporations", in *Foreign Direct Investment, Trade and Employment,* OECD, Paris, pp. 67-76.

PIORE, M. (1994), "International Labor Standards and Business Strategies", in Schoepfle, G. and Swinnerton, K. (eds.), *International Labor Standards and Global Integration: Proceedings of a Symposium,* US Department of Labor, Washington, D.C.

REDLEAF, J.L. (1992), "The Division of Foreign Policy Authority Between the European Community and the Member States: A Survey of Economic Sanctions Against South Africa," *Boston College Third World Law Journal,* Vol. 12, No. 1, pp. 97-119.

RICHARDSON, J.D. (1989), "Empirical Research on Trade Liberalisation with Imperfect Competition: A Survey", *OECD Economic Studies,* Spring.

RICHARDSON, J.D. (1995), "Income Inequality and Trade: How to Think, What to Conclude", *Journal of Economic Perspectives,* Vol. 9, No. 3, Summer.

SACHS, J.D. and SHATZ, H. (1994), "Trade and Jobs in US Manufacturing", *Brookings Papers on Economic Activity,* 1.

SACHS, J.D. and SHATZ, H. (1995), "International Trade and Wage Inequality in the United States: Some New Results", unpublished paper, Harvard University, December.

SACHS, J. and WARNER, A. (1995), "Economic Reform and the Process of Global Integration", *Brookings Papers on Economic Activity,* 1.

SAMUELSON, P. (1954), "The Pure Theory of Public Expenditure", *The Review of Economics and Statistics,* Vol. 36.

SCHOEPFLE, G. and SWINNERTON, K. (1994), "Labor Standards in the Context of a Global Economy", *Monthly Labor Review*, Vol. 117, No. 9, September.

SENGENBERGER, W. and CAMPBELL, D. (1994), *Creating Economic Opportunities: The Role of Labour Standards in Industrial Restructuring*, ILO, Geneva.

SHAO, M. (1994), "Capitalism with a Cause", *Boston Globe,* 9 January 1994.

SKELLY, J. (1995), *The Caux Round Table Principles for Business: The Rise of International Ethics,* Business Ethics, Minneapolis, Minnesota.

SOUTHERLAND, D. (1994), "Firms Cited over Imports from China", *Washington Post,* 19 May 1994.

SPARKES, R. (1995), *The Ethical Investor,* Harper Collins, London.

SRINIVASAN, T.N. (1994), "International Labor Standards Once Again!", in Schoepfle, G. and Swinnerton, K. (eds.), *International Labor Standards and Global Integration: Proceedings of a Symposium*, US Department of Labor, Washington, D.C.

Starnberg Institute (1991), *Employment and Working Conditions in Export Processing Zones*, Geneva.

STOLPER, W. and SAMUELSON, P. (1941), "Protection and Real Wages", *Review of Economic Studies*, November.

STREETEN, P. (1981), *Development Perspectives*, Macmillan, London.

SWINNERTON, K. (1995), "An Essay on Economic Efficiency and Core Labor Standards", U.S. Department of Labor, Economic Discussion Paper 47, June.

THOMAS, V. and NASH, J. (1991), "Reform of Trade Policy: Recent Evidence from Theory and Practice", *The World Bank Research Observer*, July.

UN (1993), *Transnational Corporations*, February.

UNCTAD (1994), *World Investment Report*, New York and Geneva.

UNESCO (1993), *Education for All: Status and Trends*, Paris.

US Department of Labor (1985), Draft Guidelines on 'Internationally Recognized Worker Rights", mimeo.

US Department of Labor (1989), *Reconciling Labor Standards and Economic Goals: An Historical Perspective*, Washington, D.C., September.

US Department of Labor (1994), *By the Sweat and Toil of Children, Vol. 1: The Use of Child Labor in U.S. Manufactured and Mined Imports,* Washington, D.C.

US Department of Labor (1995), *By the Sweat and Toil of Children, Vol. 2: The Use of Child Labor in U.S. Agricultural Imports & Forced and Bonded Child Labor,* Washington, D.C.

US Department of State (1994), *Country Reports on Human Rights Practices for 1993,* Washington, D.C.

US General Accounting Office (1993), "US-Mexico Trade: The Work Environment at Eight US-Owned Maquiladora Auto Parts Plants", November.

US General Accounting Office (1994), "International Trade: Assessment of the Generalized System of Preferences Program", GAO/GGD-95-9, November.

US International Trade Commission (1984), *International Practices and Agreements Concerning Compulsory Labor and U.S. Imports of Goods Manufactured by Convict, Forced, or Indentured Labor,* USITC Publication 1630, Washington, D.C.

US NAO (1994), Public Report of Review, NAO Submission No. 940001 and NAO Submission No. 940002, Bureau of International Labor Affairs, US Dept of Labor, Washington, D.C.

US NAO (1995a), Annual Report, US Department of Labor, Washington, D.C.

US NAO (1995b), Public Report of Review, NAO Submission No. 940003, US Dept of Labor, Washington, D.C.

VENABLES, A.J. (1995), "Economic Integration and the Location of Firms", *American Economic Review,* May.

WILKINSON, B. (1994), *Labour and Industry in the Asia-Pacific,* de Gruyter, Berlin.

WILLIAMSON, J. (1995), "Globalization, Convergence, and History", *NBER Working Paper 5259,* September.

WOOD, A. (1991), "How Much Does Trade with the South Affect Workers in the North?", *The World Bank Research Observer,* January.

WOOD, A. (1994), *North-South Trade, Employment and Inequality,* Clarendon Press, Oxford.

WOOD, A. (1995), "How Trade Hurt Unskilled Workers", *Journal of Economic Perspectives,* Vol. 9, No 3.

Word Bank (1995), *World Development Report*, Washington, D.C.

MAIN SALES OUTLETS OF OECD PUBLICATIONS
PRINCIPAUX POINTS DE VENTE DES PUBLICATIONS DE L'OCDE

AUSTRALIA – AUSTRALIE
D.A. Information Services
648 Whitehorse Road, P.O.B 163
Mitcham, Victoria 3132   Tel. (03) 9210.7777
Fax: (03) 9210.7788

AUSTRIA – AUTRICHE
Gerold & Co.
Graben 31
Wien I   Tel. (0222) 533.50.14
Fax: (0222) 512.47.31.29

BELGIUM – BELGIQUE
Jean De Lannoy
Avenue du Roi, Koningslaan 202
B-1060 Bruxelles   Tel. (02)
538.51.69/538.08.41
Fax: (02) 538.08.41

CANADA
Renouf Publishing Company Ltd.
1294 Algoma Road
Ottawa, ON K1B 3W8   Tel. (613) 741.4333
Fax: (613) 741.5439
Stores:
61 Sparks Street
Ottawa, ON K1P 5R1   Tel. (613) 238.8985
12 Adelaide Street West
Toronto, ON M5H 1L6   Tel. (416) 363.3171
Fax: (416)363.59.63

Les Éditions La Liberté Inc.
3020 Chemin Sainte-Foy
Sainte-Foy, PQ G1X 3V6 Tel. (418) 658.3763
Fax: (418) 658.3763

Federal Publications Inc.
165 University Avenue, Suite 701
Toronto, ON M5H 3B8   Tel. (416) 860.1611
Fax: (416) 860.1608

Les Publications Fédérales
1185 Université
Montréal, QC H3B 3A7   Tel. (514) 954.1633
Fax: (514) 954.1635

CHINA – CHINE
China National Publications Import
Export Corporation (CNPIEC)
16 Gongti E. Road, Chaoyang District
P.O. Box 88 or 50
Beijing 100704 PR   Tel. (01) 506.6688
Fax: (01) 506.3101

CHINESE TAIPEI – TAIPEI CHINOIS
Good Faith Worldwide Int'l. Co. Ltd.
9th Floor, No. 118, Sec. 2
Chung Hsiao E. Road
Taipei   Tel. (02) 391.7396/391.7397
Fax: (02) 394.9176

DENMARK – DANEMARK
Munksgaard Book and Subscription Service
35, Nørre Søgade, P.O. Box 2148
DK-1016 København K   Tel. (33) 12.85.70
Fax: (33) 12.93.87

J. H. Schultz Information A/S,
Herstedvang 12,
DK – 2620 Albertslung   Tel. 43 63 23 00
Fax: 43 63 19 69
Internet: s-info@inet.uni-c.dk

EGYPT – ÉGYPTE
Middle East Observer
41 Sherif Street
Cairo   Tel. 392.6919
Fax: 360-6804

FINLAND – FINLANDE
Akateeminen Kirjakauppa
Keskuskatu 1, P.O. Box 128
00100 Helsinki
Subscription Services/Agence d'abonne-
ments :
P.O. Box 23
00371 Helsinki   Tel. (358 0) 121 4416
Fax: (358 0) 121.4450

FRANCE
OECD/OCDE
Mail Orders/Commandes par correspondance
:
2, rue André-Pascal
75775 Paris Cedex 16 Tel. (33-1) 45.24.82.00
Fax: (33-1) 49.10.42.76
Telex: 640048 OCDE
Internet: Compte.PUBSINQ@oecd.org
Orders via Minitel, France only/
Commandes par Minitel, France exclusive-
ment :
36 15 OCDE
OECD Bookshop/Librairie de l'OCDE :
33, rue Octave-Feuillet
75016 Paris   Tél. (33-1) 45.24.81.81
(33-1) 45.24.81.67
Dawson
B.P. 40
91121 Palaiseau Cedex   Tel. 69.10.47.00
Fax: 64.54.83.26

Documentation Française
29, quai Voltaire
75007 Paris   Tel. 40.15.70.00

Economica
49, rue Héricart
75015 Paris   Tel. 45.75.05.67
Fax: 40.58.15.70

Gibert Jeune (Droit-Économie)
6, place Saint-Michel
75006 Paris   Tel. 43.25.91.19
Librairie du Commerce International
10, avenue d'Iéna
75016 Paris   Tel. 40.73.34.60

Librairie Dunod
Université Paris-Dauphine
Place du Maréchal-de-Lattre-de-Tassigny
75016 Paris   Tel. 44.05.40.13

Librairie Lavoisier
11, rue Lavoisier
75008 Paris   Tel. 42.65.39.95

Librairie des Sciences Politiques
30, rue Saint-Guillaume
75007 Paris   Tel. 45.48.36.02

P.U.F.
49, boulevard Saint-Michel
75005 Paris   Tel. 43.25.83.40

Librairie de l'Université
12a, rue Nazareth
13100 Aix-en-Provence Tel. (16) 42.26.18.08

Documentation Française
165, rue Garibaldi
69003 Lyon   Tel. (16) 78.63.32.23

Librairie Decitre
29, place Bellecour
69002 Lyon   Tel. (16) 72.40.54.54

Librairie Sauramps
Le Triangle
34967 Montpellier Cedex 2 Tel. (16) 67.58.85.15
Fax: (16) 67.58.27.36

A la Sorbonne Actual
23, rue de l'Hôtel-des-Postes

06000 Nice   Tel. (16) 93.13.77.75
Fax: (16) 93.80.75.69

GERMANY – ALLEMAGNE
OECD Bonn Centre
August-Bebel-Allee 6
D-53175 Bonn   Tel. (0228) 959.120
Fax: (0228) 959.12.17

GREECE – GRÈCE
Librairie Kauffmann
Stadiou 28
10564 Athens   Tel. (01) 32.55.321
Fax: (01) 32.30.320

HONG-KONG
Swindon Book Co. Ltd.
Astoria Bldg. 3F
34 Ashley Road, Tsimshatsui
Kowloon, Hong Kong   Tel. 2376.2062
Fax: 2376.0685

HUNGARY – HONGRIE
Euro Info Service
Margitsziget, Európa Ház
1138 Budapest   Tel. (1) 111.62.16
Fax: (1) 111.60.61

ICELAND – ISLANDE
Mál Mog Menning
Laugavegi 18, Pósthólf 392
121 Reykjavik   Tel. (1) 552.4240
Fax: (1) 562.3523

INDIA – INDE
Oxford Book and Stationery Co.
Scindia House
New Delhi 110001   Tel. (11) 331.5896/5308
Fax: (11) 332.5993
17 Park Street
Calcutta 700016   Tel. 240832

INDONESIA – INDONÉSIE
Pdii-Lipi
P.O. Box 4298
Jakarta 12042   Tel. (21) 573.34.67
Fax: (21) 573.34.67

IRELAND – IRLANDE
Government Supplies Agency
Publications Section
4/5 Harcourt Road
Dublin 2   Tel. 661.31.11
Fax: 475.27.60

ISRAEL – ISRAËL
Praedicta
5 Shatner Street
P.O. Box 34030
Jerusalem 91430   Tel. (2) 52.84.90/1/2
Fax: (2) 52.84.93
R.O.Y. International
P.O. Box 13056
Tel Aviv 61130   Tel. (3) 546 1423
Fax: (3) 546 1442

Palestinian Authority/Middle East:
INDEX Information Services
P.O.B. 19502
Jerusalem   Tel. (2) 27.12.19
Fax: (2) 27.16.34

ITALY – ITALIE
Libreria Commissionaria Sansoni
Via Duca di Calabria 1/1
50125 Firenze   Tel. (055) 64.54.15
Fax: (055) 64.12.57
Via Bartolini 29
20155 Milano   Tel. (02) 36.50.83
Editrice e Libreria Herder
Piazza Montecitorio 120
00186 Roma   Tel. 679.46.28
Fax: 678.47.51

Libreria Hoepli
Via Hoepli 5
20121 Milano   Tel. (02) 86.54.46
                            Fax: (02) 805.28.86
Libreria Scientifica
Dott. Lucio de Biasio 'Aeiou'
Via Coronelli, 6
20146 Milano   Tel. (02) 48.95.45.52
                            Fax: (02) 48.95.45.48

JAPAN – JAPON
OECD Tokyo Centre
Landic Akasaka Building
2-3-4 Akasaka, Minato-ku
Tokyo 107   Tel. (81.3) 3586.2016
                            Fax: (81.3) 3584.7929

KOREA – CORÉE
Kyobo Book Centre Co. Ltd.
P.O. Box 1658, Kwang Hwa Moon
Seoul   Tel. 730.78.91
                            Fax: 735.00.30

MALAYSIA – MALAISIE
University of Malaya Bookshop
University of Malaya
P.O. Box 1127, Jalan Pantai Baru
59700 Kuala Lumpur
Malaysia   Tel. 756.5000/756.5425
                            Fax: 756.3246

MEXICO – MEXIQUE
OECD Mexico Centre
Edificio INFOTEC
Av. San Fernando no. 37
Col. Toriello Guerra
Tlalpan C.P. 14050
Mexico D.F.   Tel. (525) 665 47 99
                            Fax: (525) 606 13 07
Revistas y Periodicos Internacionales S.A. de
C.V.
Florencia 57 - 1004
Mexico, D.F. 06600   Tel. 207.81.00
                            Fax: 208.39.79

NETHERLANDS – PAYS-BAS
SDU Uitgeverij Plantijnstraat
Externe Fondsen
Postbus 20014
2500 EA's-Gravenhage   Tel. (070) 37.89.880
Voor bestellingen: Fax: (070) 34.75.778

NEW ZEALAND –
NOUVELLE-ZÉLANDE
GPLegislation Services
P.O. Box 12418
Thorndon, Wellington   Tel. (04) 496.5655
                            Fax: (04) 496.5698

NORWAY – NORVÈGE
NIC INFO A/S
Bertrand Narvesens vei 2
P.O. Box 6512 Etterstad
0606 Oslo 6   Tel. (022) 57.33.00
                            Fax: (022) 68.19.01

PAKISTAN
Mirza Book Agency
65 Shahrah Quaid-É-Azam
Lahore 54000   Tel. (42) 735.36.01
                            Fax: (42) 576.37.14

PHILIPPINE – PHILIPPINES
International Booksource Center Inc.
Rm 179/920 Cityland 10 Condo Tower 2
HV dela Costa Ext cor Valero St.
Makati Metro Manila   Tel. (632) 817 9676
                       Fax: (632) 817 1741

POLAND – POLOGNE
Ars Polona
00-950 Warszawa
Krakowskie Przedmieácie 7 Tel. (22) 264760
                            Fax: (22) 268673

PORTUGAL
Livraria Portugal
Rua do Carmo 70-74
Apart. 2681
1200 Lisboa   Tel. (01) 347.49.82/5
                            Fax: (01) 347.02.64

SINGAPORE – SINGAPOUR
Gower Asia Pacific Pte Ltd.
Golden Wheel Building
41, Kallang Pudding Road, No. 04-03
Singapore 1334   Tel. 741.5166
                            Fax: 742.9356

SPAIN – ESPAGNE
Mundi-Prensa Libros S.A.
Castelló 37, Apartado 1223
Madrid 28001   Tel. (91) 431.33.99
                            Fax: (91) 575.39.98
Mundi-Prensa Barcelona
Consell de Cent No. 391
08009 – Barcelona   Tel. (93) 488.34.92
                            Fax: (93) 487.76.59
Llibreria de la Generalitat
Palau Moja
Rambla dels Estudis, 118
08002 – Barcelona
              (Subscripcions) Tel. (93) 318.80.12
              (Publicacions) Tel. (93) 302.67.23
                            Fax: (93) 412.18.54

SRI LANKA
Centre for Policy Research
c/o Colombo Agencies Ltd.
No. 300-304, Galle Road
Colombo 3   Tel. (1) 574240, 573551-2
                       Fax: (1) 575394, 510711

SWEDEN – SUÈDE
CE Fritzes AB
S–106 47 Stockholm   Tel. (08) 690.90.90
                            Fax: (08) 20.50.21
Subscription Agency/Agence d'abonnements :
Wennergren-Williams Info AB
P.O. Box 1305
171 25 Solna   Tel. (08) 705.97.50
                            Fax: (08) 27.00.71

SWITZERLAND – SUISSE
Maditec S.A. (Books and Periodicals - Livres
et périodiques)
Chemin des Palettes 4
Case postale 266
1020 Renens VD 1   Tel. (021) 635.08.65
                            Fax: (021) 635.07.80
Librairie Payot S.A.
4, place Pépinet
CP 3212
1002 Lausanne   Tel. (021) 320.25.11
                            Fax: (021) 320.25.14
Librairie Unilivres
6, rue de Candolle
1205 Genève   Tel. (022) 320.26.23
                            Fax: (022) 329.73.18
Subscription Agency/Agence d'abonnements :
Dynapresse Marketing S.A.
38, avenue Vibert
1227 Carouge   Tel. (022) 308.07.89
                            Fax: (022) 308.07.99
See also – Voir aussi :
OECD Bonn Centre
August-Bebel-Allee 6
D-53175 Bonn (Germany)   Tel. (0228)
                                 959.120
                       Fax: (0228) 959.12.17

THAILAND – THAÏLANDE
Suksit Siam Co. Ltd.
113, 115 Fuang Nakhon Rd.
Opp. Wat Rajbopith
Bangkok 10200   Tel. (662) 225.9531/2
                            Fax: (662) 222.5188

TRINIDAD & TOBAGO
SSL Systematics Studies Limited
9 Watts Street
Curepe
Trinadad & Tobago, W.I.   Tel. (1809)
                                 645.3475
                            Fax: (1809) 662.5654

TUNISIA – TUNISIE
Grande Librairie Spécialisée
Fendri Ali
Avenue Haffouz Imm El-Intilaka
Bloc B 1 Sfax 3000   Tel. (216-4) 296 855
                       Fax: (216-4) 298.270

TURKEY – TURQUIE
Kültür Yayinlari Is-Türk Ltd. Sti.
Atatürk Bulvari No. 191/Kat 13
Kavaklidere/Ankara
                       Tel. (312) 428.11.40 Ext. 2458
                       Fax: (312) 417 24 90
Dolmabahce Cad. No. 29
Besiktas/Istanbul   Tel. (212) 260 7188

UNITED KINGDOM – ROYAUME-UNI
HMSO
Gen. enquiries   Tel. (0171) 873 0011
Postal orders only:
P.O. Box 276, London SW8 5DT
Personal Callers HMSO Bookshop
49 High Holborn, London WC1V 6HB
                            Fax: (0171) 873 8463
Branches at: Belfast, Birmingham, Bristol,
Edinburgh, Manchester

UNITED STATES – ÉTATS-UNIS
OECD Washington Center
2001 L Street N.W., Suite 650
Washington, D.C. 20036-4922   Tel. (202)
                                      785.6323
                            Fax: (202) 785.0350
Internet: washcont@oecd.org

Subscriptions to OECD periodicals may also
be placed through main subscription agencies.

Les abonnements aux publications périodiques
de l'OCDE peuvent être souscrits auprès des
principales agences d'abonnement.

Orders and inquiries from countries where Dis-
tributors have not yet been appointed should be
sent to: OECD Publications, 2, rue André-Pascal, 75775 Paris Cedex 16, France.

Les commandes provenant de pays où l'OCDE
n'a pas encore désigné de distributeur peuvent
être adressées aux Éditions de l'OCDE, 2, rue
André-Pascal, 75775 Paris Cedex 16, France.

5-1996